1997

National Standards
A Catalyst for Reform

National Standards
A Catalyst for Reform

Edited by Robert C. Lafayette

In Conjunction with the American Council
on the Teaching of
Foreign
Languages

National Textbook Company
a division of *NTC Publishing Group* • Lincolnwood, Illinois USA

Contents

Introduction

National Standards: A Catalyst for Reform

Robert C. Lafayette
Louisiana State University

Jamie B. Draper
American Council on the Teaching of Foreign Languages

On November 18, 1995, at the annual meeting of ACTFL in Anaheim, California, the national standards for foreign language education, *Standards for Foreign Language Learning: Preparing for the 21st Century,* were officially released during a special ceremony. The event was the culmination of a three-year effort to define what all students should know and be able to do as a result of foreign language instruction.

Background

The development of national disciplinary standards was triggered by the national reform effort initiated at the 1989 Education Summit in Charlottesville, Virginia. It was at this summit that the National Education Goals were approved by the nation's governors and President George Bush. Goal Three called for students to attain high standards in challenging subject matter; at the time, foreign languages were not included. Fortunately, the action of concerned foreign language educators around the country led to correction of that omission. In 1991 the National Education Goals Panel, a congressionally approved, bipartisan commission that monitors the nation's progress toward

Robert C. Lafayette (Ph.D., the Ohio State University) is chair of the Department of Curriculum and Instruction and director of the French Education Project at Louisiana State University.

Jamie B. Draper (M.S., Georgetown University) is special projects manager and member liaison for the American Council on the Teaching of Foreign Languages. She served as project manager for the National Standards for Foreign Language Learning project.

meeting the goals, recommended the establishment of national standards and assessments that would provide solid evidence of student achievement in meeting the goals. While the notion of a national assessment system was not received with enthusiasm, the idea of standards was viewed with a great deal of optimism, particularly after the success of the standards that had been developed by the National Council of Teachers of Mathematics.

Upon learning of the U.S. Department of Education's interest in funding standards development, in the fall of 1992 the American Council on the Teaching of Foreign Languages, the American Association of Teachers of French, the American Association of Teachers of German, and the American Association of Teachers of Spanish and Portuguese began collaborating to determine standards for the profession. In January 1993 foreign language education became the seventh and final subject area to receive federal funding to develop national standards for students in kindergarten through grade 12.

Project Structure

The National Standards in Foreign Language Education Project was guided by a board of directors composed of representatives of the four collaborating organizations plus two at-large members. An eleven-member task force was given the charge of actually writing the standards. Two criteria used in appointing this group were that members must be (1) representative of the entire field of foreign language education and (2) primarily practicing teachers, individuals familiar with today's classrooms and today's students. The group that finally came together on the task force represented all levels of instruction, elementary through postsecondary, as well as teacher education. Commonly and less commonly taught languages, both modern and classical languages, the linguistics of second language acquisition, cultural education, heritage language learning, and the use of technology in foreign language education were all represented on the task force.

From June 1993 through October 1995, the task force met nine times. Between meetings a smaller writing team conducted additional work. A volunteer board of reviewers provided thorough critiques of the emerging document. A twenty-member advisory council also was appointed to review the document as it progressed. The advisory council was composed of individuals both within and outside the foreign language profession, including representatives of business, federal and state government, community service organizations, education administrators and policymakers at the state and local levels, and the related fields of bilingual education and English as a second language.

The Process

The five sections of the national foreign language standards represent the answers to five questions the task force posed to themselves and the profession:

1. What do we believe foreign language education in this country should be? *(philosophy statement)*
2. Given this philosophy, what should foreign language education prepare students to do? *(goals)*
3. What are the essential skills and knowledge students need in order to achieve these goals? *(standards and curricular experiences)*
4. How do we know students are making progress toward meeting the goals? *(progress indicators)*
5. What classroom practices will assist students in meeting the standards? *(learning scenarios)*

The task force shared each stage of the process, from the philosophy statement to the learning scenarios, with the profession. The project newsletter, conference presentations, and one-on-one conversations encouraged foreign language educators to give feedback on the work in progress. The standards became topics of discussion at departmental meetings in many schools. In the ultimate test, the task force chose six pilot sites to verify the feasibility of the standards in actual classroom settings for several months. The task force read and seriously considered all the comments received, positive and negative, and many teachers will recognize their contributions to the final product.

The process of developing the standards can be characterized by one word: collaboration. The organizations managing the project, the task force members, the members of the advisory council (more than half of whom came from outside the profession), and the thousands of teachers who reviewed the several drafts of the standards all came together in a spirit of collaboration and cooperation. The resulting document is one that can truly be said to reflect the consensus of the foreign language profession on what the field can and should offer our students. The timeline that follows helps provide some insight on the amount of collaborative effort that went into the foreign language national standards.

Project Timeline

Date	Event
September 1992	ACTFL learns of interest in the funding of standards for foreign languages.
October 1992	Meeting of ACTFL, AATF, AATG, and AATSP to discuss collaboration on the development of standards for foreign language education.
November 1992	Proposal submitted to U.S. Department of Education to develop student standards, K–16, entry-level teacher standards, teacher education program guidelines, and accomplished teacher standards.
January 1993	The four collaborating organizations receive funding from the U.S. Department of Education and the National Endowment for the Humanities to develop K–12 student standards for foreign language education.
June 1993	First meeting of the standards task force; philosophy statement developed.
August 1993	The project's first newsletter is prepared and mailed to 35,000 foreign language educators. The newsletter included a questionnaire requesting feedback on the statement of philosophy and comment on significant issues to be addressed by the task force. More than 700 responses were received. Standards task force meets on Cape Cod. Discussion centered on conceptualizing the standards framework. Issues of concern: the purposes and content of foreign language education; multiple entry points; the feasibility of standards for grades 4, 8, and 12; and standards that would be minimums and not maximums. They decided to focus first on exit standards and then determine checkpoints to evaluate progress toward the exit standard.
November 1993	Task force meets at ACTFL '93 in San Antonio, Texas, to continue refining the standards framework and developing exit standards.
February 1994	Task force meets in conjunction with SCOLT in Atlanta, Georgia. The first standards framework is presented for comment. Six goal areas of foreign language education are defined, later reduced to five with input from the advisory council.
May 1994	Writing team meets in Ogden, Utah, to further refine the standards and benchmarks.

Project Timeline *(continued)*

Date	Event
June 1994	Pilot sites requested in project newsletter. 80 districts apply to become one of the six sites ultimately selected. Task force meets in Park City, Utah, to finalize the first draft of the document.
July 1994	More than 50 state and regional leaders attend an invitational conference on standards and articulation held in Baltimore, Maryland, to begin to build links among state and regional standards-development efforts.
August 1994	First draft released for public review and comment.
October 1994	Pilot program commences. Task force meets in New York City to review comments received on the first draft and make modifications to document.
November 1994	Revised first draft released for review and comment. National Town Meeting on foreign language standards broadcast live to 250 sites around the country. The viewing audience was estimated at 3,000.
December 1994	Advisory council meets in Washington, D.C., to discuss revised draft.
February 1995	Task force meets in San Francisco to refine the standards and goals and finalize benchmarks for grades 4, 8, and 12.
April 1995	Second complete draft released for public comment.
July 1995	Task force meets to continue refinement of standards. Benchmarks are changed to progress indicators. State and local supervisors and state association leaders meet at second Invitational Workshop on National Standards in Salt Lake City, Utah. Writing team meets in Chicago to finalize front matter. The full task force works to prepare document for approval of the advisory council.
September 1995	Advisory council meets in Washington, D.C., and endorses *Standards for Foreign Language Learning: Preparing for the 21st Century.*
October 1995	The task force meets for the last time to finalize the document. Goal Four is reworked and broadened.
November 1995	*Standards for Foreign Language Learning: Preparing for the 21st Century* is presented to the profession and the public.

Overview of Volume

The purpose of this ACTFL volume is to examine how the standards might influence the various segments of the profession, including national associations and national policy, preservice and in-service professional development, state frameworks and local curriculum guides, tests and other assessment instruments, and new populations such as students from immersion programs, near-native speakers of the target language, and students in small, distant rural communities. It should be noted that in all cases, the articles were written before the final standards document was presented to the profession and the public.

In chapter 1, John F. Jennings, director of the Center on National Education Policy, explains to us why it makes perfect sense that you would be told what you are supposed to know, then helped along as you tried to master the material, and then given another chance to do so if you did not perform just right the first time. He paints a broad picture of the national standards movement and explains how an agreement about the need for this commonsensical approach in schooling began to emerge in the late 1980s and early 1990s and what this reform will mean for the improvement of elementary and secondary education in the last decade of this century.

Foreign language teaching as a profession is relatively young and is often said to lack organization. The language-specific organizations, for example, have enjoyed a relatively long history, but until recently much of their effort was spent in the literary arena. Among the more pedagogically oriented organizations such as the American Council on the Teaching of Foreign Language and the regional conferences (Central States Conference, Northeast Conference, Northwest Conference, Southern Conference, and Southwest Conference), the oldest are the Northeast and the Northwest, founded in the fifties. ACTFL itself is not quite thirty years old. In chapter 2, Helene Zimmer-Lowe, executive director of the American Association of Teachers of German, explores the efforts of the foreign language teaching field to establish itself as a profession and to develop professional policy about what is being taught and who is teaching it. It also describes the field's activities over nearly three decades to establish and foster policy at the state and national levels, activities that in tandem with other, more powerful organizations and forces will support its work to become a true profession.

Audrey L. Heining-Boynton in chapter 3 addresses the potential impact of the standards on preservice teacher-education programs. Will this new national document change the content and context of undergraduate and fifth-year certification programs? How might foreign language departments be influenced by the evolution and revolution currently taking place in the profession? What are or should be some of the criteria to assess interns and initially certified teachers? How are other disciplines coping with the national standards movement? This article addresses these questions and many more.

In chapter 4, Eileen Glisan tackles similar issues within the professional development of teachers. In the first part of the article, Glisan presents an excellent overview of the characteristics of today's foreign language teachers, the types of professional development opportunities offered to teachers of foreign languages, and the obstacles to reform in classroom teaching. Glisan concludes her article by proposing several guiding principles and suggesting new avenues for assisting in-service teachers in basing instruction on the standards by means of collaborative professional development efforts.

This volume for the most part deals with traditional elementary and secondary school foreign language programs whose traditional students are English-speaking Americans enrolled in French, German, Latin, or Spanish courses. In chapter 5, however, Russell Campbell addresses "new" learners and "new" environments. Some of the new learners, such as native speakers of Spanish enrolled in foreign language Spanish classes, might better be labeled neglected than new since they have long been present in our foreign language classes. Fortunately, as a profession we have broadened our horizons and are confronting the challenges of providing appropriate language instruction to thousands of American students who differ dramatically from traditional students—or Type T students, as Campbell calls them. The author goes on to deal with Type I (immersion), Type H (heritage), and Type HI (heritage-immersion) students. Campbell's discussion is apt to provoke reflection on foreign language learning and teaching in traditional as well as nontraditional settings.

In chapter 6 Mel Nielsen and Elizabeth Hoffman challenge the profession to adapt distance learning to reach the unreachable in small, distant rural communities. The emerging revolution in global technologies is making it possible to open new opportunities in learning for all students including, in particular, at-risk populations in urban and rural schools. They claim that rural schools are the ideal place to begin because geography is a serious equity issue affecting much of the school population in the United States. And, if core curriculum is defined as essential curriculum, then students who are ill prepared to communicate in a foreign language are at risk.

There is a significant distance between Anaheim, California, where the national foreign language standards were presented to the profession and the public, and the actual programmatic application of the standards in the typical everyday classroom. In chapter 7, Walter Bartz and Margaret Keefe Singer conjecture what the potential programmatic implications of the standards will be in the average classroom based on information gathered from the mathematics profession, the first to complete their standards (1989) and begin to acquire information on their impact in the classroom. The authors maintain that the standards will reach the classroom only if classroom practitioners are involved throughout the process of curriculum development and if an assessment component is built into the equation. The authors also report the results of three surveys that they conducted with state foreign language supervisors, school administrators, and foreign language teachers on how they perceived the role of national and state standards in the everyday classroom.

Judith Liskin-Gasparro begins chapter 8 by reviewing the current debate between the competing demands of test validity and test reliability in assessment and testing. The proposed models of authentic assessment do indeed point to the empowerment of teachers and to performance assessment of student achievement, and among the many items discussed are portfolios, oral proficiency measures, self-assessment, collaborative assessment, journals, and learning logs. Given all the pressures of the everyday classroom, the author discusses to what extent authentic assessment is possible. No doubt the most appropriate segment of this article is the discussion, with excellent classroom-based examples, on how the new standards can be assessed. The article concludes with case studies of schools and school districts that are currently experimenting with alternative assessments.

In chapter 9, June Phillips and I discuss the impact that the standards have had on foreign language publishers even before their official release. We also spend a considerable amount of time reviewing and commenting on the implications of the standards for the profession in general. Then, in order to place the foreign language standards at least on a par with national standards from other content areas, we evaluate them using the Criteria for High Quality Standards developed by the Educational Issues Department American Federation of Teachers (1994). They conclude along with Mitchell (1996) that the newly released document will serve the profession well.

References

American Federation of Teachers. 1994. "Making Standards Good." *American Educator,* Fall, pp. 15, 20–27.

Mitchell, Ruth. 1996. "Bravo, Bravissimo! The Standards for Foreign Language Learning." *Basic Education,* January, pp. 2–4.

1

Using Standards to Improve Education: A Way to Bring About Truth in Teaching and Learning[1]

John F. Jennings

Center on National Education Policy

When you learned to drive a car, or to play the piano or the violin, or to fly a plane, you were told what you needed to know. Then you were guided and corrected as you went along. If you did not drive or play or fly correctly, you were taught some more and then tried again. What could be a more logical way to learn something? It makes perfect sense that you would be told what you are to know, then helped along as you tried to master the material, and then given another chance to do it if you did not perform just right the first time.

That sensible way to learn is *not* the way that American public schools now operate in many important respects. But it is the way that students will be educated once a major reform of elementary and secondary education that has recently begun is finally implemented. This article explains how an agreement about the need for this commonsensical change in schooling began to emerge in the late 1980s and early 1990s and what this reform will mean for the improvement of elementary and secondary education in the last decade of this century.

Schooling Today

In American schools today teachers explain material to students, help them to understand what they are doing right, and correct them when they are not

John F. Jennings is director of the Center on National Education Policy in Washington, D.C. He speaks to many groups, writes for professional journals, magazines, and newspapers, and is consulted by many national education organizations and leaders in the federal government. He served for many years as General Counsel for Education for the U.S. House of Representatives.

mastering the material. And when teachers control the tests, they try to help students along so that they can do better the next time. But students, teachers, and the schools are often held accountable for performance on tests that students cannot learn to and teachers cannot teach to. Moreover, the results are not revealed to teachers or students, so there is no chance to learn from mistakes and work to do better next time.

Schools are caught in a "crap-shoot" in which teachers are teaching in the dark and students are being tested in the dark. It amounts to a "gotcha" game. Students are not told exactly what they are going to be tested on, nor are they told afterward which questions they answered wrong so that they can learn the material for another time. Is it any wonder then that high school students are not motivated to learn? They do not see the relevance of what they are taught, since that's not what they are held accountable for.

Many important decisions about students' lives are made in similar fashion. An example that is easy to understand involves the SAT I, the country's most famous assessment, which is used every year to help determine the admission of hundreds of thousands of high school students to college.

A student cannot study for the SAT because the test prides itself on not being based on any one curriculum. A student can spend money to attend an SAT preparatory course run by a private company, but all that company can do is to give some pointers on test-taking techniques and hazard some guesses about the types of questions likely to appear on the test. No one but the Educational Testing Service, which writes the SAT, knows for sure what will be on the test. And those students who cannot afford the fees for those private courses are not even given the benefit of the educated guesses of the preparatory companies.

Admission to college is not the only matter decided in this fashion. Many states also require students to pass a standardized test in order to graduate from high school, and many school districts require students to pass a test to proceed from one grade to another. All these major decisions are based on tests that cannot be taught because they consist of material that is unknown and whose results are not revealed afterward so that students can learn from their errors.

Doesn't this seem like a strange system of education? If we were to learn to drive, play a musical instrument, or fly a plane in this way, there would be many more car wrecks, discordant noises, and plane crashes than there are now. Imagine having to guess the right ways to drive, play music, or fly. Is it any wonder then that the public schools are struggling so hard to improve and, in the popular opinion, are not succeeding?

Recent School Reform

The irony is that public education has just been through a period of reform unmatched in intensity and length. During the late 1970s and throughout the 1980s many states toughened high school graduation requirements, instituted professional testing for teachers and raised their salaries, and experimented with countless ways of improving teaching and learning.

But by the end of the 1980s the general impression was that the schools had not improved that much, if at all. This view was based on the fact that SAT I scores had not increased substantially, that college professors were still complaining that students were not ready for postsecondary education, and that employers were asserting that high school graduates were unprepared for the workplace.

The American public is edgy and impatient with the schools and wants results, asserted Richard Riley, the U.S. secretary of education, in a summer 1993 speech to the nation's governors. The country will be out of business if public education does not reinvent itself—and fast, according to Louis Gerstner, Jr., CEO of IBM, in a May 1994 article in the *New York Times*. Gerstner went on to assert that, just as American business had to change in order to become competitive, so would American schools. However, he found chilling the combination of public apathy and bureaucratic obstructionism that stood in the way of the needed changes.

Since the late 1970s public education has in fact undergone reform, and evidence from the early 1990s shows that more students have been taking more difficult courses. Moreover, even though greater demands are being placed on students, the dropout rate has not increased. But there is also clear evidence that grade inflation has occurred and that a grade of C has crept up to a grade of B (Office of Educational Research and Improvement 1994). It seems that teachers and students, under pressure to improve and lacking objective measures of progress, simply allowed grades to rise to show improvement.

Ironically, the school reform movement of the late 1970s and the 1980s, which created this pressure to improve, also helped to confuse the situation further because many states instituted or expanded testing systems without linking the tests to the curriculum. By 1994 forty-five states had instituted or expanded testing programs for elementary and secondary education, but only ten or so had *any* type of mandated curriculum that would tell teachers and students ahead of time what they were going to be tested on and held accountable for.

In other words, there is no "truth in teaching or learning" in many schools. Teachers and students can only guess, sometimes with limited guidance, what they are supposed to know in order to be deemed successful. The reason for this lack of connection between the test and the curriculum is that accountability has been moved to the state level, while the decisions on what ought to be taught have been left at the local level. The politicians—governors and state legislators—have responded to public displeasure with the public schools by instituting new tests in an effort to get better results from the schools. But few policymakers have moved to define first what results are to be expected on these tests.

Local Control

The reason for this failure to connect lies in our nation's history. The U.S. Constitution embodies the idea that government should be limited in its powers and that the closer the government is to the people, the better it will function. In education this has meant that, although states have authority over the schools, the power to determine the content of education has usually been delegated to local school boards. And, since there are 14,000 or so school districts in the country, there is great variance in the education being offered to students.

The National Academy of Sciences (National Research Council 1989) undertook a searching review of mathematics in the public schools, since American students consistently rank below students in many other industrialized countries on international tests. Its report describes the way the mathematics curriculum is typically fashioned in local school districts. It concluded

> In the United States, with our traditional and legal decentralization of education, we go about things very differently (than in other countries). Every summer, thousands of teachers work in small teams for periods ranging from one week to two months, charged by their school districts to write new mathematics curricula. These teacher teams usually have little training in the complicated process of curricular development, little or no help in coping with changing needs, and little to fall back on except existing textbooks, familiar programs, and tradition. The consequence usually is the unquestioned acceptance of what already exists as the main body of the new curriculum, together with a little tinkering around the edges. Many school districts simply adopt series of textbooks as *the* curriculum, making no effort to engage the staff in rethinking curricula; in those places, the *status quo* certainly reigns.
>
> . . .

The American process of curricular reform might be described as a weak grass-roots approach. The record shows that this system does not work. It is not our teachers who are at fault. In fact, teachers should play a dominant role in curricular decision making. But teachers who work in summer curricular projects are being given an unrealistic task in an impossible time frame, with only the familiar status quo to guide them.

> In static times, in periods of unchanging demands, perhaps our grass-roots efforts would suffice to keep the curriculum current. In today's climate, in which technology and research are causing unprecedented change in the central methods and applications of mathematics, present U.S. practice is totally inadequate. (National Research Council 1989:77–78).

In other words, the decisions about curriculum that are made locally would seem to respect the national tradition of local control whenever possible, but, as the National Academy of Sciences suggests, this system may have outlived its usefulness in a rapidly changing world. And, as already noted, the problem has become further complicated, in that states have testing programs in mathematics and other subjects that do not match what teachers in local school districts teach. When the results of the state assessments come out later, the public believes that the students have not learned the material and that the schools have failed.

Readiness to Change

This does not have to be the way that education is provided. "We have a history of not training students in the material they will be tested on. Other countries don't hide the test from students," according to the New Standards Project (1994:1), which issued a report on the reasons that students in other countries do better in mathematics than U.S. children. "That doesn't mean particular questions or answers of any one test are revealed to students. It means that teachers are able to gear what and how they teach toward the kind of questions that will appear on examinations" (p. 2). In other words, students and teachers in many countries are told what they are expected to know and be able to do, and then they are held accountable for mastering that knowledge.

This kind of clarity in teaching and learning is a far cry from "the confusion that reigns in most (American) schools today where tests are generated by one vendor, textbooks by another and teachers are trained by people who don't know much about specific curriculums," according to Smith and Cortines (1993:14), the undersecretary in the U.S. Department of Education and the former chancellor of the New York City school system, respectively. Again, this system of conflicting signals is about to change, and none too soon to help teachers and students to do better than they are doing now.

The American public supports a change in education that will make teaching and learning clearer in U.S. schools. Every Phi Delta Kappa/Gallup poll since 1989 has found an overwhelming majority of citizens in favor of a basic curriculum of subject matter for all schools, or what has been called in some of the surveys a "national curriculum." Some 69 percent favored a standardized national curriculum in the local public schools in 1989, and by 1994 this percentage had increased to 83 percent. The desired change in education can be achieved without a national curriculum if states move to institute standards for their schools. Nonetheless, the poll results are interesting in that they show that the public is ready to go even further than is absolutely necessary to bring about improvements in American education.

Beginnings of Change

The process of instituting standards is already under way. During the late 1980s a movement began with the stated purpose of helping teachers to know what they are to teach and students to know what they are expected to learn. Learning and accountability are starting to be linked so that all the rules will be known ahead of time and students will be able to work toward achievable objectives.

This major change is generally labeled "standards-based" reform. It means that agreement will be achieved first on what students are to know and to be able to do. Then progress through school and graduation from high school will be determined according to mastery of this content. Teachers will know ahead of time what they are to teach, and students will know what will be expected of them.

The reforms of the late 1970s and 1980s led to this change because leaders began to recognize that the changes made in that period too often focused on such things as instituting new testing programs without paying attention to curriculum, or increasing course requirements without considering the quality of the education being offered. As the Consortium for Policy Research in Education (1994) concluded

> Although students took classes with challenging titles as a result of the reforms, the titles did not ensure quality academic content. The increased number of tests only reinforced the poor skills and rote instruction that motivated the reform in the first place. Lessons learned from this experience led federal and state governments, as well as professional associations, to define content standards and expected student outcomes. (p. 6)

This movement toward reform based on defining standards began among mathematics teachers and in some states that had strong educational leadership.

In response to the report of the National Research Council (1989) and other such studies, the National Council of Teachers of Mathematics (NCTM) initiated an effort in 1989 to develop standards for mathematics. Those standards were issued by the NCTM in 1992. Meanwhile, Bill Honig, the state superintendent of schools in California, had already begun to develop curricular frameworks for the basic subjects in the early 1980s. Other teachers' associations and other states were encouraged by these experiences and initiated their own work on developing standards and frameworks.

National Leadership

The general public, the teachers' associations, and some states were ahead of the country's leaders on this issue. But national politicians soon caught up. In 1989 President George Bush and the nation's governors agreed on the idea of establishing national goals for education, the first ever to be adopted. This movement evolved into broad agreement on the need for voluntary national standards for education in order to pursue the goals.

One important development in this evolutionary tale was the appointment by the Bush administration and the Congress of a bipartisan commission to review the issue. The National Council on Education Standards and Testing (1992), whose membership was representative of a wide cross section of political views, issued a report whose depiction of American schools is important in understanding the motivation for this reform:

> In the absence of well-defined and demanding standards, education in the United States has gravitated toward de facto national minimum expectations. Except for students who are planning to attend selective four-year colleges, current education standards focus on low-level reading and arithmetic skills and on small amounts of factual material in other content areas. Consumers of education in this country have settled for far less than they should and for far less than do their counterparts in other developed countries. (p. i)

That is the major reason that national and state leaders have coalesced around the need for defining content and student performance standards: the quality of American education must be improved, and the current system of relying on local decision making over curriculum is failing to bring about that improvement. As a result of this broad agreement, President William Clinton, building on the work started by President Bush, signed into law in 1994 Goals 2000: Educate America Act (P.L. 103-227), which places the national goals into law, supports the certification of voluntary national education standards and national skill standards, and encourages the states through grant aid to develop their own standards for education.

As standards-based reform plays out in the states, now with the assistance of the Goals 2000 legislation, complete agreement on every detail of each state's plan cannot be expected, nor is it reasonable to anticipate concurrence on every aspect of the Goals 2000 legislation itself. For instance, there is a movement afoot in the Congress to eliminate altogether or to decrease sharply the funding for the Goals program, and there is legislation to amend the Goals statute to repeal any certification of standards by any national governmental body. These efforts show that the premises of the national role in standards-based reform may have to be reargued as newly elected representatives come to their posts without knowledge of the prior debates.

But the logic that moved the nation's mathematics teachers, the National Academy of Sciences, the country's major business organizations, the national education groups, and the Bush and the Clinton administrations to endorse standards-based reform remains compelling. If American students are to do better in school, we must agree on what they are to learn, and this agreement must seek greater mastery of content than is now being achieved.

State and Local Activities

Despite the publicity around the national standards and the controversy in Congress over the Goals 2000 program, the far more important decisions on standards-based reform are being made at the state level, where the Constitution places control of education. Most states have already invested several years of work in this effort and are moving toward new agreements on what students ought to know and be able to do.

Even before the enactment of Goals 2000 in early 1994, the states were moving independently to develop their own agreements on what should be taught and learned, and they have used the federal aid since then to accelerate this work. As of May 1994 (a month after Goals 2000 became law and before any funds were released), forty-two states had already developed or were developing content standards, and thirty were developing or had already adopted student performance standards to measure mastery of content. As of January 1995, forty-two states were receiving Goals 2000 funding to help them in these efforts.

According to the American Federation of Teachers (1995), the states are strongly committed to standards-based reform. They report that every state except Iowa is developing academic standards for its students and therefore it concludes: "Whatever wrangling might be going on in Congress, this report shows that the states' commitment to standards should not be underestimated" (p. 13).

Use of National Standards

National standards are important in showing what the subject-matter teacher associations think ought to be mastered in their content areas, but the national news media's focus on national standards has blown them up out of proportion and has stirred up a fear that somehow these standards can be imposed as a national curriculum. That fear is unfounded for two reasons.

First, during the congressional debate on Goals 2000, the U.S. Department of Education was explicitly barred (as it has been in the past) from imposing in any way a curriculum on states or local school districts. State control over education was reaffirmed, as it should be under the Constitution. Consequently, no federal agency would dare to undertake the task of melding and balancing the various national standards to fashion a curriculum that it would then mandate the states and local school districts to follow.

Second, the national standards were composed in a manner that makes the task of combining them into a curriculum impossible without a great deal of editing, conforming, and choosing of appropriate expectations for students within the confines of the school day and year. Nor are the specifics of the sets of standards compatible, because there was no coordination of effort in their development. Nor are they easily melded into a curriculum, because each group of teachers thought students should know so much about their particular area. The standards are more resource documents than they are specific curricula or even curricular frameworks.

For these two reasons the states are not using the national standards in the ways that critics have feared. Ramsey Selden of the Council of Chief State School Officers (CCSSO) reported

> Some states probably won't *do* standards at all. Some other states, Kentucky and California for example, are trying to build a standards-based system, and they're taking some care to make sure that their standards are consistent with these voluntary national standards. Other states are doing different things. Vermont is organizing [its standards] into clusters. Math, science, and technology are one cluster, and the arts and the humanities are in another cluster. (O'Neil 1995:12)

These developments show a healthy federalism, with the national government funding the agreements on national standards that were reached by the subject-matter specialists, while the states choose their own approaches to the use of these resources. Teachers who know the subject matter are able to pool their knowledge and experience on what students should know and be able to do, and then the real decisions on curriculum are made at the state and local levels.

New Approaches

The movement to use standards as the basis for school reform must be seen in a broader context in order to understand its full import. Throughout the American economy companies are "downsizing" in the sense of eliminating middle management and moving decision making into the hands of employees who produce or have contact with customers. The idea is that the top management of the companies will set the general policy but that the lower levels will make day-to-day decisions because they are closer to the reality of making the products or engaging the public. Middle management is eliminated because they are perceived as an impediment in this streamlined process. The federal government is moving in the same direction of simplifying administration with President Clinton's "reinventing government" initiative, and some states and local governments are also involved in their own changes along the same lines.

Standards-based reform is part of this same philosophical shift. The idea behind the movement is that there should be agreement on the results to be achieved, usually certain levels of student mastery of subject content, then the components of the educational system are aligned with these agreements, such as through basing assessments on the content and refashioning teacher education to incorporate teaching to this material, and last and most important, freedom is given to teachers, principals, and local administrators to operate the schools as they think best, through removal of legal and regulatory requirements. So, agreement on content and levels of student mastery of content is linked with subsequent relaxing of regulations and mandates. Day-to-day decisions are moved to the school building after the overall goal of student performance is defined. *Results* and *flexibility* are the two essential and interrelated code words for this change in approach to schooling.

Another component of the philosophical shift embodied in standards-based reform is a movement away from reliance on standardized norm-referenced tests to greater use of "authentic" assessments, such as essays or performance of scientific experiments. Once subject-matter content and the levels of student mastery of that content are defined, then students should be assessed to determine if they have learned the content. Comparisons to other students are not so important because student performance will instead be measured against specified levels of mastery of content.

Standards-based reform incorporates both notions: defining the results and then easing up on the rules in the system, and using assessments based on mastery of content and not on performance compared to others. These same notions are also intrinsic to other national school reform movements. The New Standards project, involving states and school districts with approximately half the student population in the country, is fashioning a standards-based assessment system that relies heavily on development of standards and authentic assessments of content. The National Board for Teacher Certification is developing a voluntary national system of certificates for teachers who show mastery of subject matter through compilations of portfolios and submissions of videotaped demonstrations of mastery of teaching techniques.

In addition to sharing the same philosophical premises, these movements are struggling to find ways to reach voluntary agreements at the national level or at some level beyond the state or region, but which agreements will not be used as the basis for federal laws or regulations. They are experiments searching for ways for the country to agree on what needs to be done and then using those agreements to encourage, not coerce, state and local actions. A common theme is to avoid national control while trying to reach national agreement.

Cautions

The focus of standards-based reform is certainly the right one; there ought to be agreement on what should be taught and what students should master before debate starts on the means of achieving this mastery. But as states and local school districts embark on this task, certain precautions should be borne in mind.

First, the standards that are developed, whether content or student performance standards, have to be subject to change. They cannot be conceived as permanent and immutable. The enterprise of developing standards is new for many and so what is learned in implementation must be brought back to change the standards to make them better.

Second, the standards must be clear and specific enough to lead to a common core curriculum for all students in a state or school district. The American Federation of Teachers (1995) reports that only a fourth of the states have such standards and that the other states' standards are not "strong enough to carry the weight of the reforms being built upon them" (p. 13). As states refashion their assessments to conform to the new standards, those standards must be clear and specific or the new tests will not be measuring what they should. Likewise with any realignment of textbooks, reform of teacher training, mounting of in-service training for current teachers, and so forth. Every aspect of standards-based reform is geared to the standards, and those must be clear and specific to make everything else work.

Third, teachers must be the core group advising on developing the state and local standards and then giving advice on how the standards are being implemented. Others have an important role to play in standards development and modification, but no one group can equal the experience that classroom teachers have. Related to this point is the importance that must be attached to professional development of teachers as states implement their new standards. It would be self-defeating for a state to invest substantial money in writing standards and then not to spend funds to train classroom teachers in what the new standards mean for their teaching.

The fourth point is connected to the third, namely, setting standards is the first step but much more needs to be done if this reform is to have real meaning. According to the CCSSO, states understand this point and are beginning to use the standards process as a way to improve their schools overall. An agreement on what should be taught and learned is an essential step in reform because it goes to the very heart of schooling, but it is certainly not the only action that must be taken.

Assessments need to be updated, teacher training and certification need to be modified, and teachers need to know what is expected of them. In addition, much more equity needs to be introduced into the now very unequal distribution of resources in our thousands of school districts. All these steps are absolutely fundamental to making comprehensive school reform work, and without them the effort to reach agreement on what students ought to know and be able to do has much less meaning.

Conclusion

Standards-based reform efforts are even now making progress in many states, and their impact will start to appear in classrooms around the country in the next few years. By the end of the century American education may be quite different from what it has been. Teachers will know what they are to teach, and students will know what is expected of them. But students, teachers, and the general public must understand why these changes are coming about, because there is often a reluctance to change and a nostalgia for the "good old days."

Furthermore, as standards are fashioned by the states, controversy will surround them. Some states have already begun to battle over what is called "outcomes-based" education, as political forces try to defeat that change and to revert to what they call "traditional schooling." These battles stem from a misunderstanding of standards-based reform, which is meant to focus on the acquisition of academic skills and not on affective development, but a broad brush is being used to tar any reform that is based on mastering subject matter. Other controversies will undoubtedly arise as political forces use the development of standards as a wedge to bring up social issues.

But these disputes must not distract us from seeing the importance of this major change in American education. The country is moving to a new way of schooling that will not only lead to a better education, but will also be fairer to both teachers and students in that they will know what is expected of them. The country is moving in the direction of truth in teaching and learning.

Note

1. This article is a revised version of an article that appeared in the June 1995 issue of the *Phi Delta Kappan.*

References

American Federation of Teachers. 1995. "Making Standards Matter: A Fifty-State Progress Report on Efforts to Raise Academic Standards." Draft version. Washington, DC: AFT.

Consortium for Policy Research in Education. 1994. "Shortfalls in 1980s Reform: Refocused Educational Strategies on the Results of Schooling." *R & D Preview,* July.

National Council on Education Standards and Testing. 1992. "Raising Standards for American Education." Washington, DC: National Council on Education Standards and Testing.

National Research Council. 1989. "Everybody Counts: A Report to the Nation on the Future of Mathematics Education." Washington, DC: National Academy Press.

New Standards Project. 1994. "Benchmaking Globally for High Standards Locally." *The New Standard,* Sept., pp. 1–2.

Office of Educational Research and Improvement. 1994. "What Do Student Grades Mean? Differences across Schools." Washington, DC: Office of Educational Research and Improvement.

O'Neil, John. 1995. "On Using the Standards: A Conversation with Ramsey Selden." *Educational Leadership,* Mar., p. 12.

Smith, Marshall S., and Ramon Cortines. 1993. "Clinton Proposals Will Challenge Students and the School Systems." *Philadelphia Inquirer,* June 24.

2

Professional Policy in Foreign Language Education: What It Is and How We Get It[1]

Helene Zimmer-Loew
American Association of Teachers of German

Imagine the leadership of the various foreign language associations sitting together with the deans of the major teacher-education programs in foreign language. Their purpose: to collaborate on the restructuring of their preservice and in-service programs to meet the needs of their graduates in a changing world. Together they will sample the present teacher corps, leaders of business and industry, legislators, school administrators, and others to determine their new direction. They will review the standards for state licensure developed for entry-level foreign language teachers and revise them wherever necessary. They may have to revise the standards for entry into the profession. Ultimately they will generate programs for experienced teachers at all levels of instruction to ensure a continuum in the ongoing effort to maintain their professional certification.

Now imagine a product of such a continuous teacher-development program, a young teacher of French, beginning his teaching career in an urban, multiethnic elementary school. Unlike countless new teachers who have preceded him, he is unlikely to quit his job in the next five years. Instead, he stands before his classroom of third graders with the knowledge and skills

Helene Zimmer-Loew (M.A., Middlebury College; M.S., St. John's University) has served as executive director of the American Association of Teachers of German since 1985. She has been president of ACTFL, NFMLTA, and JNCL-NCLIS and chair of the Northeast Conference. She is currently a member of the board of directors of the National Foreign Language Student Standards and the American Forum on Global Education. She has worked as an associate in the Bureau of Foreign Language Education in the New York State Education Department. Her last position in the department was acting coordinator of the Office of District Superintendents and the Resource Allocation Plan. She began her career as a teacher of German, Spanish, and English in high schools on Long Island, New York.

he needs. He has graduated from a nationally accredited preparation program, where he pursued a rigorous liberal-arts program, studied research-based pedagogy, and worked with real students in real schools.

This young teacher passed a battery of exams that assessed not only what he knows but whether he can put his knowledge into action. He has just completed a year-long, supervised internship in a professional-development school, one of many requirements in his state. He understands the diversity of children in this school and how they learn, prepares lessons to meet their needs, and can explain, from research and proven practices, how and why he makes decisions. He is looking forward to continuous professional development from the program in his school district and the professional associations of which he is already an active member. He plans to apply for national accomplished teacher certification as soon as he feels ready. In short, he is a professional.

These scenarios are almost within the reach of foreign language educators as the national movement toward professionalization of teaching moves forward.

This chapter will explore the overall efforts of the foreign language teaching field to establish itself as a profession and to develop professional policy about what is being taught and who is teaching it. It will also describe the field's activities over nearly three decades to establish and foster policy at the state and national levels, activities that in tandem with other more powerful organizations and forces will support its work to become a true profession.

The Characteristics of a Profession and the Role of Policy-Making

The phrase "professional policy" is an oxymoron when referring to foreign language education, in the opinion of some. Can we call the field of foreign language teaching a profession? And if we are a profession, have we developed professional policy, and how? First, the question of whether we are indeed a profession.

Model Profession

A true or model profession has a philosophy that explains its existence, its purposes, and its objectives and that orients and directs its activities in the continuing interest of others. It develops professional policies that then govern, often through legislation—one form of public policy—the professional work of its practitioner-members. Furthermore, professions possess a universally agreed upon body of specialized knowledge and theory that undergoes modification, making essential a long period of training preceding professional practice to be mastered by their practitioners (Powers et al. 1971).

The established professions, such as law, medicine, accounting, and physical therapy, use three quality-assurance mechanisms, which embody the profession's knowledge base and standards of practice: national accreditation of professional schools, state licensing of new practitioners, and advanced board certification of experienced practitioners (Wise 1994).

These professions, led by their elected boards of directors, have over the years created professional policy usually after thorough review and approval of the policies by their delegate assemblies and their membership. Often when professional schools are considering restructuring themselves, their leadership turns to their students, alumni, clients, corporations, and others for feedback on what they are doing and for recommendations on what they should be doing in light of changes in the environments in which their graduates will be working. Through this process, they are creating professional policy to guide them in their work, policy that may ultimately find its way into state legislation (Levine 1995).

A true profession supports a significant difference between the rewards of the highest and lowest paid, the most and least competent, the main fields and the subfields of the profession. It recruits able people to its ranks, people who are capable of the rigorous preparation demanded for membership. It is highly organized at the local, state, and national levels, maintaining its strength through communication among these levels.

A profession has a code of ethics and conduct more stringent than that of the state so that policing of professional conduct may remain primarily the responsibility of the profession itself. It recognizes its responsibility to those its serves and places their interests above its own. Because state legislators long ago required these professions to regulate themselves, the public generally places relatively high confidence in the fact that their practitioners operate according to established standards of practice (Powers et al. 1971).

A "Profession in Waiting"

Is the field of foreign language teaching a profession? Although the professionalism of many individual language teachers equals that of members of the established professions, our "profession" is perhaps best described as an "amateur profession" (Powers et al. 1971:29) or a "profession in waiting" (Wolk 1990). Schrier (1993) makes the distinction between foreign language teaching as a profession and as an occupation, stating that "professionalization

describes points along a continuum representing the extent to which members of an occupation *share a common body of knowledge and use shared standards of practice in exercising that knowledge on behalf of a defined clientele"* (Schrier 1993:106, emphasis in original).

Despite the fact that we are not yet a full-fledged profession, we are on our way, as demonstrated by

- The establishment of a political advocacy and policy coalition in Washington
- The development of language proficiency guidelines
- The recent publication of national K–12 foreign language standards
- Guidelines for foreign language teacher-education programs
- The development of professional standards for accomplished language teachers

As dismayed as we in foreign language education may be about our semi-professional designation, our status is no different from that of any other discipline in education. All the same, for the first time, we have the opportunity to achieve professional status in cooperation with the other major disciplinary organizations as well as the powerful national associations such as the National Council for Accreditation of Teacher Education, the Council of Chief State School Officers, and the National Board for Professional Teaching Standards, which command the attention of gatekeepers and policymakers at all levels of government.

The Status of Language Associations in the United States

The exact number of language associations in the United States at this time would be difficult to determine. The index of the most recent edition of the *Directory of Foreign Language Service Organizations* lists more than a hundred organizations and does not include the fifty-state foreign language associations (Behrens 1985). The large number of active associations must mean that there is a perceived need for them among their members, since membership is voluntary and demands a fee. Beginning with the Modern Language Association, the oldest (founded in 1883) and, to date, the largest, each organization has found a special audience to whom it appeals. Many are region-specific or state-specific; others are language-specific; still others, level-of-instruction-specific. Their foundings, in general, arose from the desire of a core group to provide better services for their potential constituency in the form of publications, conferences, seminars, local/regional meetings, instructional materials, professional development, and student programs, for example. Were we to add up the number of members in the national organizations alone, we could easily arrive at a figure over 90,000 (ACTFL 1995).

In an effort to bring about organizational unity and thereby greater influence for foreign language education, Benseler (1980) called for a merger of all national foreign language associations and regional conferences into the American Language Association. A strong ALA would replace what now exists: "a loose confederation [that] is essentially unreliable, encourages and allows needless duplication of services, wastes available resources, and leaves this profession with no strong voice in matters which concern it" (Benseler 1980:152). The ALA would have

> an organizational and administrative structure which would:
> * reflect the changing needs of the profession;
> * set standards of performance for itself and for those who gain entry to it; and
> * be comprehensible to its members." (Benseler 1980:153)

Benseler cites the success of the Joint National Committee for Languages (JNCL) as a sign that such unity is possible, and when such cooperation exists, success follows. His admonition to the field has, however, not even been seriously debated in the fifteen years since its publication. Perhaps it is time to consider his recommendations.

The Interaction of Public Policy and Professional Language Policy

Definitions

In order to understand professional policy, it is important to define public policy and its influence on professional policy. But first, we define professional policy here as a course or method of action that guides and determines the future direction of a profession, usually developed from within the profession itself with information and guidance from those making use of the services of its members.

Public policy can be defined as the implementation of laws, statutes, regulations, executive or administrative decisions, Supreme Court decisions, and treaties that determine public behavior. These laws, regulations, and decisions, especially when accompanied by appropriations, cause action.

In recent years there has been considerable discussion about a language policy for the United States similar to that of the Netherlands or Australia. In the Netherlands, the Ministry of Education and Science published *National*

Action Programme on Foreign Languages (Van Els et al. 1992). Because Dutch society has become increasingly international in outlook and supports the "vital importance of a knowledge of foreign languages," various government ministries cooperated to develop and implement a plan to include the study of foreign languages for all students at all levels. In Australia, a similar government policy is in effect. *A National Statement on Languages Other Than English for Australian Schools* (1993), which includes the official ratification by the Australian Education Council in 1989 of the place of languages other than English (LOTE), sets targets for an increase in participation rates of learners in LOTE by the year 2000.

Since the United States does not have a single, comprehensive foreign policy, a national health policy, or an environmental policy, discussions about a national education policy, much less a national language policy, are perhaps futile. Given the democratic, pluralistic, and diverse nature of American politics, we are governed by a variety of national, state, and local policies. They are the result of federalism's insistence on differentiating federal, state, and local authority and responsibility and a pluralistic democracy's give and take between competing interests as recognized in James Madison's *Federalist Paper #10*. In addition, the Constitution's separation of powers brings different perspectives from the executive, legislative, and judicial branches to all issues. Finally, the fluidity of our regular elections, new appointments, regulatory changes, influential interest groups, and media attention creates not only many policies but regular policy fluctuation.

Language Policy

What has this to do with professional language policy? A great deal over the last fifteen years. More often than not, public policy decisions influence or determine professional policy decisions. A recent example is the inclusion of foreign languages among the core subject areas in *Goals 2000* (1994), legislation that seeks to stimulate and support national educational reform efforts. As a result, federal funding was made available for the development of K–12 student standards for foreign languages. These standards will eventually have an impact on public policies affecting assessments and professional development.

Other public policy decisions that have influenced language policy include

- The *administrative* decision to close or realign certain military facilities for financial considerations that almost resulted in the elimination of the Defense Language Institute, one of the largest and most intensive language training facilities in the world

- Operation Desert Storm, which helped convince the Senate Intelligence Committee to develop *legislation* creating the National Security Education Program (NSEP), which supports institutions of higher education, undergraduate scholarships, and graduate fellowships in foreign language and international studies (A professional policy issue arose when a few area studies associations objected to the program's location in the Department of Defense.)
- The *Supreme Court*'s making of national language policy in the area of bilingual education and English as a Second Language with the *Lau vs. Nichols* (1974) decision, which insisted on the rights of students who spoke a language other than English to equal educational opportunities

The President's Commission

The report of the presidential commission *Strength through Wisdom* (President's Commission 1979) was perhaps the most dramatic recent event to influence foreign language teaching. National support for languages and international education was deemed inadequate. The importance of languages to such public policy concerns as national security, diplomacy, economic competitiveness, quality of life, humanitarian issues, international services, and rapidly changing global communications was called to the nation's attention by this presidentially appointed commission of language and area studies professionals, prominent educators, political leaders, and national policymakers.

The response to the report by language associations has taken the form of development of

- A set of guidelines to assess the proficiency of language learners by the American Council on the Teaching of Foreign Languages in 1986
- Guidelines that outline the necessary components of a model teacher-education program for entry-level foreign language teachers by the American Council on the Teaching of Foreign Languages in 1988 and a parallel document by the American Association of Teachers of Spanish and Portuguese in 1990
- Standards for entry-level and accomplished teachers by the American Association of Teachers of French in 1990 and the American Association of Teachers of German in 1992
- Content standards for foreign language learning by ACTFL, AATF, AATG, and AATSP in 1995

These efforts demonstrate the will of the foreign language occupation to move ahead on the continuum of professionalization (Schrier 1993).

The History of the JNCL-NCLIS

One of the President's Commission's major recommendations was the creation by the language and area studies associations of "a Washington presence." Language educators could no longer afford the luxury of isolationism and disinterest in national politics and its inherent policy process. The language and international studies community speaking with a unified voice had to become involved in shaping national policy, an important first step in addressing our nation's scandalous situation in these fields. The associations were to create a national coalition to address national policies and then engage in public advocacy on behalf of those policies. They were to become a *special interest group*. The commission recommended that the group organize and speak out in the public interest as far as it is consistent with its members' first amendment responsibilities to promote the national interest.

The Creation of JNCL-NCLIS

A year after the commission's report, the Joint National Committee for Languages (JNCL), a loose coalition of eight language associations that had already existed for four years to discuss professional foreign language association concerns, created a Washington office. In 1981, in collaboration with four additional language associations including English as a Second Language, bilingual education, and the classics, JNCL created a sister organization that was to eventually become the National Council for Languages and International Studies (NCLIS)—a public advocacy and action arm for the language and international studies associations.

Today the JNCL-NCLIS membership comprises more than sixty national, regional, and state associations dealing with the commonly taught languages, the less-commonly taught languages, English-as-a-second language, bilingual education, international education, international business education, translation and interpretation, and the classics.

Over the years, an effective strategy for shaping language policies has evolved in JNCL. This broad coalition serves as the forum in which the associations can discuss and develop unified public policy positions on professional issues affecting the schools, higher education, research, technology, teacher development, governmental programs, and business, among many others. NCLIS then seeks to mobilize the necessary support and influence policymakers to create the actual national (and recently state and local) laws, regulations, and administrative decisions that constitute public policies.

Legislative Accomplishments

The accomplishments of JNCL-NCLIS over the last decade testify to what a unified profession suggesting specific public policies can accomplish. At first, the organizations' positions were primarily reactive. They were seeking to protect the fewer than half-dozen federal programs from elimination or budget reduction. These included Title VI of the Higher Education Act, the National Endowment for the Humanities (NEH), the Fund for the Improvement of Postsecondary Education (FIPSE), and educational exchange programs such as Fulbright-Hays and the International Visitors Program. Initiatives recommended by the commission's report produced such legislative proposals as the National Security through Foreign Language Assistance Act or National Awards for Excellence in Foreign Language Teaching. Unfortunately, these met with little support from members of Congress and administration officials.

By the mid-1980s, however, consistent communication with national policymakers, testimony before numerous congressional and administrative hearings, the courting of legislative and executive policymakers, and the persistence of friends such as Senators Paul Simon, Christopher Dodd, and Claiborne Pell and Representative Leon Panetta began to show results.

Funding for international educational exchanges increased dramatically with a congressional mandate to quadruple them within four years. Some of the new exchange programs created were the Christa McAuliffe Fellowships, Samantha Smith Scholarships, the Congress-Bundestag Exchange, Central American Program of Undergraduate Scholarships, and the People-to-People Youth Initiative. Funding for Title VI—which had fallen to $17 million— began to increase until it was a $56-million-a-year program in 1995. Title VI was amended to include Centers for International Business Education and Research, and other programs were added for intensive summer language programs, foreign language periodicals, international internships, proficiency provisions, and entrance and exit language requirements. The NEH launched a new series of language-focused seminars for teachers at all levels of instruction and increased the number of foreign language initiatives. The Bilingual Education Act was amended to include a two-way development language program. The Education for Economic Security Act was passed, providing grants to the states for math, science, and foreign languages.

From 1985 to 1994 more than four dozen new national language and international studies programs came into existence, and in excess of $1 billion in new federal funding was awarded to kindergarten through postgraduate language programs. In many instances, the new programs were amendments to existing legislation. The new International Public Policy Institute and the National Foreign Language Resources Centers were added to Title VI in the 1991 reauthorization, and the Development of Language and Cultural Materials Program and the Critical Languages and Area Studies Consortia were added to Title V of HEA that same year. State Department reauthorization bills were amended to coordinate federal translation services, to centralize responsibility for foreign language training within the government, and to create model embassies where every staff member spoke the language of the country. Defense Department bills were amended to create a national linguistic reserve and military bonuses for learning another language. A Japanese Technical Literature Translation Center was added to the Commerce Department.

Entirely new programs addressing specific and pressing national needs were created as new legislation and then integrated into existing laws. The Foreign Language Assistance Act, for example, was first introduced by Representative Panetta and Senator Dodd as independent legislation. It was then integrated into the International Education for a Competitive America, part of a larger bill dealing with economic competitiveness. Foreign Language Assistance eventually became law as part of an Omnibus Trade Act. It then took two years to get the program funded in appropriations legislation, and it is now part of Title VII of the Elementary and Secondary Education Act. Other major legislative initiatives that benefited language study in one way or another were the Freedom Support Act, the National Writing Project Act, the National Literacy Act, the Soviet and East European Training Act, the National Endowment for Democracy, the U.S. Peace Institute, and the $150 million trust fund that is the National Security Education Program. Further legislation was negotiated in which languages and international education were major components but shared support with other professional and disciplinary areas, such as the Star Schools and the Fund for the Improvement of Education (FIE).

During the first two years of the Clinton administration, languages became a central component of sweeping educational reform acts. As mentioned above, foreign languages were added as one of the core subject areas in Goals 2000. Goals 2000 also created a new International Education Exchange program that included languages and ESL in provisions for technology and research. The Improving America's Schools Act reauthorized the federal commitment to elementary and secondary education and strengthened the ESL component in compensatory education. It also included ESL and foreign languages in the provisions for professional development and strengthened and broadened the Foreign Language Assistance Program.

Reasons for Success

In the public arena, JNCL-NCLIS activities have been successful because of a number of factors:

- Association unity
- Proactive strategies pursuing specific policy goals
- A JNCL-NCLIS staff well-versed in the national policy process
- A commitment of energy and resources by the member associations

These policy successes have also created new challenges. The most recent *Federal Funding Guide for Languages and International Education,* compiled by JNCL-NCLIS in 1995, now lists 105 national programs. Every year during the appropriations process, funding for these programs has to be protected. As the programs are reauthorized, suggestions from associations for changes and improvements are solicited, discussed, revised, and ultimately drafted in the form of amendments to the legislation. As national language and international education policies have developed, so have discussions (and sometimes disagreements) within the associations about the value of these programs, the best way to implement them, necessary programmatic changes, the use of resources, and a variety of other legitimate concerns. This far, JNCL and its members have been quite successful in keeping differences "within the family" and not having them spill over into the public policy realm. Professional unity has been a major factor in these successful efforts.

Developing Professional Policy through JNCL

In order to achieve and maintain JNCL unity, the member associations voice their opinions about what programs to create and defend to JNCL-NCLIS and receive information from JNCL-NCLIS about programs, their nature, the challenges they face, and their need for support and advocacy.

The JNCL policy committee serves as the organizer for policy discussions among its members, the JNCL-NCLIS board of directors, and, most important, the delegate assembly. At the meeting of the latter, delegates determine their preference for the professional topics to be discussed and acted upon during the upcoming year. Then, from intensive discussion of previous years' topics and other stimuli, they arrive at a consensus on a public policy statement. The policy committee works in consultation with the JNCL staff to organize that portion of the delegate assembly related to professional issues and public policy. The policy committee also encourages professionwide discussion of the topics identified by asking the delegates to return to their organizations and to encourage debate of the topics during workshops and seminars at state, regional, and national meetings. The committee provides the delegates with information and guidelines for such meetings.

Once policy has been agreed upon, the committee sends the policy statements to all organizations, which in turn publish the statements in their regular newsletters, bulletins, and bulletin boards on Internet or the World Wide Web. In addition, the national foreign language standards project has made possible the use of video conferences to stage forums in numerous locations throughout the country.

Finally, broader constituencies in education, business, the media, international organizations, and the public at large are being informed about the needs of the foreign language field.

The Role of the National Foreign Language Center

Another vehicle for developing policy is the National Foreign Language Center (NFLC), established in 1986 at the Johns Hopkins University. The NFLC, located in Washington, D.C., is this country's only comprehensive foreign language policy institute. Initial funding for the center was provided by four private foundations: the Exxon Education Foundation, the Ford Foundation, the Andrew W. Mellon Foundation, and the Pew Charitable Trusts. NFLC's overall mission is to improve the foreign language competency of Americans so that they are able to participate effectively in the global exchange of ideas and to compete in world trade and finance (NFLC n.d.). The purpose of its various activities is to play a leading role in formulating public policy that will make language teaching both within and outside the formal educational system more responsive to critical national needs. Through collaborative efforts with representatives from education, business, and government, the NFLC is involved in developing innovative strategies in language education reform. The NFLC draws on the expertise of individuals within the United States and abroad: educators and scholars, government officials, and corporate executives are involved in the center's seminars, conferences, and research projects.

According to a brochure published by the NFLC (n.d.), the primary focus of the center in its early days was the development of national foreign language policy. In its most recent brochure, however, it describes itself as a "non-profit research and policy institution focused on issues relating to language competency." The center's research supports "the informed allocation of resources for the improvement of U.S. capacity in languages other than English." Its agenda comprises a variety of complementary and mutually reinforcing endeavors, each of which is intended to contribute essential information to the discussion of language policy.

Although the center's research grants, study visits, seminars, and publications have no doubt benefited the professional leadership, the broad impact that it was expected to have had on the development of professional or public policy has yet to materialize. Under its new leadership, the center has made a notable effort to include more of those in the field who are politically engaged and who support the notion of a new context for language learning. The new leaders advocate the practical utility of knowing foreign languages and cultures, especially those essential to our future needs in national security, domestic concerns, and technology.

The center needs to play a leading role in developing policy by convening colloquia that will encourage constructive discussion of the educational mission of foreign and second languages and determine the most effective means to coordinate its work in critical areas of national need. The NFLC could then disseminate the results of such discussions to key members of the various language associations and the JNCL-NCLIS. Association leaders would, in turn, disseminate a policy statement for discussion and request endorsement or ratification as described in the section above. Ultimately, the NCLIS staff would transform the endorsed policy statement into legislation for Congress to consider.

Professionalism through Accreditation, Licensure, and Advanced Certification

Surely the greatest advance in professionalizing foreign language teaching can be achieved by developing the three components that characterize a profession: accreditation, licensure, and advanced certification.

For almost ten years, thousands of educators representing dozens of national organizations and disciplines have been developing two sets of national standards—one for experienced teachers and one for students. The two parallel movements are now being brought together by leaders who are convinced that all efforts to define what students should know and be able to do in various subject areas will be for naught if teachers themselves don't know the subject matter and aren't prepared to teach it.

The National Board for Professional Teaching Standards launched the teacher standards movement for advanced certification in 1987. Since then, it has made major strides in creating a voluntary national system to certify expert teachers. The board has approved assessments for eight certificates for the 1996–97 school year with almost thirty more planned over the next five years. The board recently named 176 National Board Certified Teachers for the Early Adolescence/Generalist and Early Adolescence/English Language Arts certificates (National Board for Professional Teaching Standards 1995).

In addition, standard setting for beginning teachers is well under way through a project supported by the Council of Chief State School Officers (CCSSO) called the Interstate New Teacher Assessment and Support Consortium (INTASC). This effort could affect licensure in most states, since thirty states are already represented on its board of directors (CCSSO 1995). The standards set for entry-level teachers by INTASC are compatible with the standards set by the National Board of Professional Teaching Standards. In both cases, the emphasis is on assessing teachers' actual performance, not in counting how many hours of course work they have completed.

Furthermore, proponents of professionalization are arguing that teachers should graduate from a nationally accredited program that meets vigorous standards and that they should continue to learn and grow on the job in order to qualify for accreditation by the National Board of Professional Teaching Standards. At present, 500 of the 1,300 current teacher-education programs are accredited by the National Council for Accreditation of Teacher Education (NCATE). This number, however, represents more than 80 percent of the teacher-education graduates who complete their work each year (Wise 1995). Since standards for licensure vary greatly among states, a national standard for accreditation of schools of education is a critical part of the professionalization of education.

Vision to Reality

The efforts of the foreign language field to establish itself as a profession have been accelerated by two recent events: the inclusion of foreign languages as part of the basics in Goal 3 of the National Goals and the recent publication of the national K–12 foreign language content standards. The issue of standards has begun to interest not only those teachers in our elementary and secondary schools, but also those in institutions of higher education. The sessions on standards at major national conferences such as ACTFL and MLA are filled to capacity. Furthermore, the five regional conferences and many state meetings have added major sessions dedicated to presenting and discussing the standards.

These efforts are, however, at the beginning of a long-term commitment to professionalization. Every opportunity for discussion and consensus must be used to determine professional policy. Our field will have to change to meet the higher standards it sets for its students and itself as well as those defined in collaboration with other organizations involved in the reform movement such as INTASC, NCATE, and the NBPTS.

With the creation of JNCL, foreign language organizations have made progress toward collaborating on the development of a common policy agenda. The National Foreign Language Center serves as yet another agent for discussion of professional and public policy as well as for planning and coordination of language programs at all levels. Working together, JNCL and the NFLC could prove to be a powerful force toward the goal of professional policy development.

Our image to the outside world is no longer characterized as lacking in focus and without communication and coordination among groups. It is a sign of progress and hope for the future that we have been able recently to overcome these barriers, to exchange, to discuss, and yes, to compromise when necessary in order to establish professional policy. Using the expertise of those within the field from kindergarten through the Ph.D., and adding to that strength the recommendations of parents, scholars, school and college administrators, elected officials, business executives, and the community at large, we may yet realize that professional vision of the young teacher of French described in the introduction of this chapter. We have at last the support and will necessary to move from the occupation end of the continuum to true professionalism.

Note

1. The author wishes to thank Dr. J. David Edwards, executive director of JNCL-NCLIS, for his assistance with the sections on public policy and legislation.

References

American Association of Teachers of French. 1989. "The Teaching of French: A Syllabus of Competence." *AATF National Bulletin* 15, Special Issue, October.

American Association of Teachers of German. 1993. "Professional Standards for Teachers of German." *Die Unterrichtspraxis* 26:80–96.

American Association of Teachers of Spanish and Portuguese. 1990. "AATSP Program Guidelines for the Education and Training of Teachers of Spanish and Portuguese." *Hispania* 73:785–94.

American Council on the Teaching of Foreign Languages. 1986. *Proficiency Guidelines*. Yonkers, NY: ACTFL.

American Council on the Teaching of Foreign Languages. 1988. "ACTFL Provisional Program Guidelines for Foreign Language Teacher Education." *Foreign Language Annals* 21:71–82.

American Council on the Teaching of Foreign Languages. 1995. *Desk Book*. Yonkers, NY: ACTFL.

Behrens, Sophia A. 1985. *Directory of Foreign Languages Service Organizations,* 3d ed. Orlando, FL: Harcourt, Brace Jovanovich.

Benseler, David P. 1980. "The American Language Association: Toward New Strength, Visibility, and Effectiveness as a Profession," pp. 143–56 in Thomas H. Geno, ed., *Our Profession: Present Status and Future Directions.* New York: Northeast Conference.

Council of Chief State School Officers. 1995. *States' Status on Standards: Findings from the Conference on Standards-focused Collaboration to Improve Teaching and Learning.* Washington, DC: CCSSO.

Goals 2000: Educate America Act. 1994. Washington, DC: Department of Education.

Lau vs. Nichols. 1974. United States Supreme Court. no. 72-6520.

Levine, Marsha. 1995. "21st Century Professional Education: How Education Could Learn from Medicine, Business and Engineering." *Education Week* 14,21, pp. 33–34.

National Board for Professional Teaching Standards. 1995. Press release, November. Detroit: NBPTS.

National Foreign Language Center. n.d. "Responding to America's Foreign Language Needs." Baltimore: National Foreign Language Center at the Johns Hopkins University.

National Statement on Languages Other Than English (LOTE) for Australian Schools. 1993. Carlton, Victoria: Curriculum Corporation.

Powers, James R., et al. 1971. "Professional Responsibilities," pp. 26–29 in James W. Dodge, ed., *Leadership for Continuing Development.* New York: Northeast Conference.

President's Commission on Foreign Languages and International Studies. 1979. *Strength through Wisdom: A Critique of U.S. Capability.* Washington, DC: Superintendent of Documents.

Schrier, Leslie L. 1993. "Prospects for the Professionalization of Foreign Language Teaching," pp. 105–23 in Gail Guntermann, ed., *Developing Language Teachers for a Changing World.* Lincolnwood, IL: National Textbook.

Van Els, T. J. M., et al. 1992. *The Dutch National Action Programme on Foreign Languages. Recommendations and Policy Reactions.* Nijmegen: Ministry of Education and Science.

Wise, Arthur. 1994. "Professionalization and Standards: A Unified System of Quality Assurance." *Education Week* 12,40, pp. 37,48.

———. 1995. Personal communication.

Wolk, Ronald A. 1990. "Profession in Waiting." *Teacher Magazine,* April, p. 3.

3

Standards and Foreign Language Teacher Education: Developing New Professionals during a Time of Reform

Audrey L. Heining-Boynton
University of North Carolina at Chapel Hill

Since 1989 when the National Council of Teachers of Mathematics published the first standards document, *Curriculum and Evaluation Standards for School Mathematics,* twelve other content areas have brought together professionals from their ranks to formulate content standards for their disciplines. In addition, numerous state education agencies have undertaken the development of standards and the means of assessing them for their K–12 students.

In the past, teachers have often been underinvolved participants in a broader educational policy. They have performed tasks and followed curriculum that for the most part has been written by someone else. For a long time, top–down management has been the norm, and the voice of teachers in policy development has been virtually nonexistent.

Suddenly, site-based management has plunged teachers into a leadership role, often with very little training on how to be a team member of a group larger than their grade level or subject area. Many teachers are now being asked to construct, write, and disseminate curriculum and policy, when before,

Audrey L. Heining-Boynton (Ph.D., Michigan State University) is an associate professor of education and Romance languages at the University of North Carolina at Chapel Hill. She has served as president of the National Network for Early Language Learning, vice president of the Michigan Foreign Language Association, and board member of the Foreign Language Association of North Carolina. She is a frequent presenter and curriculum consultant both nationally and internationally. She has written numerous articles for *Modern Language Journal, Foreign Language Annals, SCOLT Dimensions,* and *Central States Reports.* She is coauthor of *¡Animate! Content-Based Beginning Spanish* and has served as author and project director of federal grants. The North Carolina State Board of Education appointed her to its Professional Practices Commission.

the most extensive policy they had designed was that of their own classroom. Unlike at any time in the past, teachers are being held accountable for what and how well they teach. Today, classroom teachers are members of state and national standards-writing teams and committees, so along with greater accountability has come an increase in teachers' input on what students should know and be able to do as well as the subsequent assessments of these standards.

In addition, teachers have been used to either "covering the book," or following the department's or school's syllabus. Recently, though, these notions, concepts, duties, and beliefs have been turned upside down. Veteran teachers will admit that times have changed dramatically, and that their comfort zones are often violated. Today, a teacher's repertoire demands a knowledge not only of one's content area, but also of how to deal with students with special learning needs, how to address the multicultural issues of both school and community, and how to integrate into learning and teaching the many technological advances.

Therefore, if the teacher's role has changed, the assumption is that the way we train teachers must change. Also, if states, the federal government, and the content areas have reviewed, revised, and rewritten their standards to identify student expectations, should it not be assumed that the teacher-training profession should be doing the same?

What impact does the standards movement have on teacher education? What must universities do to keep pace with the evolution of and revolution in the profession? What role should professional organizations take in the development of future foreign language teachers? What are or should be some of the criteria to assess interns and initially certified teachers? What are other disciplines doing about the process? This article will explore the impact that national standards have had and will have on initial teacher-development programs in the field of K–12 foreign language teacher education.

Standards for Teacher Education

Before this most recent educational reform movement, teacher-education programs felt no pressure to change. Except for some minor fine tuning and updating, teacher development has remained relatively the same for decades. Then, quite suddenly, beginning in the mid to late 1980s, teachers were asked to participate in experiences and perform duties in which they had never been asked to participate before. In addition, student demographics have changed dramatically and radically. Up until recently, teachers have received little formal training to become decision makers, policymakers, and public-relations officials and to deliver instruction to a highly diverse population in a technologically explosive world. With the changing demands on the field has come the need to review and revise teacher education.

Research has revealed other serious reasons to reform teacher education. Goodlad (1991) called for the complete redesign of teacher education because of the following findings: a debilitating lack of prestige in the teacher-education enterprise; a lack of program coherence; the gulf between theory and practice; a stifling regulated conformity.

These facts may well contribute to the poor retention and recruitment of new teachers that the profession has experienced over the past decade. For example, in 1993–1994, nearly 20 percent of all beginning teachers in North Carolina did not return to the classroom the next year. In fact, nearly half of all first-year teachers will leave the classroom within four years (*Keystone* 1994).

The Need for Standards in Teacher Education

Until the end of the 1980s, teacher development had changed relatively little since the advent of the normal school. Beginning in the 1960s, though, researchers began to investigate teacher-education students. They discovered time and again that teacher-education students were among the least academically able of all college students (Carnegie Forum 1986; Koerner 1963; Vance & Schlechty 1982; Weaver 1979). Policymakers tend to blame institutions of higher education (IHE) for the problem, claiming that IHEs are not recruiting the most academically able candidates for the teaching profession (Boyer 1983; National Center for Education Statistics 1990; National Commission for Excellence in Teacher Education 1985). Also, in the 1970s, few states mandated examinations of teacher competence, such as the National Teacher Exam (NTE). The profession was attracting poorly qualified individuals, and there was little in place to act as a quality control. In foreign languages, reports proliferated of teachers who barely were able to speak the target language.

Reform in Teacher Education

Finally, in the mid to late 1970s, the teaching profession began to confront the problem. Teacher educators awakened to the fact that something had to be done to correct years of neglect and complacency. The profession needed ways of assessing the competence of future teachers. For example, by 1984 all but nine states had either adopted the NTE or a similar exam, were going to do so within three years, or were considering the adoption of one (Plisko & Stern 1985). The American Council on the Teaching of Foreign Languages (ACTFL) developed the Oral Proficiency Interview (OPI), which provided a way to ascertain the oral ability of an individual.

Besides requiring national testing as a way of assuring content competence, the American Association of Colleges of Teacher Education (1986) recommended a revamping of teacher education. AACTE proposed that IHEs, in partnership with school districts, develop alternative training programs that meet the following criteria:

1. Selective admission standards including but not limited to (a) a baccalaureate degree, (b) assessment of subject-matter competence, (c) assessment of personal characteristics, and (d) assessment of communication skills
2. A curriculum that provides candidates with the knowledge and skills essential to the beginning teacher
3. A supervised internship in which candidates demonstrate pedagogical competence
4. An examination that assures competence in the subject field and in professional studies

Concurrent to the publication of the AACTE's criteria, a group of concerned deans of schools and colleges of education founded the Holmes Group in 1985. The group, now including approximately ninety research universities across the country, formed a consortium dedicated to the improvement of teacher education and the upgrading of the teaching profession in general. In its first report, the group called for a more coherent link between the arts and sciences and teacher education (Stoddart and Floden 1995).

Professional Development Schools

Another development instituted to improve the training of teachers was the creation of Professional Development Schools (PDS). PDSs take teacher education into the schools, making the K–12 classroom the main site for preservice instruction rather than the university. PDSs also provide in-service instruction for participating school districts, and they also may confer clinical professor status upon classroom teachers who provide instruction for the preservice students. With PDSs, future teachers are present in and involved with the schools much more than they are during the early observational experiences and student teaching assignments of traditional teacher-education programs.

Professional Development Schools are an outgrowth of the national revision of teacher education and the implementation of higher standards in the profession. These programs of teacher training are also called "Fifth Year" programs. Five of the programs in place the longest, each with a different format, are at the University of Virginia, Stanford University, Louisiana State University, Michigan State University, and the University of Florida. When initially certified teachers graduate from these programs, they receive a master's degree in education from that institution. The programs differ in the number of credit hours they require, in when they admit students to begin the program (the most common entry point is either in the junior year of an undergraduate degree or at the beginning of the fifth year), and in their selection of a basic philosophy of teaching. What all PDS programs have in common is that a portion (if not all) of the teacher training that used to take place on campus now takes place in the schools. PDSs also elicit the assistance of classroom teachers in instructing the teacher interns.

Since the PDS model of teacher education is relatively new, no longitudinal research data is available. Future studies must ascertain the effectiveness of these programs and determine whether any model is more effective than the others. However, even though no empirical data are presently available, there appear to be a number of advantages to the PDS model. First, the extended period of time in the schools for preservice teachers should provide for a more thorough and realistic introduction into the profession. In addition, the universities create an agreement with local school districts to develop sites that will place and work with the PDS universities' student teachers before they accept student teachers from another university. This is extremely important in areas where many universities are vying for a few student teacher placements. Also, cooperating teachers, or clinical adjunct professors as they are sometimes called, go through extensive training before receiving a student intern. This provides an excellent opportunity for universities to introduce state-of-the-art teaching techniques to practicing teachers in a much more comprehensive way than in the past. It is hypothesized that the cadre of cooperating teachers will enhance their own classroom performance, and the students will receive better instruction.

Alternative Paths to Teacher Certification

Besides reworking traditional teacher-education programs, another popular option has been the creation of alternative certification programs now found in most states. These programs have evolved in response to the national teacher shortage in math, science, foreign language, and ESL, as well as from a concern about the caliber of new teachers coming from colleges and universities. Alternative path programs hope to address the main criticisms of traditional teacher-education programs: the novice teachers' lack of content knowledge and their inability to control and cope with today's students. Alternative certification streamlines teacher training by (1) recruiting individuals who already have a strong knowledge of their subject area and (2) providing these individuals with what is felt to be essential pedagogical information so that they may succeed in the classroom. Alternative certification provides a quick supply of teachers for areas in critical demand.

Nearly every state has alternative routes to teacher certification. They are typically administered by state departments of education or school districts. They allow college graduates a short preservice training and purport to provide continued training and support during the first year of teaching. There were eighteen states in 1986 that offered alternative paths to certification; in 1992, there were forty (Feistritzer 1993).

Alternative paths to certification have added a substantial number of teachers across the country. For example, between 1986 and 1991, more than 10,000 new teachers were recruited via alternative routes in nine states in the Southern Regional Board: Alabama, Florida, Georgia, Maryland, Mississippi, North Carolina, South Carolina, Texas, and Virginia (Corbin 1991). Texas enrolled 1,064 new teachers via the alternative path in 1989–1990 (Texas Education Agency 1990). The Los Angeles Unified School District recruited 1,100 new teachers into their alternative certification program between 1984 and 1990, many in the fields of bilingual education, math, and science (Stoddart 1992).

School districts, state departments of education, state legislatures, and universities have all been involved in the process. For example, in Los Angeles the district hires uncertified teachers, selected certified teachers in the school district deliver instruction to the certification candidates, and the district grants licenses to the candidates who meet the requirements of the Los Angeles Unified School District (LAUSD). An individual who has a baccalaureate degree and demonstrates subject-matter competence is given a fifteen-day orientation on policies, practices, and procedures of the LAUSD. They also take a two-year curriculum of course work and a one-week seminar on multicultural education. These courses and seminars are offered at a district training center and are taught by district teachers and administrators (Stoddart and Floden 1995).

In New Jersey, the teacher candidates spend twenty days in a classroom, supervised by an experienced teacher. The teacher candidate gradually assumes responsibility for the classroom. The candidates then participate in twenty weeks of professional education at a state regional training center, taught by university teacher-education faculty (Stoddart and Floden 1995).

Traditional versus Alternative Routes to Teacher Certification

The main differences between university-based and alternative teacher-training programs are the context and the content of the programs. With university-based programs, most of the instruction takes place on university campuses, while alternative paths provide training and instruction either exclusively in the schools or at a combination of sites, such as at a university, a state training center, and the school district.

The content of a university-based program requires more hours of formal instruction, but alternative certification programs typically require more hours of supervised field experience as a full-time teacher. Alternative routes focus more on teaching methods and classroom management than on subject matter, since the alternative-route candidate was deemed to be knowledgeable in their content area upon hiring (Darling-Hammond, Hudson, & Kirby 1989).

Traditional routes to teacher education and alternative paths are based on different philosophical beliefs. Those who believe in the traditional path feel that an individual requires several years of supervised preservice training. Those who believe in the alternative route maintain that individuals with subject-matter expertise can learn on the job with in-service training and support (Stoddard and Floden 1995).

Information on the effectiveness of alternative routes to teacher certification is lacking, even though the number of certificates via this path is proliferating. For example, no empirical data report whether these on-the-job trained teachers become effective teachers, or how long they stay in the profession. What has been noted is that alternative paths to certification are not always a solution to the teacher shortage. Darling-Hammond (1994) forcefully criticizes Teach for America, an organization that takes excellent arts and sciences graduates, and with minimal training, puts them in the classroom. Darling-Hammond notes that an individual with content knowledge, commitment, and sincerity still may lack important pedagogical skills needed to be an effective teacher.

Standards for Initially Certified Teachers

Up to this point, this article has explored the need for standards in teacher education. Are specific standards established for teacher education? ACTFL developed provisional program guidelines for foreign language teacher education in 1988. ACTFL formulated these guidelines before the standards movement took hold. How do these guidelines compare with more recent efforts of states and content areas? Who has created standards that are being used as the model for what initially certified teachers need to know? The group recognized as the model for teacher-education standards is the Interstate New Teacher Assessment and Support Consortium.

The Interstate New Teacher Assessment and Support Consortium

The Interstate New Teacher Assessment and Support Consortium (INTASC) was formed in 1987 to enhance collaboration among states interested in reforming teacher development and teacher assessment for licensing. Now sponsored by the Council of Chief State School Officers (CCSSO), thirty-six states are actively involved in the mission of creating standards for initially certified teachers. INTASC focuses on standards-based licensing of new teachers and works in collaboration with a number of other institutions and organizations that are involved with the creation of standards for teachers and the delivery of both preservice and in-service instruction for teachers. INTASC primarily collaborates with state education agencies, which includes state boards of education and professional standards boards. INTASC also includes members from key organizations such as the National Board for Professional Teaching Standards (NBPTS), the American Association of Colleges of Teacher Education (AACTE), the National Council for the Accreditation of Teacher Education (NCATE), the National Association of State Boards of Education (NASBE), the National Association of State Directors of Teacher Education and Certification (NASDTEC), the National Education Association (NEA), and the American Federation of Teachers (AFT.

INTASC's goal is to provide direction in the creation of teachers who are able to nurture, support, and encourage *all* learners. INTASC believes there is more to teaching than just covering the curriculum. To achieve these goals, teachers must have a deeper understanding of their subject, how knowledge is acquired and nurtured, and how individual differences affect learning (CCSSO 1994).

In 1992 INTASC proposed ten core standards that promote a systemic, performance-based approach to education, licensing, and the support of continued professional growth of teachers (CCSSO 1994).

The ten core standards for new teachers proposed by INTASC are

1. The teacher understands the central concepts, tools of inquiry, and structures of the discipline(s) he or she teaches and can create learning experiences that make these aspects of subject matter meaningful for students.

2. The teacher understands how children learn and develop and can provide learning opportunities that support their intellectual, social, and personal development.

3. The teacher understands how students differ in their approaches to learning and can create instructional opportunities that are adapted to diverse learners.

4. The teacher understands and uses a variety of instructional strategies to encourage students' development of critical thinking, problem solving, and performance skills.

5. The teacher uses an understanding of individual and group motivation and behavior to create a learning environment that encourages positive social interaction, active engagement in learning, and self-motivation.

6. The teacher uses knowledge of effective verbal, nonverbal, and media communication techniques to foster active inquiry, collaboration, and supportive interaction in the classroom.

7. The teacher plans instruction based on knowledge of subject matter, students, the community, and curriculum goals.

8. The teacher understands and uses formal and informal assessment strategies to evaluate and ensure the continuous intellectual, social, and physical development of the learner.

9. The teacher is a reflective practitioner who continually evaluates the effects of his or her choices and actions on others (students, parents, and other professionals in the learning community) and who actively seeks out opportunities to grow professionally.

10. The teacher fosters relationships with school colleagues, parents, and agencies in the larger community to support students' learning and well-being (CCSSO 1994).

These ten standards embody three essential characteristics. First, they are performance-based, describing what teachers should be able to do, not what courses need to be taken to receive a license. Second, they reflect the knowledge and skills required to develop learner-centered education. And third, they interlink with the standards created by the National Board for Professional Teaching Standards (NBPTS) for experienced teachers. The first standard addresses the requisite content-area knowledge; standards two through ten describe the pedagogical base that enables such teaching.

The INTASC standards furnish teacher-education professionals with the basis for revising both the content and the structure of their teacher-preparation programs. These standards focus on what teachers need to know and how they must translate that knowledge into effective practice in the classroom. They also contribute a framework between state teacher-education program review and approval and national program accreditation. The INTASC standards also provide a framework for institutions of higher education and state departments of public instruction to create performance-based assessments that lead to the initial certification of teachers (CCSSO 1994).

Mathematics was the first content area to work with INTASC to develop specific teacher-training standards for their discipline. They were also the first content area to begin and complete the writing of K–12 content standards for their field.

ACTFL has met with members of the INTASC board. The present plan is that ACTFL will use the INTASC guidelines as a basis for the revision of its teacher-education standards. In addition, ACTFL maintains conversations with the AACTE and intends to join the National Council for the Accreditation of Teacher Education (NCATE) to further strengthen the profession's ties with the production of high-quality initially certified teachers.

Beyond the Initially Certified: Standards for Career Teachers

In the spirit of total reform, the teaching profession is reviewing not only preservice and initially certified individuals. The NBPTS was instituted to certify highly proficient members of the field.

The National Board for Professional Teaching Standards

The NBPTS was founded in 1987. It resulted from a recommendation by the Carnegie Forum on Education and the Economy's Task Force on Teaching as a Profession (1986), which proposed the creation of national examinations for experienced teachers that would license them as other professions such as medicine, law, and accountancy are licensed.

In the 1994–95 school year, exams were completed in early adolescence, English language arts, and early adolescence/generalist. Presently, draft standards are approved for public comment and critique in eight more areas, and committees are finishing the standards for nine more fields. By the end of the 1990s, more than thirty certificates will be available or under development for all areas of K–12 teaching. Some of the areas under development at the present are science, mathematics, art, social studies, history, vocational education, and English as a new language (NBPTS 1994a). Foreign languages are slated to be included by 1997.

The NBPTS will not replace state licensure and the setting of criteria for initially certified teachers. Rather, it is establishing advanced standards for experienced teachers. It is offered on a voluntary basis (NBPTS 1994b). The NBPTS will collaborate with institutions of higher education to develop teacher-education programs that support the NBPTS (1994a).

The NBPTS's hope is that by making the career of teaching more professional, schools will be able to retain the best in the field as well as attract promising new teachers.

As was stated previously, the INTASC standards come from the work of the National Board for Professional Teaching Standards. There are a number of incentives for teachers successfully completing National Board Certification. Full or partial credential reciprocity exists between Alabama, Iowa, Oklahoma, New Mexico, and North Carolina. NBPTS fulfills professional development activities for licensure renewal in Colorado, Massachusetts, North Carolina, and Ohio, and in the local districts of Fairfax County, Virginia, and the District of Columbia. Mississippi and North Carolina provide salary supplements for National Board Certified teachers. New Mexico and North Carolina as well as Marlborough County, South Carolina, and Fairfax County, Virginia, provide release time for teachers to work on their portfolios or prepare for the assessment center (NBPTS 1995).

Recommendations for Improving Teacher-Education Standards

The U.S. Department of Education offered a series of recommendations based on a two-day meeting in March 1992 when K–16 educators from all fields came together to discuss ways of reforming teacher education along with school reform. Recommendations were made for state education agencies, districts and schools, institutions of higher education, professional organizations, U.S. Department of Education, and researchers. Many of their recommendations relate directly to the field of foreign language education and its effort to create content standards and revise existing teacher-education standards. The recommendations that pertain directly to initial certification programs in foreign language education are as follows:

State Education Agencies

- Support teacher-education programs that emphasize collaborative relationships among university and school staffs and clinical teaching experiences with diverse student populations
- Support efforts to improve the quality of teaching in institutions of higher education, especially in programs related to the preparation of teachers (Achieving World Class Standards 1993)

Institutions of Higher Education

- Develop strong liberal arts programs as prerequisites for teacher education
- Involve arts and science faculty in improving teacher education through integrating innovative teaching ideas in the arts and science courses themselves (Achieving World Class Standards 1993)

Professional Organizations

- Establish standards and assessments of student and teacher performance at school, state, and national levels
- Participate in decisions affecting preservice and in-service education, mentoring, and advanced professional development
- Support subject-area associations' efforts to establish standards-related teacher-education and licensing programs
- Collaborate across professional organizations to develop general and subject-specific pedagogical methods
- Use new technologies for education and encouraging collaboration among teachers (Achieving World Class Standards 1993)

U.S. Department of Education

- Support projects that establish and study the effectiveness of professional development schools
- Support efforts to develop professional teaching standards for initial licensure and for advanced certification of teachers (Achieving World Class Standards 1993)

Researchers

- Conduct research to test the influence of world class standards on improving teacher education, teaching, and student achievement
- Conduct research on characteristics of excellent teacher education, excellent teaching, and high levels of student achievement
- Research successful teachers and how they become educated
- Research models of productive collaboration among arts and science and education faculty to distinguish between real barriers and those that are myths (Achieving World Class Standards 1993)

Assessing Teacher Education

How do we know whether teacher educators are training quality teacher candidates? One way is by an outside evaluation of teacher-education programs at IHEs. One such review is done by the National Council for the Accreditation of Teacher Education (NCATE). NCATE is a rigorous accreditation group that thirty-six states use to approve teacher-education programs. Departments/schools/colleges of education spend at least a year before an on-site visitation by NCATE preparing written documentation to demonstrate that their institution is in compliance with the stringent standards that NCATE maintains. Teacher-education programs must describe and then demonstrate such things as linkage to arts and sciences, incorporating multicultural education in the curriculum, and a thorough advising program, both preservice and after licensure. NCATE has been working with the CCSSO and the NBPTS to develop a system of complementary standards so that accreditation, licensure, and certification demonstrate a progression of teacher mastery.

NCATE's revisions incorporate more performance-oriented accreditation standards, a state partnership framework linking accreditation of IHE programs to licensing results, teacher-preparation standards geared to specific content areas, and participation with other quality-assurance agencies in discussions about building the profession of teaching through a stronger quality-assurance system (Wise 1995).

NCATE standards are becoming more explicit and performance-oriented. For example, teachers should be able to use strategies for developing critical thinking and problem solving among their students. They should also be able to utilize both formal and informal evaluation strategies. Prospective teachers should be versed in technology and classroom management. They should be able to effectively collaborate with colleagues, parents, and others in the community. Prospective teachers must also be able to state why they have selected a particular teaching strategy. "In short, prospective teachers should demonstrate competence, needed knowledge, and acceptable proficiency" (Wise 1995:6). These skills come directly from the INTASC principles and those of the NBPTS.

Besides assessing general knowledge of teaching and learning, NCATE also reviews content-area preparation in fifteen disciplines such as mathematics and English. Guidelines are provided by specialty organizations, yet, to date, none are available for foreign languages.

Assessing Preservice Teachers

Evaluating the knowledge of preservice teachers has changed radically in the recent past. Many universities require student teachers to compile portfolios of what they have learned during their experiences toward initial certification. Some states are moving toward this model as a way of reviewing certification candidates, rather than only assessing college transcripts and courses taken.

Another revision is that of the National Teacher Examination (NTE). The series of exams has evolved into the Praxis series. The Praxis I assesses academic skills of basic proficiency in reading, mathematics, and writing. The Praxis II measures content-area knowledge. Preservice candidates in foreign languages may choose among tests on pedagogy as well as a variety of language-specific tests. Five exams exist in Spanish, four in French, two in German, and one each in Italian, Japanese, and Latin. Of the tests available in Spanish and French, each language provides a test entitled Productive Language Skills that is one hour in duration and requires the examinee to speak.

Over the past years, the Educational Testing Service has developed the Praxis III. This exam took seven years to develop, and currently six states use the system for licensing, preservice assessment, or beginning teacher support. This performance-based assessment employs trained local observers who use a common framework of criteria to evaluate the skills of teachers in their own classrooms. The assessment is administered during the teacher's first year of teaching. The criteria and the program for training assessors enable state officials to ascertain which provisionally licensed teachers merit a continuing license. There are nineteen criteria in four domains. The domains are

• Organizing content knowledge for student learning
• Creating an environment for student learning
• Teaching for student learning
• Teacher professionalism (Danielson and Dwyer 1995)

Foreign Language Content Standards and
Foreign Language Standards for Teacher Education

What connection do the foreign language content standards have with standards for preservice teachers and teacher-education programs? The answer can be summed up by Standard 5.2, which states that "students show evidence of becoming life-long learners by using the language for personal enjoyment and enrichment." Teacher-education programs must impart in the preservice teacher the desire to become a lifelong learner. In addition, initially certified teachers must themselves achieve strong proficiency in the four language skills and a strong knowledge of the target culture if they are going to assist their students in achieving foreign language Standards 1, 2, 3.1, and 4. And finally, it is through strong teacher-education programs that novice teachers will understand the need to cooperate with and reinforce subject areas other than foreign languages, thus helping their students see the relevance of foreign language study and fulfill Standard 3.1.

Conclusions and Recommendations

Never before has American education been subjected to such extensive review and revision. And in order for students to achieve the types of standards that we hold for them, teachers must exhibit an in-depth understanding of their subject matter, and they must model an investigative spirit. Teachers must also interact with others about teaching and have a clear focus on educational outcomes (Achieving World Class Standards 1993). All parties involved with teacher education are responding to the demands of K–12 schools and the kinds of individuals they require to provide instruction for our changing population.

What follows are a series of recommendations that we as foreign language educators should consider as we look to improve the profession. These recommendations reflect the ideas put forth in this article.

1. It is recommended that ACTFL and other foreign language associations pursue or continue to maintain close ties with INTASC, AACTE, NBPTS, NCATE, and any other national organizations concerned with the standards for teacher education and teachers.

2. It is recommended that we study, interact with, and benefit by the experiences of other successful K–12 disciplines such as mathematics, who are leading the way in standards projects for teacher education. By dialoging with individuals from other content areas, we can learn about successful techniques used to mount national reviews and assessments of not only content-area standards but also standards for teachers and teacher educators.

3. It is recommended that the AATs, NNELL, state foreign language organizations, and any other affiliated foreign language organizations join ACTFL in the review of ACTFL Provisional Program Guidelines for Foreign Language Teacher Education, on the basis of the work of the NBPTS and INTASC.

4. It is recommended that teacher-education programs be revised to incorporate training for K–12 foreign language educators.

5. It is recommended that we not only incorporate in our teacher-education programs a strong component of content knowledge, methodology, and developmental psychology, but also prepare our future foreign language teachers to become effective political activists who can defend the rights of all students to study a foreign language in a long, uninterrupted sequence.

References

Achieving World Class Standards. 1993. *The Challenge for Education Teachers. Proceedings.* Barbara Lieb, comp. Washington, DC: United States Department of Education; Office of Educational Research and Improvement.

American Association of Colleges of Teacher Education. 1986. "Alternative Certification: A Position Statement of AACTE." *Journal of Teacher Education* 36,3:24.

Boyer, Ernest. 1983. *High School: A Report on Secondary Education in America.* New York: Harper and Row.

Carnegie Forum on Education and the Economy's Task Force on Teaching as a Profession. 1986. *A Nation Prepared: Teachers for the Twenty-first Century.* New York: Carnegie Corporation.

Corbin, W. 1991. *Facts and Figures for South Carolina's Critical Needs Certification Program.* Rock Hill, SC: Winthrop College.

Council of Chief State School Officers. 1994. *Model Standards in Mathematics for Beginning Teacher Licensing and Development: A Resource for State Dialogue.* Washington, DC: Interstate New Teacher Assessment and Support Consortium, Mathematics Sub-Committee.

Danielson, Charlotte, and Carol Dwyer. 1995. "How Praxis III Supports Beginning Teachers." *Educational Leadership* 59,6:66–67.

Darling-Hammond, Linda. 1994. "Who Will Speak for the Children? How 'Teach for America' Hurts Urban Schools and Students." *Phi Delta Kappan* 76,1:21–34.

Darling-Hammond, L., L. Hudson, and S. Kirby. 1989. *Redesigning Teacher Education: Opening the Door for New Recruits to Science and Mathematics Teaching.* Santa Monica, CA: Rand Corporation.

Feistritzer, C. E. 1993. "National Overview of Alternative Teacher Certification." *Education and Urban Society* 26,1:18–28.

Goodlad, John. 1991. "Why We Need a Complete Redesign of Teacher Education." *Educational Leadership* 49,3:4–7.

Keystone: A Newsletter for Business & Personnel Administrators. 1994. Nov.

Koerner, J. 1963. *The Miseducation of American Teachers.* Baltimore: Penguin.

National Board for Professional Teaching Standards. 1994a. *Teacher Pioneers.* National Board for Professional Teaching Standards 1993 Annual Report. Detroit, MI: NBPTS.

National Board for Professional Teaching Standards. 1994b. *What: What Teachers Should Know and Be Able to Do.* Detroit, MI: NBPTS.

National Board for Professional Teaching Standards. 1994c. *Why: Why America Needs the National Board for Professional Teaching Standards.* Detroit, MI: NBPTS.

National Board for Professional Teaching Standards. 1995. *The Candidate Connection: A Newsletter for Candidates Seeking National Board Certification.* Detroit, MI: NBPTS.

National Center for Education Statistics. 1990. *New Teachers in the Market, 1987 Update.* Washington, DC: U.S. Department of Education.

National Commission for Excellence in Teacher Education. 1985. *A Call for Change in Teacher Education.* Washington, DC: American Association of Colleges of Teacher Education.

Plisko, V. W., and J. D. Stern. 1985. *The Condition of Education.* Washington, DC: United States Department of Education, Office of Educational Research and Improvement, National Center for Educational Statistics.

Stoddart, Trish. 1992. "The Los Angeles Unified School District Intern Program: Recruiting and Preparing Teachers for an Urban Context." *Peabody Journal of Education* 67,3:84–122.

Stoddart, Trish, and Robert E. Floden. 1995. *Traditional and Alternate Routes to Teacher Certification: Issues, Assumptions and Misconceptions.* East Lansing, MI: National Center for Research on Teacher Learning, Michigan State University.

Texas Education Agency. 1990. *1990 Alternative Teacher Certification in Texas.* Austin, TX: TEA.

Vance, V., and P. C. Schlechty. 1982. "The Distribution of Academic Ability in the Teaching Force: Policy Implications." *Phi Delta Kappan* 64,1:22–27.

Weaver, T. M. 1979. "The Need for New Talent in Teaching." *Phi Delta Kappan* 61:29–46.

Wise, Arthur. 1995. "NCATE's Emphasis on Performance." *Quality Teaching: The Newsletter of the National Council for Accreditation of Teacher Education* 4,3:3–6.

4

A Collaborative Approach to Professional Development

Eileen W. Glisan

Indiana University of Pennsylvania

> the present pattern of professional development activity reflects an uneven fit with the aspirations and challenges of present reform initiatives in subject-matter teaching, equity, assessment, school organization, and the professionalization of teaching. . . . Professional development must be constructed in ways that deepen the discussion, open up the debates, and enrich the array of possibilities for action. (Little 1993:148)

If the new standards are to have a significant impact on the foreign language profession, language teachers who are currently in the classroom must play a key role in bringing about the necessary reform. Many studies dealing with implementation of standards cite professional development as one of the most important vehicles for helping teachers to deal with changing educational needs of the American public (Leighton and Sykes 1992; Sparks 1994; Wagner 1993). Professional development has also been highlighted as a key factor in current reform efforts underway by the states. In a survey conducted by Inman and LaBouve (1994) for the Joint National Committee for Languages, forty-three states reported including professional development as a part of their reform plans, while twenty-four states reported that professional development and teacher training are among the most important elements of reform. The professional literature has also stressed the value of involving teachers *themselves* in setting high standards, reconceptualizing the school curriculum, designing new assessments, and training new teachers (Laws 1991; Ravitch 1992).

Eileen W. Glisan (Ph.D., University of Pittsburgh) is professor of Spanish and coordinator of the Secondary Education/Spanish Program at Indiana University of Pennsylvania. She is coauthor of *Teacher's Handbook: Contextualized Language Instruction* and *Enlaces* (an intermediate Spanish program), author of many chapters and articles on language pedagogy, and a frequent workshop presenter and consultant to school districts. She is certified by ACTFL as an oral proficiency tester of Spanish. Currently on the board of directors of the Northeast Conference on the Teaching of Foreign Languages, she will be chair of the 1997 Northeast Conference.

While the need for professional development in today's era of standards may be clear to most, the manner in which in-service help might best be delivered is still unclear, partially because of the number of factors to be addressed. For example, Mesicek (1993) cites the following new roles of the classroom teacher that are essential today in raising standards and realizing educational reform:

- Teachers must meet the needs of an increasingly diverse student population.
- Teachers must keep up with an ever-expanding body of research-based information on effective teaching and effective schools.
- The role of the teacher is changing from that of a "dispenser of knowledge" to that of a "facilitator of learning."
- The role of the teacher is expanding beyond the scope of the classroom.
- Universities and teacher-education programs must become more collaborative (pp. 8–9).

Several subject-matter areas have recognized the paramount role of professional development in implementing new standards and reform. The National Council of Teachers of Mathematics (NCTM) has initiated a network of grant-funded projects in order to disseminate information about the new mathematics standards for students and teachers and to provide the training and support teachers need to initiate reform changes in the classroom (Carlson 1992; Hala 1995). The math and science professions have suggested that school leaders give teachers time to participate in in-service programs and that universities offer courses when teachers are free to take them, such as in the late afternoons and evenings (U.S. Dept. of Education 1993). In the opinion of many science professionals, the standards may provide more opportunities for team teaching and should free teachers to explore subjects in greater depth and reflect on the significance of the content (Speece 1993). The National Council for the Social Studies (NCSS), in an effort to promote systematic professional development opportunities for teachers, has developed an advanced certification procedure that requires teachers to provide evidence of continued learning and professional involvement (Biemer 1993). Similarly, the American Association of Teachers of French (AATF) and the American Association of Teachers of German (AATG) have proposed a procedure whereby teachers could receive a national license in addition to state certification. The advanced certification procedure being developed by the AATG is based on the model developed by the National Board for Professional Teaching Standards (NBPTS) (Lafayette 1993).

How will in-service foreign language teachers be equipped with the skills necessary for addressing the new standards? The present article attempts to respond to this important question that must be answered if the standards are to serve as a catalyst for reform in how languages are taught in the classroom. Before exploring the question, the article examines several issues that affect the way in which professional development is designed: characteristics of today's foreign language teachers, the internal and external obstacles to reform in classroom teaching, and current types of professional development opportunities offered to teachers of foreign languages. The article then explores new considerations for making a better fit between professional development and reform efforts. Using several guiding principles, the article suggests new avenues for assisting in-service teachers in basing instruction on the standards by means of collaborative professional development efforts at various levels.

Who Are Today's Foreign Language Teachers?

Identifying the characteristics of today's foreign language teachers can enable us to understand the professional development needs of the in-service sector of the profession.[1] According to data compiled from Wolf and Riordan's (1991) survey of foreign language teachers associated with a state foreign language organization, today's language teacher is likely to be a white, middle-aged woman who has taught for some twenty-one years and has earned both bachelor's and master's degrees. Brickell and Paul's (1981) study reflected some disturbing findings on the type of preservice preparation that teachers were reporting: only 50 percent of teachers surveyed had ever studied in a foreign country and the teachers indicated that they had spent at least half their time in college foreign language classes studying literature. One would hope that a more recent survey would yield much different results. However, Schrier's (1989) study of foreign language teacher-preparation programs in four-year colleges and universities indicated that preservice preparation has changed very little in recent years. For example, she found that 56 percent of the 500 responding institutions still placed a heavy emphasis on the study of literature. Further, within pedagogical course work, only 23 percent of preservice teachers reported having the opportunity to explore instructional techniques that include modern technology. These studies point to the likelihood that a large number of beginning teachers are graduating from institutions that fail to provide the type of preparation they need in linguistic skills, cultural awareness, and pedagogical expertise. This lack of preservice preparation magnifies the importance of in-service training and continued professional development opportunities for beginning teachers. Clearly new studies are needed in order to continue to verify these findings and to examine the characteristics of foreign language teachers who will be in the classroom as we move into the next century.

Present Obstacles to Reform: A Case Study Approach

In order to clarify the scope of the task to be undertaken in in-service programs, it is necessary to explore the obstacles that must be overcome so that extensive reform may occur. The principal obstacles are presented below in the form of case studies that represent *true* scenarios experienced by this author. The obstacles are divided into (1) internal factors (those created within the foreign language teaching community) and (2) external factors (those brought about by individuals or situations outside the realm of foreign language teaching).

Internal Factors

Unfortunately, many times our profession is its own worst enemy. Often individuals enter the teaching profession for the wrong reasons: they perceive the job to be easy; it's a "fall-back" profession in case another career isn't successful; it's nice to have summers off from work. What is the result? Classrooms across the country are staffed by many language teachers who do not take their profession seriously enough to want to continue their own professional development. They perceive little need for updating their pedagogical knowledge or language skills. Since they are sometimes not required by the state or school district to update their skills, they become entrenched in the approach to teaching they learned as undergraduate education majors or experienced as students and choose not to change. They delude themselves into thinking that what they have been doing in the classroom for many years is satisfactory; besides, it's too much work to change the textbook, the tests, the work sheets!

Case Study 1: Teacher Beliefs about Professional Development. Perhaps this problem relates to the perceptions that teachers have about their roles as professionals. Schrier (1993) distinguishes between teaching as an *occupation*, a way of making a living, and teaching as a *profession*, a vocation that involves a system of advanced learning. This difference in perception can clearly be seen in the following case study of two foreign language teachers.

Ms. Drummond is a German teacher at a mid-sized urban high school, where she has been teaching for fifteen years. She has kept up to date with current teaching trends and is considered to be an effective teacher. She has developed a communicative approach to teaching and now teaches grammar as a tool for meaningful interaction rather than as an end in itself. Ms. Drummond attends conferences and workshops regularly, most of them on her own time such as on weekends and in the summer. She often becomes discouraged, however, since she has experienced difficulty in working with many of her colleagues to strengthen their language program. Some of her colleagues do not share Ms. Drummond's enthusiasm for teaching and her desire to continue learning. They feel that they have learned all there is to know about teaching; since they are often not paid to attend workshops, they don't feel they should have to give up their free time for professional development.

One day in the foreign language office, Ms. Drummond was talking to Mrs. White, a veteran Spanish teacher of twenty-two years, who hasn't changed her teaching much over the years. Mrs. White was very upset, as she was quite often, because she claimed that her students weren't able to use descriptive adjectives appropriately in Spanish. She began a ten-minute monologue, blaming students because they don't have any commitment to learning these days. When Ms. Drummond attempted to share some ideas with Mrs. White concerning innovative approaches to teaching grammar, Mrs. White pulled out a work sheet and defensively explained how she has students practice using descriptive adjectives so that they can see the difference between their native language and the target language. Ms. Drummond read the following work sheet:

> Translate the following into Spanish, keeping the proper word order.
>
> 1. I have a car red.
> 2. Do you have a sister tall?
> 3. I'm wearing a sweater blue.
> 4. She buys gloves black.
> 5. I like books interesting.

Ms. Drummond, who was more than confused at seeing the work sheet, asked Mrs. White why the English word order wasn't correct. Mrs. White explained that students just can't remember to put the adjective after the noun in Spanish, and that, in this way, they'll be reminded. Ms. Drummond nodded in disbelief and excused herself from the room. She felt a sense of despair as she wondered how Mrs. White and teachers like her could ever be convinced to change their approaches to teaching when they seem reluctant to learn new ideas.

This scenario illustrates a key internal problem among many foreign language teachers: the lack of commitment to teaching as a *profession.* This dilemma is particularly apparent in foreign language classrooms, given that language teaching has changed so dramatically over the past ten years, while in many cases, teachers' knowledge and skills have not changed. Perhaps this lack of professional commitment is the result of the many obstacles teachers face daily, identified by Leinwand (1992) as collegial isolation, professional isolation, lack of confidence and fear of change, fear of failure, lack of support, and insufficient time. How do we assist teachers in overcoming these obstacles? How do we help teachers to develop a more professional attitude toward change? How can teachers be given greater responsibility for their own professional growth? These are among the questions to be considered as we examine the possibilities for developing a collaborative professional development effort.

External Factors

Foreign language teachers themselves have the power to change the internal problems described in the previous section. However, there are many obstacles to reform that come from outside the teaching community itself and over which we have less control. They include level of preservice preparation, state policies, lack of collaboration between universities and school districts, and school-level misconceptions about foreign language pedagogy. A case study illustrates each of the above factors.

Case Study 2: Level of Preservice Preparation. Preservice foreign language teachers are at the mercy of their preservice preparation programs. As the following case study illustrates, undergraduate education majors may not even realize that their teacher-preparation programs are less than adequate until they enter the classroom as certified teachers.

Dr. Winston is a professor of Spanish and teaching methodology at a mid-sized state university. She coordinates the Spanish education program and provides in-service and professional development opportunities for area foreign language teachers. She and her colleague, Dr. Echeverría, a professor of Spanish language and literature, teach a two-week institute for Spanish teachers each summer. Dr. Winston teaches the morning session devoted to pedagogical innovations while Dr. Echeverría teaches the afternoon session, which features immersion in Spanish through exploration of cultural concepts. Participating teachers have the opportunity to interact with native Spanish speakers, use Spanish to speak to one another about interesting topics, expand their cultural awareness, update their knowledge about effective pedagogical practices, present practice teaching lessons, and prepare materials for use in their own classes.

This past summer twenty-two teachers enrolled in the Spanish institute. Most of the participants were teachers who had attended the institute in previous years, while a few were newcomers to this workshop format. During the first morning session, Dr. Winston engaged teachers in thinking about their individual approaches to teaching and imagining how a visitor would react to what they see happening in their classrooms. The discussion that ensued enabled Dr. Winston to review some basic pedagogical principles with the teachers while involving them in self-reflection. At the conclusion of the first morning session, one of the teachers asked to speak to Dr. Winston privately. Lauren Pistella, a beginning teacher of Spanish, had just finished her first year of teaching in a rapidly expanding suburban school district. One of her colleagues, who was a former student of Dr. Winston, had convinced Lauren to participate in the institute with him. Lauren was extremely upset after experiencing the first three hours at the institute. She confessed to Dr. Winston that, although she had just graduated from her teacher-training program one year ago, the only training she had received was in the audiolingual methodology (ALM). She learned to do pattern drills, help students to memorize dialogs, and create multiple choice and translation tests. Her student teaching experience provided additional experience in teaching with ALM, as her cooperating teacher was a firm believer in the method. Lauren acknowledged, somewhat embarrassingly, that ALM was the only way she knew how to teach and that she had used this method throughout her first year of teaching. One would have assumed that Lauren, having just graduated, would have known more about innovation in teaching than her peers who had graduated much longer ago. The sad fact was, however, that she had invested in a four-year teaching preparation program that had enabled her to graduate in 1993 and had prepared her to teach in the 1960s.

Heining-Boynton, in this volume, discusses in detail the preservice preparation of foreign language teachers. The impact of new teacher preparation is mentioned here again, since it has an effect on the need for in-service teacher training. Fortunately, Lauren in the previous case study recognized the need for professional development. Many teachers who receive the same type of teacher preparation, however, do not seek professional renewal either because they fail to realize the magnitude of their professional inadequacies or they are too embarrassed to interact with more capable peers.

Case Study 3: State-Level Policies. Another external obstacle to reform involves state policies, perhaps the most important of which are the certification policies. Some states have tended to be less than rigorous in their standards for teacher certification and professional development. A common problem encountered today, particularly as former teachers reenter the profession, is the issue of second certification and granting of emergency teaching certificates. The following case study describes this problem and the difficulties that can arise between school administrators and foreign language teacher-preparation programs.

Dr. Andrew Beecher is a professor of French and foreign language education at Greensburg State University, where he also coordinates the French education programs. During his ten years at the university, he has worked diligently to raise standards in order to ensure that those students who obtained teacher certification were well qualified and would be excellent teachers. He developed outcomes for each year of the program, together with an oral proficiency requirement that must be attained prior to student teaching. In recent years, Dr. Beecher has seen an increasing number of graduate students who have returned for a second certification in French. These returning students must adhere to the same requirements as those in the undergraduate program, with the exception that in some cases they are required to complete only a half semester of student teaching, depending on the extent of their teaching experience. When Dr. Beecher came to Greensburg State, the language departments had had an agreement that students who were completing certification requirements in a second foreign language would need to complete only twenty-four course credits instead of thirty-six. Dr. Beecher managed to change this, recognizing that many students took advantage of this loophole and were not developing the necessary level of proficiency in the second foreign language. Now the requirements are the same for each area of language certification, including the proficiency requirement, no matter how many languages the student chooses to pursue. Dr. Beecher feels that it is better for a student to have one area of certification and be very strong in that area than to have a mediocre level of proficiency in two languages.

Today Dr. Beecher received a telephone call from Dr. Regis Cilo, an assistant superintendent of one of the local school districts. Dr. Cilo was seeking information about certification requirements for one of his teachers, whose first area was Spanish and who wanted to be certified in French. According to Dr. Cilo, this teacher had been granted emergency certification in French so that she could teach a few French classes. The teacher had completed twelve credits of French a few years ago and had never visited a French-speaking country. Dr. Cilo wanted to know how she could obtain "quick certification" so that she could continue to teach both French and Spanish for the district. Dr. Beecher explained to Dr. Cilo that Greensburg State did not support quick avenues to certification because they believe in teacher education of high quality. He suggested that the teacher take a leave and return to the university full-time to complete the certification requirements, including perhaps a summer study-abroad program. Dr. Cilo was astonished that the university couldn't provide independent study courses to satisfy the requirements, for after all, if you teach one foreign language, you could certainly teach another. Further, he added, the university should require students to major in two languages, because teachers with only one area of certification are useless to school districts. He told Dr. Beecher that he intended to call the dean of the College of Education to discuss this matter with him.

According to a recent fifty-state survey of legislative and administrative actions, forty-six states permit individuals to apply for emergency or shortage-driven credentials (AACTE 1993). Studies of teachers who enter the profession through quick alternative routes have found that these teachers experience difficulties with curriculum development, pedagogical content knowledge, students' learning styles and levels, classroom management, and student motivation (Darling-Hammond 1991; Lenk 1989). Beginning teachers who lack full training show more ignorance about student differences and needs and about basic methodology than do fully trained beginners (Rottenberg and Berliner 1990). Clearly, in-service preparation is particularly important for foreign language teachers entering the profession without the necessary knowledge base and teaching experiences. Our profession must confront the issues of emergency certification and requirements for teachers seeking certification in a second foreign language, while educating school administrators about the effect of these issues on the quality of instruction in foreign language classrooms.

A related problem at the state level involves the decline in the number of foreign language specialists who are equipped with the skills necessary for providing in-service opportunities. In Inman and LaBouve's (1994) survey of state activities, most state supervisors reported that their states were beginning to use education generalists instead of curriculum specialists in various content areas. Only twelve supervisors reported working only on foreign languages; twenty-three were in charge of foreign languages and other disciplines; three were called "education generalists"; and twelve states have eliminated the foreign language supervisor position or have no individual assigned to work on foreign language education.

Case Study 4: Lack of Collaboration between Universities and School Districts. Much of the literature dealing with reform in education has stressed the importance of collaboration between faculty in schools and in higher education (Goodlad 1991; Olson 1992). The following case study illustrates why collaboration between university and school faculty in foreign languages is often not possible.

Dr. Brian Monaghan is a second-year assistant professor in the Department of German at a major research university. The department is housed in the College of Arts and Humanities. Since his primary area of research is applied linguistics and foreign language pedagogy, he was given the task of training and supervising the department's teaching assistants. He expressed an interest in supervising student teachers as well, but that responsibility lies with the university's College of Education. During the end of his first year as an assistant professor, Dr. Monaghan became involved with a local collaborative made up of foreign language teachers in secondary and postsecondary instruction. He conducted a few workshops for some local school districts and was asked to serve as editor of the state language journal. In a discussion with the dean of the College of Education, he expressed his interest in working on the student teaching program with the college and the public schools.

Today Dr. Monaghan was asked to see the dean of his college, Dr. Brenda Radica, for his second-year evaluation. Dr. Monaghan wasn't worried, for he knew that he had been working around the clock to prove himself as a new professor in the department. He was much surprised, however, by these comments from his dean: "Now, Brian, you've published a few articles over the past two years, which is great. But I also see that you've become involved in various efforts with public school teachers. Well, I need to be honest with you. If you expect to receive tenure and promotion, you'll need to focus your efforts on the areas that count here, that is, scholarly work, publications. You're wasting your time on these other activities that will not matter to the tenure and promotion review board." An astonished Dr. Monaghan replied, "But, Dr. Radica, I think that collaboration with the public schools is so important in bringing about more effective instruction on both sides." "But that's not your concern," interrupted the dean. "You just worry about your tenure and promotion," she reiterated sternly. As Dr. Monaghan left the dean's office, he wondered if he really belonged in an institution that only valued scholarly publications.

This scenario is more common than one would like to believe. Major research institutions have faculty and resources that could be very helpful to public school districts and teachers. Closer collaboration could benefit faculty and programs in both sectors. However, many faculty in higher education are told that this type of collaboration will result in negative faculty evaluations and failure to receive tenure and promotion. It behooves our profession to attempt to convince institutions of higher learning that the efforts of faculty with public school personnel are significant contributions to the field. We need to think carefully about whether we will be able to accomplish the goals of the standards without the support and assistance of university faculty.

Case Study 5: School-Level Misconceptions about Foreign Language Pedagogy. Quite often school districts themselves pose obstacles to reform. The following case study illustrates the conflict between an assistant principal and a Spanish teacher over innovations in teaching.

Ms. Barbara Sullivan is a Spanish teacher at a suburban multicultural high school. The district, which has a 40 percent minority student population, is the result of a merger of three districts that were combined under a federal court order in order to achieve greater racial and socioeconomic equity of the student body. Ms. Sullivan, one of four Spanish teachers at the high school, has been teaching for some twenty years. Unlike her colleagues, however, she has kept abreast of teaching innovations, attending conferences regularly, participating in the state foreign language association, and serving as a cooperating teacher for the local university. Over the years she has changed her approach to teaching in order to involve her students in more communicative language use and hands-on learning.

Last week Ms. Sullivan was observed by Mr. MacDonald, newly appointed assistant principal, who had been transferred from one of the junior high schools in the district. Mr. MacDonald had a reputation among the teachers for not having a great deal of expertise in current classroom practices; in fact, his classroom observation reports were described as "being a joke." The class that Mr. MacDonald observed was a Spanish IV class that was working on epic poetry. As always, Ms. Sullivan used Spanish throughout the entire period, engaged students in small-group work to perform comprehension tasks dealing with a new poem, elicited class discussion in Spanish about the poem, and had students brainstorm ideas in pairs for composing their own epic poems. Students' desks were arranged in groups of four in order to facilitate group work. After the class had concluded, Ms. Sullivan felt very good about the class, since students were on task, spoke in Spanish, and accomplished the lesson objective. Later in the day, Mr. MacDonald had a postobservation conference with Ms. Sullivan, at which time he told her that her class was the worst class he had ever visited because there was too much chaos, students were talking out of turn without raising their hands, the lesson objective wasn't obvious, and the atmosphere was too informal; to make matters worse, students didn't even use the textbook or workbook! Ms. Sullivan attempted to offer a rationale for what she had done with the students; however, Mr. MacDonald refused to listen and told her that he would visit the class again next week.

So today Mr. MacDonald returns to Ms. Sullivan's Spanish IV class. Ms. Sullivan decides to play the game Mr. MacDonald's way in order to receive a positive evaluation. She places the students' desks back in rows and gives students work sheets that deal with a grammar point to be reviewed. For much of the class period, Ms. Sullivan has students complete the review sheet, read back their answers (one student at a time), and then do some exercises from the textbook. After class, with a smile on his face, Mr. MacDonald says to

Ms. Sullivan: "Now this is the type of class I wanted to see. Students were on task, you had control, and there was a clear focus. I guess I just saw you on a bad day last week, right? A great class today!"

Many school administrators such as Mr. MacDonald still hark back to their own language learning experiences of many years ago as they observe today's classrooms.[2] Teachers often feel pressured to conform to administrators' expectations in order to receive a positive evaluation, even if the expectations are completely unfounded. Hammadou and Schrier (1988) conducted a survey of the attitudes of secondary school administrators from California, Iowa, Maryland, and Ohio toward the supervision of foreign language teachers. Supervisors reported that the two most important elements of effective teaching were the ability to motivate students and maintaining a positive classroom environment. The least important element was teachers' fluency in the foreign language. Administrators had some difficulty in distinguishing between performance evaluation of teachers and the nonevaluative type of supervision for strengthening instruction.[3]

Huling-Austin (1992) cites another difficulty with evaluations by school administrators: they fail to differentiate between beginning and experienced teachers, which violates the natural progression of learning to teach. Beginning teachers often receive very high ratings on evaluation instruments that are intended for use with all teachers. This, according to Huling-Austin (1992), reinforces the idea that teaching skill is developed primarily in a preservice program and that the level of teaching expertise developed by the novice teacher is adequate and not in need of further development.

Other actions taken by school districts also impose threats to reform, such as class size, scheduling of two levels of language students in the same class (for example, French IV and V together during the same period), variable scheduling, and lack of time for team teaching and collaboration among teachers.[4] All these factors have serious implications for teachers who attempt to institute the classroom changes suggested by the new standards.

The profession must address the internal and external obstacles just described if teachers are to implement the new standards with any success. The present article will return to these obstacles later when an approach to professional development is explored.

Present In-Service Opportunities for Foreign Language Teachers

What is the present state of in-service instruction for foreign language teachers? Draper (1991) surveyed members of the National Council of State Supervisors of Foreign Languages and others responsible for foreign language education at the state level. The survey was designed to elicit the "dreams, realities and nightmares" for foreign language education as perceived by survey participants (p. 1). The following was cited as one of the most frequent nightmares about in-service opportunities for language teachers:

> If preservice education is dismal, in-service preparation is worse. University methods people and state consultants generate models and methods of instruction which are discussed at regional and national conferences. Very little of this trickles down to the classroom teacher who tends to be overloaded with large classes and multiple preparations. Thus, while a dozen or so movements have come and gone, a large percentage of teachers still have had no training in dealing with anything but formal grammar and explication of written texts. . . . For most schools, there is simply no delivery vehicle for updating knowledge and skills. In-service education of teachers is delegated to 16,000 autonomous school boards, and most of them are unwilling or unable to generate funds for teacher in-service. (Draper 1991:3)

Draper's (1988) earlier survey had unexpectedly revealed that 55 percent of the responding state supervisors reported having no access to information on foreign language teacher supply and demand, recruitment initiatives, and in-service opportunities. In their follow-up study of foreign language teachers affiliated with one state professional association, Wolf and Riordan (1991) discovered that the local education agency provides practically no in-service opportunities and that there are few opportunities offered by regional and state government agencies. Most in-service training is sponsored by the state's professional language association and by methods classes offered by local colleges and universities.

Fifteen years ago, Jorstad (1980) made several recommendations concerning in-service development for language teachers at the ACTFL Professional Priorities Conference. She proposed a variety of in-service programs, including study abroad, that address language skill development, heightening of cultural awareness, and review of current pedagogical research and classroom applications. Our professional literature includes few descriptions of in-service programs for foreign language professionals, either because few program models exist or because program developers have failed to disseminate information about the types of models. Also, much in-service work is likely to be short-term workshops offered by local collaboratives and foreign language organizations, which do not tend to get reported formally.

What types of in-service projects have been documented? The literature contains several descriptions of collaborative projects carried out by university and basic education professionals. Curland (1987) describes the University of Oregon's series of summer institutes that brought together high school foreign language and social studies teachers to explore the history and literature of a given region and period. According to Curland (1987), the grant-funded institutes brought about a new emphasis on the study of language and other cultures in the Oregon schools while creating a new level of collaboration between university and public school educators. Similarly, the Department of Romance Languages at the University of North Carolina at Greensboro conducted a series of four-week graduate-level summer institutes that offered foreign language teachers the opportunity to revitalize their language skills, increase their knowledge of literature and culture, strengthen their teaching abilities, and encourage stronger ties between the public schools and the university (Smith 1985). In 1988 the Modern Language Association, in collaboration with the University of Texas and the Texas Education Agency, conducted a summer institute for university coordinators of foreign language instruction and supervisors of language programs in schools at state and local levels (Hayden 1989); this was to be the first in a series of three institutes held in different states. Among the results of the Texas institute were the development of a vision document to guide foreign language education in the state, the creation of a proficiency-oriented textbook evaluation form, and the design of individual projects for implementation at the school district level.

Other types of in-service work have been the by-product of collaborative projects between basic education and higher education faculty to strengthen teacher-education programs in foreign languages (Glisan and Sullivan 1993; Mellgren and Caye 1989). The University of North Florida AT&T Alliance Project developed a model to improve the preparation of urban teachers by integrating preservice and in-service educational delivery systems (Fountain and Evans 1994). The project identified five critical points along the continuum as benchmarks around which to design professional activities: (1) early field experiences; (2) preinternship experiences; (3) internship experiences; (4) beginning teacher experiences; and (5) professional educator experiences. One of the important indicators of this project's success is that in-service teachers are more willing to experiment in order to improve their teaching practices.

In a federally funded in-service project, Indiana University of Pennsylvania introduced some forty foreign language teachers to the concept of proficiency by addressing teachers' own language skills and their teaching abilities. The project featured Saturday total immersion workshops in order to strengthen teachers' own oral proficiency, a three-week summer institute that included training in conducting and rating the ACTFL Oral Proficiency Interview, the design of postinstitute implementation projects, and dissemination of the projects by the teachers (Glisan and Phillips 1989).

In the 1980s, the foreign language profession responded to the idea of teachers teaching teachers and of teachers assuming more responsibility for their own professional growth and that of their fellow teachers. Both the Central States Conference and the Northeast Conference on the Teaching of Foreign Languages have conducted extension or outreach programs in an effort to disseminate valuable information to teachers not in attendance at the conferences (Riordan 1989). Selected conference attenders participate in an intensive workshop at the conference designed to introduce them to innovative ideas for teaching and to train them in taking the workshop on the road to their colleagues. Participants must present at least one outreach workshop to their colleagues within some fifteen months and must submit a written project report. The goal of the outreach concept is to disseminate important information to a wider audience while helping teachers to accept responsibility for professional development (Riordan 1989).

Another type of collaborative project has created professional development opportunities. The College Board, the American Council on the Teaching of Foreign Languages, and the New England Network of Academic Alliances in Foreign Languages and Literatures have been collaborating in an effort to create articulated standards and student achievement levels for foreign language education in grades 7–14. Their work has focused on student transitions between middle school and high school and between high school and postsecondary education. The project includes the development of an articulation framework that defines learning outcomes for each level, includes expectations for cultural and literary competence, and describes matching classroom assessment strategies. The project is being piloted at secondary and postsecondary sites in New England, and professional development workshops are being conducted to enable teachers to put the standards into practice by means of actual classroom work with students (*Provisional Learning Outcomes Framework* 1993).

New Considerations in Approaching Professional Development

Principles of Professional Development

If the foreign language profession is to initiate effective changes to address the new standards, the nature of the professional development efforts that have been carried out in the past must be reevaluated in the light of current reforms. According to Little (1993), the design of professional development continues to be affected by (1) the complexity of the reform tasks in the absence of tested principles and practices, (2) the problem of the fit between the task of reform and the existing models of professional development, and (3) the lack of attention to teachers' opportunities to learn and grow professionally within the workday and work year.

Little (1993:138–39) has offered the following principles of professional development that address the complexity of current reforms in classroom teaching:

1. *Professional development offers meaningful intellectual, social, and emotional engagement with ideas, with materials, and with colleagues both in and out of teaching.* Teachers do not take on active professional involvement by simply participating in a "hands-on" activity as part of a workshop. Instead, they must be engaged in the study of their disciplines, given access to new ideas in university and business settings, and provided with systems of consultation and support with fellow teachers.

2. *Professional development takes explicit account of the contexts of teaching and the experience of teachers.* One-way "training and coaching" of teachers usually offers superficial treatment of the fit between new ideas and old habits. Modes of professional development such as focused study groups, teacher collaboratives, and long-term partnerships help teachers to adapt new ideas to fit their individual and institutional practices and circumstances.

3. *Professional development offers support for informed dissent.* Closer collaborations and partnerships often provide for more open discussion and well-informed dissent that can strengthen group decisions and individual choices.

4. *Professional development places classroom practice in the larger contexts of school practice and the educational careers of children.* It enables teachers to understand and act upon the connections among students' experiences, teachers' classroom practice, and schoolwide organization and cultures. More traditional approaches to professional development have tended to treat teachers nearly exclusively as classroom decision makers independent of the larger world of practice around them. An important part of professional growth is the teachers' ability to assume leadership or assistance roles in their schools or districts.

5. *Professional development prepares teachers (as well as students and their parents) to employ the techniques and perspectives of inquiry.* It enables teachers to conduct their own research, generate new

knowledge, and assess the knowledge claimed by others. Thus, rather than simply consuming existing research, they learn how to conduct their own.

6. *The governance of professional development ensures bureaucratic restraint and a balance between the interests of individuals and the interests of institutions.* Teachers have traditionally had little influence over and played few leadership roles in formal professional development programs in school districts. A revised system of resource allocation might provide more balanced support for professional development efforts initiated by teachers.

The Foreign Language Standards and Professional Development: Areas to Be Addressed

What areas do future in-service efforts need to address in order to help teachers address and disseminate information about the foreign language standards? In-service programs often focus on the development of pedagogical techniques rather than on the strengthening of subject-matter knowledge, for many assume that teachers know the content they are to teach. Mosenthal and Ball (1992) remind us that good teaching depends on, although is not guaranteed by, the teacher's subject-matter knowledge.

1. *Language proficiency and cultural awareness.* In order to engage students in the types of communicative activities suggested in the benchmarks of the standards, current teachers must develop a satisfactory level of proficiency in the languages they teach. Particularly in the areas of listening and speaking, students need to hear and interact with fluent teachers if language acquisition is to occur. Typically teachers whose linguistic skills are low tend to use the foreign language very little in their classrooms because they feel inadequately prepared to do so. Hand in hand with the development of language proficiency is the heightening of cultural awareness. Teachers cannot teach culture effectively from a textbook: they must be able to bring their own real-life cultural experiences to the classroom. If students are to develop cultural sophistication, they must perceive that culture and language are intertwined and they must use the language as a tool for exploring not only other cultures, but also other subject matter as stipulated in Standards 3.1 and 3.2 (see Appendix A). Hence, it is imperative that teachers keep abreast of current happenings in the cultures of the languages they teach and benefit from travel and study abroad experiences continually.

2. *Self-reflection about teaching.* Teachers who continue to update their knowledge and teaching approaches usually engage in ongoing self-reflection about their teaching. To gain an understanding of the approach that might effectively address the standards, today's in-service teachers must reflect on their own philosophies about the learning and teaching processes in light of current research findings. Observations of their own teaching, reflection, and discussion are effective avenues for effecting a change in philosophy. As the quote at the beginning of this article illustrates, the only way to realize reform (and pay attention to the new standards) is by altering the way in which teachers think about teaching.

3. *Collaboration with colleagues.* Foreign language teachers need time to work together at the departmental level in order to develop carefully articulated programs that are built upon the new goals and standards. Teachers must decide together what they can expect from students at each level and how instruction can be spiraled from one level to the next so that students are not constantly starting language study from the beginning. Curricula must be goal-oriented, centered on high standards for student performance. Curricula that consist of lists of grammar points to be "covered" have no place in programs that address the standards. Teachers must share ideas about teaching and testing strategies that will best enable students to use the language in ways suggested by the standards. Further, language teachers need time to collaborate with fellow teachers in other disciplines in order to find ways in which foreign languages and other subject areas can be integrated so that students can use the foreign language meaningfully to learn content.

4. *Experimentation with new classroom strategies.* Teachers must constantly learn about and try innovative techniques for helping students to use the foreign language effectively to meet their needs. Strategies that are outmoded, ineffective, and no longer reflect current research must be abandoned in favor of exciting new approaches, if students are to acquire a foreign language and learn to use it for communication.

5. *Use of modern technology as a tool for teaching language.* One of the goals in the standards framework is for students to access new information and knowledge in the foreign language. Modern technology is a key vehicle for helping students to acquire new information and knowledge. Therefore, teachers must use the various

technological means for bringing language and culture into the classroom and for teaching students how to use technology to access new information continually.

6. *The needs of today's students.* The foundation of the standards framework is that *all* students should develop and maintain proficiency in more than one language and, further, that language should be taught as a basic subject at all grade levels. This underlying principle means that foreign language teachers will be faced with the challenge of teaching *all* students, not just those in the college-bound group. In-service teachers will need to develop the skills necessary for teaching students with physical, emotional, and cognitive disabilities and those with low motivation and other difficulties.

7. *Selection and adaptation of instructional materials.* Teaching a foreign language through a page-by-page textbook approach is not likely to produce students who can participate actively in multilingual communities and the global society. Teachers need opportunities to incorporate a wide variety of instructional materials into their teaching and to adapt them to fit the needs of their students. To address the five broad goal areas of the standards framework, teachers must integrate authentic language samples (e.g., E-mail, audiotapes, video, newspaper articles, literary excerpts) into classroom activities. The effort to introduce current authentic language into the classroom should continue.

Most of the areas described above are also included in the teacher standards recently developed by AATF (1989) and AATG (1992) and the teacher guidelines designed by ACTFL (1988) and AATSP (1990).[5]

A Model of Professional Development from the Mathematics Profession

As our profession prepares to deal with addressing the new standards through reformed classroom instruction, we have much to learn from our counterparts in mathematics, who developed their *Curriculum and Evaluation Standards* (NCTM 1989) and their *Professional Standards for Teaching Mathematics* (NCTM 1991). Before beginning professional development efforts on the standards, the NCTM launched a widespread dissemination effort in order to create an awareness of what the standards were within the teaching community and to foster a positive climate for discussing them. With the initial mailing of over 200,000 copies of the standards document to members of the mathematics-education community and individuals involved in educational policy at state and federal levels, the NCTM began a series of regional meetings designed in a "turnkey" fashion so that teachers began informing other teachers about the standards (Crosswhite, Dossey, and Frye 1989; Dolan 1995). The NCTM also commissioned a public relations firm to develop a videotape for public use, a speaker's kit for local adaptation, and a marketing strategy (Frye 1989). More than 200 affiliated groups have been instrumental in promoting the standards by designing implementational strategies that meet local needs. A series of grant-funded projects is underway to assist teachers in addressing the standards in the various mathematical areas of the curriculum.

QUASAR Project

One of the key projects designed to assist the development of teachers' capacity for mathematics instructional reform is the QUASAR (Quantitative Understanding: Amplifying Student Achievement and Reasoning) project, begun in 1991 (Brown and Smith 1994). The primary goal of this national educational reform project is to assist teachers in developing and implementing enhanced mathematics programs for students in middle schools located in economically disadvantaged communities. At six middle-school-based sites of the project, teams of mathematics teachers, school administrators, and "resource partners" (mostly university mathematics educators) are working in collaboration to implement innovative mathematics instructional programs for all students at each school. At each site, work is guided not only by general principles from the reform literature, but also by the complex and dynamic local conditions, as a collaborative community of practice for teachers is designed. The foundation of the QUASAR project is the creation of networks of activities in which teachers learn and work together in order to achieve the reform goals. A key principle of this task is the notion of teacher "assistance," a term used by Tharp and Gallimore (1988), who claim that it is more appropriate to assist teachers to make changes than to assess them on their progress. The challenge for the QUASAR project was to design opportunities for teachers to develop and use their knowledge about mathematics, pedagogy, and students in cycles of planning, implementing, and reflecting in order to bring about innovative instruction (Shulman 1987).

Teachers at each of the sites have been engaging in a network of six professional activities:

1. *Course work* that provides a foundation for teaching or serves a particular need identified by the teachers and resource partners as important to their efforts to reform mathematics instruction
2. *Ongoing workshops* that address a need as identified by the teachers and resource partners and are integrated with follow-up classroom application
3. *Professional meetings* of city, state, and national mathematics organizations, in which teachers participate in sessions of interest and share information with colleagues on the work in which they are engaged, thus enabling teachers to see themselves as part of a national network of teachers
4. *Time for individual reflection* in order to analyze and adapt teaching approaches and examine the impact of instruction on student learning, accomplished through journal writing and viewing of videotapes
5. *Time for collaborative pedagogical thinking,* which includes "tagging up" opportunities for teachers to consult with each other on difficulties they have experienced in implementing a particular teaching strategy, ask for advice, and share effective ideas; common planning time; regularly scheduled extended planning sessions; and summer sessions
6. *Classroom-based support,* through which resource partners and others observe teachers' classes, and at times coteach or model-teach the teachers' classes, in order to provide assistance to teachers rather than the traditional type of evaluation that accompanies classroom observations (Brown and Smith 1994)

Various types of data have been compiled from the QUASAR project such as program development interviews, social context interviews, self-documentation, site-developed reports and proposals, telephone records, and visit reports. Data analysis has indicated, among other phenomena, that the project has assisted most of the domains of teachers' professional knowledge, that the activities and ongoing support available to teachers are closely connected, and that easier accessibility to human and material resources has enabled teachers to respond more positively to assistance activities (Brown and Smith 1994).

PBS MATHLINE

The mathematics profession is also breaking new ground with its MATHLINE telecommunications highway, the first discipline-based educational service offered by the Public Broadcasting Service (PBS), which is based on the mathematics standards set by NCTM. MATHLINE's first initiative currently underway is the Middle School Math Project, a year-long professional development opportunity for teachers of middle school mathematics that offers

1. A video series featuring classroom teachers modeling NCTM standards-based instruction
2. Two national interactive teleconferences
3. Online learning groups of teacher participants, each mentored by an experienced practicing teacher (PBS MATHLINE 1995)

This program enables teachers to join a community of teachers who are striving for excellence in teaching mathematics. Teachers take responsibility for their own professional development by watching the videotapes on their own schedules and then interacting with fellow teachers and experts in the field by means of teleconferences and online programing. Each teacher becomes a member of an electronic learning community of twenty-five to thirty fellow teacher-participants, which have a practicing teacher as an online facilitator and resource leader for the group. More than 2,000 teachers of mathematics in thirty-eight states will participate in this initiative this year. The MATHLINE project has been recognized and praised by the Clinton administration and NCTM.

PBS MATHLINE's second service, which will be operational next year, is the Math Online Resource Center (MORC). MORC will provide a wealth of opportunities and services for teachers of mathematics, including

• A subscription service for professional resources via the Internet
• Curricular materials for classroom use
• Reference materials delivered with video, audio, print, and interactive components
• Online groups for seminars, discussion, and collaboration
• News items of interest to math teachers changed daily and archived
• Customized searches of professional resources based on individual user profiles (PBS MATHLINE 1995)[6]

MORC will provide an exciting new dimension to professional development, enabling mathematics teachers to access virtually any type of information and resources without leaving the classroom.

Professional Development for the Foreign Language Teacher: New Directions and Shared Responsibilities

The approach to professional development presented below is based upon five primary considerations, as synthesized from the information presented earlier in this article:

1. Current research in educational reform indicates that teacher preparation and ongoing professional development should be a continuum that begins early in the college career and extends through the experiences of professional educators (Fountain and Evans 1994).

2. An important factor in professional development is collaboration among educators at various levels. The Holmes Group (1990), for example, suggests restructuring education through the development of professional development schools that function as collaboratives between institutions of higher education and the public schools. Under this plan, a college/school partnership would create a new institution that would plan and operate exemplary teaching schools and improve teaching and learning for students and preservice and in-service teachers while providing the opportunity for basic and higher education faculty to collaborate on research to improve their teaching (Holmes 1990; Kennedy 1990).

3. The university, with its resources in staffing and research, has a key role to play in professional development activities at various levels. Schnur and Golby (1995) stress the fact that viable colleges of education must "reconsider their research agendas in the context of the fundamentals of practice" and "engage in collaborative research with interested parties internal and external to the university" (p. 18). They also suggest close collaboration between the university teacher-education faculty researcher and the classroom teacher.

4. Small-scale ("one shot") in-service programs, such as one- or two-hour workshops, have limited value in helping teachers to strengthen instruction (Goldenberg and Gallimore 1991; Mosenthal and Ball 1992). Little change in teaching practice actually results from attendance at this type of in-service programs, which do not usually provide sufficient impetus for self-reflection and implementation of new ideas. Professional development opportunities of a long-term nature that engage teachers in extensive self-reflection, action research, and design of innovative strategies are more likely to produce significant reform in teaching and adherence to standards.

5. University course work offered as professional development is often disconnected from the realities of the teachers' school and classroom situations and is often inconsistent with the ways in which students construct adequate knowledge (Brown and Smith 1994).

National Level

National Voluntary Certification. The National Board for Professional Teaching Standards (NBPTS) is attempting to bring professionalism back into teaching through its voluntary certification process, which many envision to replace state certification (Earley 1993). According to James R. Smith, senior vice-president for the NBPTS, board certification will provide "professional growth unlike any now available to teachers" (cf. Sparks 1994:59). In an interview, Smith explains the role of professional development at the school district level:

> School districts that are serious about National Board certification will encourage groups of teachers to work together to assess themselves against the standards and to prepare for the formal assessment. These districts will provide released time, equipment and facilities for preparing and sharing videos of instruction, assistance in developing and critiquing portfolios, resources for improving specific areas of practice that need improvement, and general support that makes it clear that they value highly accomplished teaching. (Sparks 1994:59)

The certification process consists of a three-part system that features the standards of excellence that teachers in each certification area must meet, the exemplary practices that measure the standards, and the professional development activities that help teachers to understand the standards and practices constituting highly accomplished teaching (Baratz-Snowden 1993). The National Board certification process features two modules, one requiring data collected at the teacher's school site and the other requiring data gathered at an assessment center. In order to earn a professional teaching certificate, teachers will need to demonstrate teaching effectiveness through data collected from their school sites, including components such as videotapes of teaching, instructional materials prepared, letters from parents and colleagues, and students' work. In addition, they will need to demonstrate knowledge of the content area and pedagogy by responding to interviews, simulations, and written testing at an assessment center.

As a part of the data collection, foreign language teachers might be required to demonstrate how they are addressing the standards in their instruction and collaboration with colleagues. What proof is there that students are developing skills based upon the standards? ACTFL and the foreign language teaching organizations would play a key role in helping teachers work toward this certification.

Federally Funded Institutes. Given that the development of standards in foreign language education is part of a national effort to raise standards for student achievement, there should be a national effort to equip teachers with the knowledge and skills they need to address the standards. Indeed, in the audiolingual era of the 1950s and 1960s a large number of in-service teachers were retrained to teach oral skills by means of summer institutes funded by the National Defense Education Act (NDEA). Federally funded institutes could address pedagogical innovation and the development of language skills and cultural awareness. Strasheim (1991) urges the profession to lobby for structured month-long overseas study opportunities similar to those provided by the NDEA Overseas Institutes of several decades ago, except with possibilities for matching funds from foundations and businesses. ACTFL and the foreign language teaching organizations could collaborate in seeking federal funding for in-service institutes, as could universities, state departments of education, and state foreign language organizations.

Paramount to the success of institutes of the NDEA type is what the participants do afterward. How many teachers attend workshops and institutes, pay lip service to the helpfulness of the experience, and never do anything to use what they have learned in their own teaching? Institute participants, therefore, must agree to return to their school districts and implement change as a result of what they have accomplished in the in-service program. It is the responsibility of project directors of grant-funded programs to provide for reporting and dissemination of postinstitute work by the participants. Higher education faculty should be included in such institutes, particularly those who prepare new teachers and provide professional development opportunities for in-service teachers. This would allow for better articulation and collaboration across levels.

Online Professional Development. With the development of new standards and the need to reach more teachers, the time is right to examine more innovative avenues for professional development. The projects begun by the PBS MATHLINE described earlier are exciting initiatives that might be explored by the foreign language profession. The formation of online communities of teachers and administrators who continue to learn and grow professionally together is likely to bring a new meaning to the concept of collaboration and professional growth. A key issue in considering this type of large-scale project, of course, is funding. Of great importance in securing grant support would be the collaboration among the various language constituencies (ACTFL, foreign language teaching organizations, regional conferences, JNCL-NCLIS, state departments of education, state foreign language organizations), all of which would need to work together to develop the project and seek monetary support from public and private sectors.

State Level

Collaboration between State Departments of Education and State Foreign Language Organizations. Foreign language education at the state level could be much more effective if state departments of education and state foreign language organizations would collaborate on issues such as in-service opportunities for language teachers. Since many states now have no foreign language specialist, state departments often lack the expertise to secure grant funding and provide the necessary professional development opportunities in the foreign language instruction. The following are some ways in which the two groups might come together:

- Participation by a department of education representative (ideally, the foreign language specialist) in meetings held by the language organization's board or officers
- Joint planning of conferences and workshops
- Special meetings to discuss current issues such as the new standards
- Joint design of state-level standards for teachers and students
- Joint grant writing
- Copublication of language newsletters

Certification Requirements. A key issue that should be addressed by state departments of education and state foreign language organizations is teacher certification, which should be a concern not only of preservice teachers. Leighton and Sykes (1992) propose that states establish requirements for license renewal that encourage them to continue their professional development. They acknowledge that, while many states have flexible options for continuing education, their options are often inadequate and unrelated to the development of teaching skill. Vermont has attempted to address this problem by creating district-development councils that oversee the development of individual growth plans for teachers. These plans require ongoing assessment of professional development and collaboration with peers and administrators (Leighton and Sykes 1992).

The Holmes Group (1986) has suggested that the teaching force consist of three levels of personnel, each with different job descriptions: instructors, professional teachers, and career professionals. Instructors' teaching certificates would be available to those teachers with bachelor's degrees, and they would be valid for five years and nonrenewable. Beginning instructors would be closely supervised and enrolled in intensive professional development programs. The professional teacher certificate requires a master's degree based upon advanced study in the certification area and pedagogy, as well as supervised classroom experience with at-risk students. Teachers in this group would need to demonstrate their teaching skills, gather documentation of their effectiveness, and be observed in various learning situations. Approximately one-fifth of teachers would receive certification as career professionals, after extensive, outstanding teaching performance and specialized study, primarily at the doctoral level. Career professionals would assume supervisory roles in the education of pre- and in-service teachers, in instructional design, and in assessment of students and teachers.

This three-tier certification system would address the problem of teachers failing to keep their skills and knowledge current and would bring a higher level of professionalism to teaching. The professional development program offered to level-one foreign language instructors would include assistance to teachers in designing instruction based on the new standards. Professional and career teachers would need to demonstrate how they are addressing the standards in providing challenging content matter in foreign languages. In addition, the present system of granting emergency certification would need to be reconceptualized so that this type of certification is granted only when absolutely necessary and to teachers who are seriously enrolled in a viable certification program.

Regional Supervision. One of the difficulties that foreign language teachers often experience as they attempt to grow professionally is that they seldom receive feedback and suggestions about their teaching from individuals who have the expertise to do so. In fact, seldom are teachers observed for any reason other than evaluation of their teaching skill (Tharp and Gallimore 1988). School principals may observe classes once or twice a year but are not knowledgeable enough about foreign language teaching to offer valid observation and assistance. Indeed, as seen in Case Study 5, principals often hark back to their own language learning experiences of many decades ago as they try to reflect on sound classroom practices. Few school districts have the funds to employ supervisors in each subject area, whose job is to observe classrooms and help teachers to improve their teaching. Perhaps what would be more feasible is for regions of each state, or groups of nearby school districts, to employ supervisors, who would then supervise foreign language programs in specific regions (four or five school districts, for example). The role of foreign language regional supervisors might be to

- Observe classes in their regions and provide suggestions for updating teaching
- Help teachers to understand the new standards and to base instruction on them
- Arrange for in-service programs in foreign languages
- Offer input to school principals on the performance of teachers in the classroom
- Direct induction/mentoring programs
- Serve as liaisons between schools and state departments of education and state foreign language organizations and universities
- Direct and facilitate the communities of online learning groups of foreign language teachers
- Disseminate information about current issues in the field (such as the standards), new pedagogical ideas, and information about professional development activities

Regional supervision can be the link that is currently missing in providing helpful site-based assistance to foreign language teachers as they attempt to address the new standards and effect reform in their teaching.

School Level

Teacher Induction/Mentoring. Recent studies have illustrated the special needs of beginning teachers as they learn to become professionals in the school system (Huling-Austin 1992). Some states are establishing an induction or mentoring program in an effort to raise teacher standards. As Phillips (1989:19–20) stated, induction is viewed "as a means of preventing incompetent teachers from taking root as a result of too quickly awarding permanent certificates and tenure." In the induction system, university personnel interact with classroom teachers and assist them in developing effective teaching strategies. Mentoring involves the veteran or career teachers serving as models and helping novice teachers one-on-one. According to a 1992 report, some ten states have induction programs, while seventeen states offer some type of assistance for beginning teachers (Leighton and Sykes 1992). Minnesota and California are examples of states that have developed performance-based certification programs that include an induction experience (Leighton and Sykes 1992).

Induction/mentoring is exemplified in a move by the Oklahoma legislature, which established the Oklahoma Commission for Teacher Preparation in 1992. Its purpose was to design a new "competency-based" teacher preparation and professional development system that could be implemented by fall 1996 (Earley 1995). One of the eight recommendations of the commission was that professional development institutes be established to prepare P–12 and college/university educators to be teacher mentors and to help those who have left teaching and want to reenter the field. The commission also suggests that the entry-year induction program be replaced with a three-year residency and that classroom teachers be given more opportunities for professional growth (Earley 1995).

In foreign language education, induction and mentoring could be designed to give attention to the new standards by guiding teachers in developing strategies for addressing them in instruction. For induction to be successful, however, it is imperative that only *qualified* university personnel and master teachers be selected to serve as teacher mentors.

Team Teaching. The mathematics profession has acknowledged the need for teachers to connect with one another and with educators in other communities to watch them teach, talk with them about their work, and share ideas. Avenues such as the formation of networks that make ongoing professional exchanges feasible and the accessing of video footage from various types of classes would open classroom doors and help to build a sense of professional community (Ball 1992). Foreign language teachers need to be given time for collaborating with each other to address the standards, explore curricular implications, and develop strategies for basing instruction on them. Given the current organization of most school systems, teachers are seldom afforded the opportunity to observe other classrooms, much less design lessons and teach with colleagues. Team teaching could be used to provide time for collaborative pedagogical thinking identified as being so important by the QUASAR project described earlier (Brown and Smith 1994). As a tool for professional development, team teaching could foster learning and collaboration between colleagues while encouraging collaboration and articulation within the foreign language teaching staff as well as between teachers of foreign language and those of other subject areas. This could be the avenue for bridging foreign language and content by engaging foreign language teachers in collaborative teaching tasks with their counterparts in social sciences, English, math, art, and music. Through this type of cross-curricular professional development, foreign language teachers could address the standard that suggests that students use the foreign language to acquire new information in other fields. Further, teachers would acquire new skills and knowledge continually.

Teacher Level

Action Research in the Classroom. Historically classroom teachers have had little involvement in research into language learning and teaching, which has been the domain of university professors. Recent attempts to bring a higher level of professionalization to the teaching field have included the suggestion that teachers should be involved in research and development as they relate to their own classrooms, and further, that a primary goal for in-service teacher education is to offer teachers ways of exploring their own classrooms (Nunan 1990). Kemmis and McTaggart (1982) explain the concept of action research:

> The linking of the terms "action" and "research" highlights the essential feature of the method: trying out ideas in practice as a means of improvement and as a means of increasing knowledge about the curriculum, teaching and learning. The result is improvement in what happens in the classroom and school, and better articulation and justification of the educational rationale of what goes on. Action research provides a way of working which links theory and practice into the one whole: ideas-in-action. (p. 5)

Johnson (1993) stresses the value of action research as a means of helping teachers make informed decisions about implementing policies, programs, and practices; identify program needs; and evaluate program outcomes and changes implemented in the classroom. Action research enables teachers to acquire knowledge and skill in research methods and applications to become more cognizant of the possibilities for change. Studies have shown that teachers who engage in action research become more critical and reflective about their own teaching approaches and practices (Oja and Pine 1989).

Nunan (1990) describes an action research in-service program for second language teachers. The goals of this program are to introduce teachers to the procedures for investigating classroom processes, enable them to apply techniques to their own teaching, assist them in identifying their own attitudes and beliefs about language and learning, and help them to identify areas for further investigation within their own classrooms. There are five stages to the program: in the "theory and practice" stage, teachers identify the aspects of the classroom that interest them, discuss the preconceptions they have about classroom observation, observe a video segment of a classroom lesson, and engage in small-group discussion about the segment; in the "methods and techniques" stage, teachers use observational techniques and instruments to analyze video segments of classroom lessons; in the "issues for investigation" stage, teachers explore what lends itself to investigation in the classroom; in the "investigating your own classroom" stage, teachers analyze a video segment of their own teaching; in the "developing an action research proposal" stage, from what they discovered about their own teaching teachers formulate research questions to guide their postworkshop action research in their classrooms (pp. 65–75).[7]

Tucker and Donato (1995) have recently proposed a model for apprenticing preservice teachers to doctoral candidates in foreign language education for classroom-based research. They describe the development of an elementary school Japanese program and how preservice and in-service teachers in the program have engaged in several research projects through an apprenticeship model. Their classroom research has both benefited from and contributed to the Japanese program itself, to participants in the teacher-education program at the University of Pittsburgh, and to foreign language education practice and policy in Pennsylvania. Tucker and Donato have found that students in this project have learned many research skills and analytic tools while acquiring a firsthand appreciation for the benefits of documenting and reflecting upon their teaching practices.

Action research could be a valuable tool for helping foreign teachers to design programs and procedures based upon the foreign language standards. The development of online collaboration would make action research even more accessible to them. Unlike "one-shot" in-service workshops, action research provides ongoing professional development and the impetus for reflection and change. In addition, it can serve as an important avenue for gathering evidence on how the standards might be most effectively addressed through classroom practices.

The Role of Local Organizations and Collaboratives. Little (1993) has stressed the importance of teacher collaboratives in helping teachers to locate new ideas about their individual and institutional practices and circumstances. Phillips (1989) has suggested the development of stronger collaboratives, consortia, and alliances as vehicles for providing ongoing in-service opportunities for foreign language teachers. The Academic Alliance Project has spawned a national network of more than 130 local collaboratives made up of school and college foreign language faculty (Silber and Waterfall 1988). Collaboratives can serve professional development on yet another level by providing opportunities for faculty from basic and higher education to address professional issues such as the standards and to articulate program goals across levels. They can also enable foreign language faculty to benefit from the expertise of one another as they continue to strengthen their linguistic skills and keep abreast of current events in the regions where their target languages are spoken. Collaboratives can be the bridge between state and school district efforts in the area of in-service work by bringing professional activities, such as workshops, to foreign language teachers at a local level.

Foreign language collaboratives will certainly have an exciting new role to play if online communities of teachers become a reality.

Conclusion: A Look Forward

Because the issue of professional development of in-service teachers presents so many challenges and encompasses so many factors, our efforts must be made at several levels. This article has described an approach to professional development that involves collaboration of educators and institutions at national, state, school district, and local levels. As summarized in table 4-1, this approach addresses various internal and external obstacles to basing teaching on the new standards and to creating reform.

The widespread professional development that will address the new standards undoubtedly requires closer collaboration among ACTFL, the foreign language teaching groups, the regional conferences, state departments of education, and state foreign language organizations. National voluntary certification, more rigorous state certification requirements, teacher induction/mentoring programs, online collaboration, and opportunities for team teaching and action research will bring greater professionalism to teaching, which may, in turn, give teachers a greater sense of responsibility about their own ongoing professional development. Innovative standards for teacher certification that provide for multiple levels of professionalism will have a positive effect on preservice teacher preparation and will serve as a catalyst for ongoing professional renewal. Closer collaboration between state departments of education and state foreign language organizations is paramount in creating more effective state policies on certification and professional development issues. Regional supervision and teacher mentoring will help school district administrators who are not knowledgeable about foreign language teaching to develop a better understanding of current approaches to language teaching and the important role of the new standards. The university has an important contribution to make in collaborating on the components of professional development at all levels. The resources and expertise of university faculty can help in writing grants, introducing current research and innovation, collaborating with teachers to address the standards, and engaging teachers in ongoing action research projects. Local foreign language organizations and collaboratives can play a key role in bringing professional development activities to local teachers and bridging the gap between in-service work offered at the school district and state levels.

The approach described here is not meant to be presented as a simplistic solution to a multifaceted problem that faces the profession as we attempt to deal with the new standards. The problem facing us is a challenging one

Table 4-1. A Collaborative Approach to Professional Development

Level	Professional Development Activities	Partnerships/ Collaborations	Obtacles Addressed
National	National voluntary certification; federally funded institutes	National Board for Professional Teaching Standards; ACTFL; foreign language teaching organizations; universities; state departments of education; state foreign language organizations	Teacher beliefs; preservice preparation; state policies; lack of collaboration between basic and higher education
State	Collaborative projects (design of standards, conference planning, copublication of newsletters, joint grant writing, special meetings); certification requirements; regional supervision	State departments of education; state foreign language organizations; foreign language teaching organizations; school districts; universities	Teacher beliefs; preservice preparation; state policies; lack of collaboration between basic and higher education
School	Teacher induction and mentoring; team teaching	School districts; teachers; universities	Teacher beliefs; preservice preparation; state policies; lack of collaboration between basic and higher education; school-level misconceptions about foreign language teaching

to which there is no simple answer or solution. What we know, however, is that we cannot attempt to face the challenge alone. Our foreign language profession must look in new directions and develop strategies for engaging our many constituencies in closer collaboration if we are to have any success in adhering to the new standards and to effect reform. Perhaps the most important outcome of these efforts is the creation of a "collaborative, supportive and collegial process of sharing and experimenting in the context of mutual respect and reflection," which has been identified in the mathematics literature as a key goal in the reform movement (Leinwand 1992:468). Table 4-2 depicts the resulting process of systematic professionalism, which encompasses ongoing opportunities to share, to support, and to take risks in an environment designed to overcome the obstacles to change (Leinwand 1992). The types of collaborative networks suggested in this article would assist foreign language professionals in becoming curious, self-confident, flexible, and empowered decision makers who are equipped to face the obstacles to change. The new directions presented here offer opportunities for greater collaboration and resulting professionalism as we search for ways to unify our approach to professional development and therefore enable the standards to have a significant impact on the teaching of foreign languages.

Table 4-2. Transforming the Reality of One Classroom within a Supportive Environment

Stage	Key Action	Dispositions	Professional Attributes
		Sharing	
Awareness	Hears about it	Positioned to find out about new things	Curiosity
	Sees it		Currency in the field
	Reads about it		
Familiarity	Learns about it	Willing to learn	Ongoing learning
		Risk Taking	
Experimentation	Tries it out	Comfortable trying out new things	Self-confidence
	Experiments with it		Semiautonomy
Integration	Sees where it fits in	Able to link new with existing conditions	Decision making
Routine	Builds it into instruction	Willing to adjust routines	Flexibility
			Self-improvement

Source: Steven J. Leinwand, "Sharing, Supporting, Risk Taking: First Steps to Instructional Reform." *Mathematics Teacher* 85,6 (1992):468.

Many questions remain to be answered as we continue to face this challenge. Will federal and state governments provide the necessary funds to support innovative professional development opportunities for foreign language teachers? How long will it take for new certification requirements to be instituted? Will universities begin to recognize the importance of collaborating with their counterparts in basic education? Will teachers become more actively involved in these new professional endeavors such as action research and team teaching? How will we measure the success of professional development efforts in addressing the foreign language standards? There is no doubt that the challenge we face is a huge one, but it will not be insurmountable if we have the courage to work collaboratively to search for new answers and to follow new directions.

Notes

1. See Schrier (1993) for a comparison of known data on foreign language teacher characteristics with information compiled by the NEA (1987) on the characteristics of U.S. public school teachers. Brickell and Paul were commissioned by ACTFL in 1979 to conduct a national survey of foreign language instruction in secondary schools. Their data reflect responses from eighty school districts in ten states and from twenty teacher-training institutions. Wolf and Riordan (1991) conducted a survey of teachers who were involved with a state foreign language organization.
2. Morain (1990) shares the story of a similar evaluation by a helpful administrator.
3. For earlier studies dealing with attitudes of school administrators, see Baranick and Markham (1986) and Beard (1984).
4. Many school districts are adopting variable schedules for classes. In the "4 × 4 block" option, four classes are offered for a 90-minute block during each semester. Generally, there is a balance of academic and elective classes offered during the year, which often means, for example, that foreign language level II is one of four course offerings in semester 1, with level III being offered some thirteen months later in semester 4 of high school. Another alternative is the Copernican schedule, in which foreign language level I is offered as one of two 3½-hour block courses (i.e., for first trimester in year 1 of high school) and foreign language level II as one of two courses in first, second, or third trimester of year two (Baskerville 1994).
5. See Lafayette (1993) for a detailed comparison of the teacher standards and guidelines prepared by the foreign language teaching organizations.
6. For more information on the Middle School Math Project and MORC, write Mary Harley Kruter, Director, PBS MATHLINE, 1320 Braddock Place, Alexandria, Virginia 22314.
7. See Nunan (1990) for sample work sheets, checklists, and schedules used in the inservice workshop for lesson observation and analysis.

References

American Association of Colleges for Teacher Education. 1993. *Teacher Education Policy in the States: A 50-State Survey of Legislative and Administrative Actions.* Washington, DC: AACTE.

American Association of Teachers of French. 1989. "The Teaching of French: A Syllabus of Competence." *AATF National Bulletin* 15 (special issue, Oct.).

American Association of Teachers of German. 1992. "Professional Standards for Teachers of German." Draft version. Cherry Hill, NJ: AATG.

American Association of Teachers of Spanish and Portuguese. 1990. "AATSP Program Guidelines for the Education and Training of Teachers of Spanish and Portuguese." *Hispania* 73:785–94.

American Council on the Teaching of Foreign Languages. 1989. "ACTFL Provisional Program Guidelines for Foreign Language Teacher Education." *Foreign Language Annals* 21:71–82.

Ball, Deborah Loewenberg. 1992. *Implementing the NCTM Standards: Hopes and Hurdles.* East Lansing, MI: National Center for Research on Teacher Learning.

Baranick, William A., and Paul L. Markham. 1986. "Attitudes of Elementary School Principals toward Foreign Language Instruction." *Foreign Language Annals* 19,6:481–89.

Baratz-Snowden, Joan. 1993. "Assessment of Teachers: A View from the National Board for Professional Teaching Standards." *Theory into Practice* 32,2:82–85.

Baskerville, Jane J. 1994. Personal correspondence to Judith Shrum.

Beard, Joe Leonard. 1984. "Attitudes of Secondary School Counselors and Superintendents toward Foreign Language Teaching: A Descriptive Study." *Foreign Language Annals* 17,1:29–32.

Biemer, Linda. 1993. "Advanced Preparation of Social Studies Teachers and NCSS Certification." *International Journal of Social Education* 7,3:81–85.

Brickell, Henry M., and Regina H. Paul. 1981. *Ready for the '90's? A Look at Foreign Language Teachers and Teaching at the Start of the Decade.* New York: Policy Studies in Education.

Brown, Catherine A., and Margaret Schwan Smith. 1994. *Building Capacity for Mathematics Instructional Innovation in Urban Middle Schools: Assisting the Development of Teachers' Capacity.* Paper presented at the annual meeting of the American Educational Research Association, New Orleans, LA.

Carlson, Carol G. 1992. *Focus 27: The Metamorphosis of Mathematics Education.* Princeton, NJ: Educational Testing Service.

Crosswhite, F. Joe, John A. Dossey, and Shirley M. Frye. 1989. "NCTM Standards for School Mathematics: Visions for Implementation." *Mathematics Teacher* 82:664–71.

Curland, David J. 1987. "The University of Oregon's Summer Institute for the Combined Study of History and Literature." *ADFL Bulletin* 18,3:52–54.

Darling-Hammond, Linda. 1991. "Are Our Teachers Ready to Teach?" *NCATE Quality Teaching Newsletter* 1,1, pp. 6–7, 10–11.

Dolan, Dan. 1995. Personal correspondence.

Draper, Jamie B. 1988. *State Activities Up-Date: Focus on the Teacher.* Yonkers, NY: American Council on the Teaching of Foreign Languages.

———. 1991. *Dreams, Realities, and Nightmares: The Present and Future of Foreign Language Education in the United States.* Washington, DC: Joint National Committee for Languages.

Earley, Penelope. 1993. "The Teacher-Education Agenda: Policies, Policy Arenas, and Implications for the Profession," pp. 7–22 in Gail Guntermann, ed., *Developing Language Teachers for a Changing World.* Lincolnwood, IL: National Textbook.

————. 1995. "Commission Releases Report on Educator Preparation." *AACTE Briefs* 16,3, pp. 2.

Fountain, Cheryl A., and Donna B. Evans. 1994. "Beyond Shared Rhetoric: A Collaborative Change Model for Integrating Preservice and Inservice Urban Educational Delivery Systems." *Journal of Teacher Education* 45,3:218–27.

Frye, Shirley M. 1989. The NCTM Standards—Challenges for All Classrooms." *Mathematics Teacher* 82:312–17.

Glisan, Eileen W., and June K. Phillips. 1989. "Immersion Experiences for Teachers: A Vehicle for Strengthening Language Teaching." *Canadian Modern Language Review* 45,3:478–84.

Glisan, Eileen W., and Valerie J. Sullivan. 1993. "Strengthening Foreign Language Teacher Preparation through Teacher-Supervisor Exchange. *Foreign Language Annals* 26,2:217–25.

Goldenberg, Claude, and Ronald Gallimore. 1991. "Changing Teaching Takes More Than a One-Shot Workshop." *Educational Leadership* 49,3:69–72.

Goodlad, John. 1991. "Why We Need a Complete Redesign of Teacher Education." *Educational Leadership* 49:4–10.

Hala, Marilyn. 1995. Personal communication, NCTM.

Hammadou, JoAnn, and Leslie L. Schrier. 1988. "A Four-State Survey of Secondary Administrators' Perceptions of Foreign Language Supervision." *Foreign Language Annals* 21,3:259–67.

Hayden, Rose L. 1989. "The UT-TEA-MLA Summer Institute for Foreign Language Professionals: Background Report and Evaluation." *ADFL Bulletin* 20,3:13–19.

Holmes Group. 1986. *Tomorrow's Teachers: A Report of the Holmes Group.* East Lansing, MI: Holmes Group.

————. 1990. *Tomorrow's Schools: Principles for the Design of Professional Development Schools.* East Lansing, MI: Holmes Group.

Huling-Austin, Leslie. 1992. "Research on Learning to Teach: Implications for Teacher Induction and Mentoring Programs. *Journal of Teacher Education* 43,3:173–80.

Inman, Julie E., and Robert LaBouve. 1994. *The Impact of Education Reform: A Survey of State Activities.* Washington, DC: Joint National Committee for Languages.

Johnson, Beverly. 1993. *Teacher as Researcher.* Washington, DC: American Association of Colleges for Teacher Education.

Jorstad, Helen L. 1980. "Inservice Teacher Education: Content and Process," pp. 81–86 in Dale L. Lange, ed., *Proceedings of the National Conference on Professional Priorities.* Boston: ACTFL.

Kemmis, Stephen, and Robin McTaggart. 1982. *The Action Research Planner.* Victoria, Australia: Deakin Univ. Press.

Kennedy, Mary M. 1990. "Professional Development Schools." *National Center for Research on Teacher Education Colloquy* 3,2. (ERIC Document Reproduction Service No. ED 326516).

Lafayette, Robert C. 1993. "Subject-Matter Content: What Every Foreign Language Teacher Needs to Know," pp. 124–58 in Gail Guntermann, ed., *Developing Language Teachers for a Changing World.* Lincolnwood, IL: National Textbook.

Laws, Barbara Boswell. 1991. "Why Teachers Must Play a Role in Setting National Standards." *Educational Leadership* 49,3:37–38.

Leighton, Mary S., and Gary Sykes. 1992. *The Professionalization of Teaching: Centerpiece of Kentucky Reform.* Charleston, WV: State Policy Program, Appalachia Educational Laboratory.

Leinwand, Steven J. 1992. "Sharing, Supporting, Risk Taking: First Steps to Instructional Reform." *Mathematics Teacher* 85,6:466–70.

Lenk, Harriet Anne. 1989. *A Case Study: The Induction of Two Alternate Route Social Studies Teachers.* Unpublished Ph.D. diss., Teachers College, Columbia University.

Little, Judith Warren. 1993. "Teachers' Professional Development in a Climate of Educational Reform." *Educational Evaluation and Policy Analysis* 15,2:129–51.

Mellgren, Millie Park, and Leslie Ann Caye. 1989. "School-University Collaboration in Second Language Teacher Education: Building a Successful Partnership." *Foreign Language Annals* 22,6:553–60.

Mesicek, Kris. 1993. "Quality in the Teaching Profession and Our Schools." *NCATE Quality Teaching Newsletter* 2,2, pp. 8–9.

Morain, Genelle. 1990. "Preparing Foreign Language Teachers: Problems and Possibilities." *ADFL Bulletin* 21,2:20–24.

Mosenthal, James H., and Deborah Loewenberg Ball. 1992. "Constructing New Forms of Teaching: Subject Matter Knowledge in Inservice Teacher Education." *Journal of Teacher Education* 43,5:347–56.

National Council of Teachers of Mathematics. 1989. *Curriculum and Evaluation Standards for School Mathematics.* Reston, VA: NCTM.

———. 1991. *Professional Standards for Teaching Mathematics.* Reston, VA: NCTM.

National Education Association. 1987. *Status of the American Public School Teacher, 1985–1986.* Washington, DC: NEA.

Nunan, David. 1990. "Action Research in the Language Classroom," pp. 62–81 in Jack C. Richards and David Nunan, eds., *Second Language Teacher Education.* Cambridge, Eng.: Cambridge Univ. Press.

Oja, Sharon N., and Gerald J. Pine. 1989. "Collaborative Action Research: Teachers' Stages of Development and School Contexts. *Peabody Journal of Education* 64,2:96–115.

Olson, Lynn. 1992. "Teacher's Guide to School Reform." *Teacher Magazine* 3,8:26–45.

PBS MATHLINE. 1995. Personal correspondence and announcements.

Phillips, June K. 1989. "Teacher Education: Target of Reform," pp. 11–40 in Helen S. Lepke, ed., *Shaping the Future: Challenges and Opportunities.* Middlebury, VT: Northeast Conference.

Provisional Learning Outcomes Framework. A Report by the Articulation and Achievement Project. 1993. College Board, ACTFL, The New England Network of Academic Alliances in Foreign Languages.

Ravitch, Diane. 1992. "National Standards and Curriculum Reform: A View from the Department of Education." *NAASP Bulletin* 76,548:24–29.

Riordan, Kathleen M. 1989. "Teachers Teaching Teachers: An InService Model That Works." *Foreign Language Annals* 22,2:185–88.

Rottenberg, Claire J., and David C. Berliner. 1990. *Expert and Novice Teachers' Conceptions of Common Classroom Activities.* Paper presented at the annual meeting of the American Educational Research Association, Boston, MA.

Schnur, James O., and Michael J. Golby. 1995. "Teacher Education: A University Mission." *Journal of Teacher Education* 46,1:11–18.

Schrier, Leslie L. 1989. "A Survey of Foreign Language Teacher Preparation Patterns and Procedures in Small, Private Colleges and Universities in the United States." Ph.D. diss., Ohio State University.

————. 1993. "Prospects for the Professionalization of Foreign Language Teaching," pp. 105–23 in Gail Guntermann, ed., *Developing Language Teachers for a Changing World.* Lincolnwood, IL: National Textbook.

Shulman, Lee S. 1987. "Knowledge and Teaching: Foundations of the New Reform." *Harvard Educational Review* 57,1:1–22.

Silber, Ellen, and Beth Waterfall. 1988. "Academic Alliances: School/College Faculty Collaboratives." *Foreign Language Annals* 21,6:587–90.

Smith, Roch C. 1985. "Meeting the Professional Needs of Teachers: A Graduate-Level Institute in Language and Literature." *ADFL Bulletin* 16,2:22–24.

Sparks, Dennis. 1994. "Staff Development Implications of National Board Certification: An Interview with NBPTS's James Smith." *Journal of Staff Development* 15,1:58–59.

Speece, Susan. 1993. "National Science Education Standards: How You Can Make a Difference." *The American Biology Teacher* 55,5:265–67.

Strasheim, Lorraine A. 1991. "Preservice and Inservice Teacher Education in the Nineties: The Issue Is Instructional Validity." *Foreign Language Annals* 24,2:101–7.

Tharp, Roland G., and Ronald Gallimore. 1988. *Rousing Minds to Life: Teaching, Learning, and Schooling in Social Context.* Cambridge, Eng.: Cambridge Univ. Press.

Tucker, G. Richard, and Richard Donato. 1995. "Developing a Research Component within a Teacher Education Program," pp. 453–70 in James E. Alatis, ed., Georgetown University Round Table on Languages and Linguistics. Washington, DC: Georgetown Univ. Press.

U.S. Department of Education. 1993. *Improving Math and Science Teaching: A Report on the Secretary's Second Conference on Mathematics and Science.* Washington, DC: Office of Educational Research and Improvement.

Wagner, Ellen D. 1993. *New Directions for American Education: Implications for Continuing Educators.* Washington, DC: Office of Educational Research and Improvement.

Wolf, W. C., Jr., and Kathleen M. Riordan. 1991. "Foreign Language Teachers' Demographic Characteristics, In-Service Training Needs, and Attitudes toward Teaching." *Foreign Language Annals* 24,6:471–78.

5

New Learners and New Environments: Challenges and Opportunities

Russell N. Campbell

University of California, Los Angeles

> Communication is at the heart of the human experience. The United States must educate students who are linguistically and culturally equipped to communicate successfully in a pluralistic American society and abroad. This imperative envisions a future in which ALL students will develop and maintain proficiency in English and at least one other language, modern or classical. Children who come to school from non-English backgrounds should also have opportunities to develop further proficiencies in their first language. (National Standards in Foreign Language Education 1995:1)

The noun *challenge,* as in "Solving this problem will be a major challenge," suggests a test of one's abilities, while the verb *challenge,* as in "I challenge you to solve this problem," suggests a dare but with an underlying assumption that there is a degree of obligation for the challenged to assert an effort toward the resolution of the problem. In the title of this article, both interpretations seem to apply.

The word *opportunities* is unambiguous in its positive connotation that there are rewards to be garnered if action is taken to seize the moment. In this case, the title is intended to suggest that those of us in the modern language teaching profession have a chance to make even greater contributions than we are currently making toward building a nation with significantly

---

Russell N. Campbell (Ph.D., University of Michigan, Ann Arbor) is director of the Language Resource Program, professor emeritus, and former chair of the TESL/Applied Linguistics Department at UCLA. He has served as president of TESOL and is a member of the board of trustees of the Center for Applied Linguistics in Washington, D.C. He was instrumental in the establishment of the first bilingual immersion program (Culver City Spanish Immersion Program) in the United States.

greater multilingual, multicultural resources. These challenges and opportunities are to be found in the development and implementation of appropriate instructional programs for a significant number of nontraditional students who await our professional attention. We will refer to these nontraditional students as "new learners," although some of these student populations have been in our schools for many decades. We will also consider some of the "new environments," or nontraditional instructional formats for teaching these "new learners."

Traditional Foreign Language Learners: Type T Students

An estimated 90 to 95 percent of all foreign language courses taught in the United States are designed for young adult native speakers of English. Typically the students are monolingual speakers of English enrolled in high school and university courses with little, if any, prior instruction in a foreign language. Given the predominance of this type of student, referred to hereafter as Type T (for traditional) students, it reasonably follows that the universities and colleges that train future teachers of modern languages, curriculum developers, textbook writers, publishers, and language test developers and administrators should dedicate the vast majority of their intellectual and fiscal resources to the service of this population. It is also the case that the bulk of research and development activities in foreign language teaching, learning, and testing reported in journals and presented at professional conferences reflect primary concern with the design, implementation, and evaluation of courses with Type T students in mind.

The investment of national foreign language education resources in this population is not in question: Clearly, provision of opportunities for typically monolingual anglophones to acquire proficiency in foreign languages is an admirable, worthwhile objective for both students and, ultimately, the nation and should not be diminished in any way. On the contrary, if we are to remedy the "scandalous" situation that was referred to in the 1980 presidential commission report (President's Commission 1980), then it behooves us to vigorously continue the search for the optimal conditions for the teaching of foreign languages to Type T students. It is lamentable, perhaps still "scandalous," that more than ten years later, Dolson and Lindholm (1995) could still venture the following assessments of one population of anglophone Americans.

As a group, English-speaking students in California tend to graduate from secondary schools with the following characteristics:

1. They are able to speak only one language, English. Even if they know something of another language, it is at a minimal, nonfunctional proficiency level;
2. They are menacingly ethnocentric, possessing little knowledge or appreciation of other cultural groups;
3. They have pronounced shortcomings in the academic, linguistic and social skills necessary to compete in an international economy;
4. Since little or no attention is given to the development of their crosscultural competencies, they are not well suited to participate in cooperative efforts to address global concerns of commerce, ecology, poverty or peace;
5. They are often unable to recognize racism and prejudice when these behaviors are manifested by their own group. Furthermore, they are not predisposed to stand up collectively or individually against such practices.

It is clearly important that modern language educators continue to seek more effective, more efficient, and more productive strategies for the teaching of foreign languages to Type T students. This article, however, will bring into focus another set of opportunities and challenges that teacher educators, teachers, curriculum developers, language examiners, textbook authors, publishers, and researchers face if they are to provide appropriate language instruction to untold thousands of American students who differ dramatically from Type T students.

Three types of "new learners" will be presented under the headings of *Type I* (for Immersion), *Type H* (for Heritage), and *Type HI* (for Heritage-Immersion).

New Foreign Language Learners: Type I Students

An anecdote will help introduce the discussion of Type I students. Spanish courses have been offered in a middle school in a Los Angeles suburb for many years. One Spanish teacher in this school is a woman; we will give her the fictitious name of Ms. Robinson. She has had more than twenty years of experience successfully introducing monolingual anglophone students to the linguistic features of this great language and, of equal importance, to many of the salient features that define the culture of the people who speak it. To Ms. Robinson's credit, her students have consistently performed well on local and state Spanish language examinations and she is well respected by her colleagues and students.

A few years ago, a group of new students from a particular elementary school in her district enrolled in one of Ms. Robinson's elementary Spanish classes. Although these young students were clearly representatives of the middle class neighborhood in which the school was located and appeared similar in every way to the students she was accustomed to teaching, they were in fact significantly different, and, much to her dismay, she found herself ill prepared to teach them as she had taught hundreds of other students in that school. Very little in her experience or her repertoire of teaching methods, materials, and assessment instruments were relevant to these "new learners."

Unlike her typical students, these anglophone children, monolingual English speakers when they began their formal schooling, were not neophytes to the Spanish language. In fact they had participated in a Spanish immersion program (SIP) (Campbell 1984) since they entered elementary school at the kindergarten level. Although they had never enrolled in traditional Spanish courses, they had studied approximately 65 percent of the elementary school curriculum through the medium of the Spanish language. As one student reported, "We don't study Spanish, we study in Spanish."

The Spanish immersion program in which these students had participated was a replication of an innovative approach to foreign language education first introduced in a suburb of Montreal in the late 1960s.

The Canadian Experiment

Responding to a group of anglophone parents' insistence that their children must be provided opportunities to attain a high proficiency in French, a language of great political and economic importance in the Canadian province of Quebec, school officials and McGill University scholars first studied and then rejected a number of Foreign Language in the Elementary School (FLES) curricula and sought a model of foreign language education that held greater promise. Ultimately, having exhausted their search for an existing, highly productive model, these educators posed this question: "What if we taught our monolingual English-speaking elementary school children *in* French *as if* they were French?"

This was deemed an intuitively acceptable question given the observations by the interested parties that many children in Europe, Africa, Asia, and elsewhere are routinely enrolled in schools in which the language of instruction is different from the students' home language and that there was evidence that they not only succeeded academically but acquired the language of instruction as well. It was noted, however, that in those schools it was typically the case that attention to the development of the students' competence in their home languages was not a critical part of the school curriculum. For the

Canadian parents and school officials, the experimental program had to promise opportunities: as the first priority, for normal development of English language skills; second, for normal scholastic achievement; and third, for high proficiency in French.

With these demands in mind, a kindergarten through sixth grade bilingual curriculum was designed, and in 1968 the first French immersion program (FIP) kindergarten class was inaugurated. Since 1968 hundreds of school districts in Canada and the United States have adopted the principles and procedures that emerged from this experimental program. The efficacy of the model has been substantiated by hundreds of research and evaluation projects with the results reported in numerous theses, dissertations, articles, and books (cf. especially Genesee 1987; and California State Department of Education 1984). Here a brief description of the model will suffice.

Details of the French Immersion Program

To accommodate the acquisition and development of both languages, the division of instructional time in the two languages was approximately as follows:

Kindergarten	100% in French
First grade	100% in French
Second grade	80% in French, 20% in English
Third grade	60% in French, 40% in English
Fourth, fifth, and sixth grades	50% in French, 50% in English

The subject matter taught in the two languages was completely consistent with the standard elementary school curriculum taught in all Canadian public schools. However, instruction in English language arts (reading and writing) was delayed until the second grade. It should also be noted that no course or subject, or portions of courses, were ever duplicated or repeated, i.e., first in French and then in English or vice versa.

Goals

The designers of the first FIP established the following goals for the bilingual curriculum:

- To provide the participating students with functional competency in the second language (French)
- To promote and maintain normal levels of first language (English) development

- To ensure achievement in academic subjects commensurate with the students' academic ability and grade level
- To instill in the students an understanding of and appreciation for the target language group and their language and culture without detracting in any way from the students' identity with and appreciation for the home language and culture (Genesee 1984:12)

Results

At the end of their elementary school studies, students participating in the immersion program consistently perform scholastically—as measured by standardized achievement tests administered in English—as well as or better than their peers who are enrolled in English-only curricula. In addition, these students have shown no retardation in the development of English language skills; are measurably less ethnocentric; and acquire levels of "functional" (Genesee 1987) competence in the target languages that are superior to students in any other known foreign language programs designed for elementary school students (Campbell et al. 1985). In brief, all the program's goals and expectations were met by the pilot group of students, and subsequently, by many thousands in other schools in the United States and Canada who have now participated in French, Spanish, German, Cantonese, Mandarin, Russian, Arabic, and Hawaiian immersion programs.

Krashen (1984) has described the success of immersion programs as follows:

- Immersion students do as well in English language skills as students educated entirely in English.
- Immersion students do as well in subject matter as students who are educated entirely in English.
- Immersion students acquire a great deal of the second language. Canadian immersion students easily out perform students enrolled in traditional French classes, and, after several years of immersion, approach native speakers of French on some measures. Immersion students do not typically achieve full native competence in French while they are in the programme; they have an "accent" and make some grammatical errors when they speak.

The comment in this quotation that immersion students make "some grammatical errors when they speak" can be extended to all attempts at production, as contrasted with comprehension, of the target language, whether spoken or written. Following is a sample of unedited, unplanned writing produced by a sixth-grade Spanish immersion student.

Deportes

A mi megusta las deportes. Yo coleciona cartas de muchos deportes y yo juege a unos tambien. El deporte que megusta mas es la Baseball. Yo juge un equipo para 3 anos y you tengo mas de mil cartas de Baseball. Ami tambaien megusta el Football Eurpana. No colecione cartas de Footbasll pero juge en un equipo para unos anas.

Los deportes son bueno para you porque me da excerciso y me hace furte. Los deportes tambien da un cosa comun para muchos mino y pueden hablar de deportas o jugar. You pienso que deportes son buenas para todos personas viejo o no viejo. Da personas also en comun y da excersio a todos.

Los deportes tiene also para todos, para personas que lefustan el frio, hay el ski. Para personas que legustan el agua, hay nadar y barcos. Y para personas que legustan bolas, hay football, baseball, tennis y muchas mas. Ultimo, para personas que no quier agua, or frio, hay juegos de pensar como chess y cartas. Los deportes tien algo por todas.

An analysis of this writing sample reveals a high frequency of grammatical error including deviation from rules of agreement (gender, number, person), selection of articles and prepositions, spelling and punctuation, and vocabulary usage. On the other hand, it also reveals the student's ability to communicate a complex body of information that reports preferences, arguments, and choices. It further reveals an extensive vocabulary, as well as correct usage of many grammatical conventions and standard orthographic representations. Clearly, if one takes the "half full" view of the student's achievements, one sees an individual ready to take the next steps toward becoming a mature, literate user of the Spanish language.

As will be repeated below, the opportunities and challenges such students present for foreign language teachers are exceedingly great. The question: How can the modern language teaching profession exploit the wealth of communicative competence that Type I students bring to our classes to produce a substantial number of American children with high competence in foreign languages?

It is important to note again that students in the type of immersion program described here receive approximately 65 percent of all their elementary (K–6) school instruction in the target foreign language (ostensibly taught as if they were native speakers of the target language). This requires students to comprehend and learn from their teachers' oral instruction; comprehend and learn from reading material presented in their textbooks and other written materials; and produce oral and written discourse in fulfilling both social and scholastic functions in the classroom.

Theoretical Underpinnings

Krashen (1984) argues that immersion works because the underlying principles that define the pedagogical and structural features of immersion programs are consistent with his second language acquisition hypotheses, especially the hypothesis that claims that "we acquire language in only one way: when we understand messages in that language, when we receive comprehensible input" (p. 62). It is quite true that immersion education, as described here, exhibits many aspects of accepted current psycholinguistic theory related to second language acquisition. It is not surprising, therefore, given the stamp of approval of leading second language acquisition theoreticians and the reported success of thousands of students in the acquisition of foreign languages, that the immersion model has now been implemented in a large number of American schools.

Since the inauguration of a single Spanish immersion kindergarten class of about thirty students in Culver City, California, in 1971, the number of schools offering immersion programs in the United States alone has grown so that now there are approximately 33,000 students enrolled in immersion programs in 187 schools in 25 states and Washington, D.C.: of these 118 are Spanish immersion, 58 French, 18 Japanese, and 13 German (Center for Applied Linguistics 1995). There is every reason to believe that this number will continue to grow, thus providing modern language teachers with increasing opportunities and challenges to guide these students to higher levels of competence in their chosen foreign languages.

It was students from one such school in Culver City, California, who presented themselves to "Ms. Robinson" for continued instruction in Spanish in the aforementioned middle school. Clearly, to her considerable consternation, the syllabus that she designed for Type T students, the textbooks chosen to teach them, and the achievement goals established for the course were not compatible with the needs of Type I students.

Summary of Type I students

For subsequent comparison with other types of "new learners," we provide the following summary of characteristics of Type I students who have completed a typical elementary school language immersion program. Type I students demonstrate

- Very good comprehension of both spoken and written discourse
- Low to low-intermediate production proficiency in both spoken and written performance

- Extensive vocabulary acquisition that is limited to social and scholastic experiences in school contexts
- Restricted knowledge of sociolinguistic rules that govern choice of registers in both spoken and written discourse
- Near complete acquisition of target-language phonology
- Above-average (when compared with nonimmersion peers) knowledge and appreciation of cultural characteristics of speakers of target languages

Research on Immersion Foreign Language Education

The characteristics given here reflect the results currently being derived from immersion programs. It should be noted that a substantial number of research scholars and language teachers are dedicated to improving the model so that the results will be even more favorable in the years to come. Lapkin, Shapson, and Swain (1990) have defined a number of research and development questions on French immersion in Canada that can be generalized to other target language programs. A selected subset of their questions follow:

- How can the vocabulary component of existing immersion programs be strengthened?
- How can we work toward the early detection of students having language-related difficulties in immersion? What types of remedial activity are effective in minimizing such difficulties?
- How can grammatical and discourse knowledge (including vocabulary) best be integrated with immersion content teaching?
- Does extended expressive second language use significantly alter immersion learners' proficiency? What are the most effective ways of encouraging extended expressive second language use by students?
- Can the usefulness of productive second language activity, such as computer writing networks, be empirically established, and, if so, what are the implications for implementation?
- Do certain subject areas lend themselves more readily than others to being offered in the second language (in terms of content learning, second language learning, and the integration of content and language)?

Resolution of these and other questions will, over time, positively modify the language development characteristics of Type I students, thus providing modern language teachers with a different, higher-level set of teaching/learning variables to take into consideration as they plan for these students. It is apparent that the most significant research on these questions will result from sustained, active participation of modern language teachers.

A significant opportunity and challenge for the traditional foreign language teacher is to help find ways to accommodate Type I students in middle and secondary school foreign language curricula.

New Foreign Language Learners: Type H Students

The traditional foreign language teachers' opportunities and challenges are not limited to the influx of Type I new learners into their comfortable world of Type T students.

The results of the spring 1993 language census, compiled by the Statewide Education Demographics Unit of the California State Department of Education (Greco 1994), identified 1,151,819 students as limited English proficient (LEP). This was an increase from 488,000 such students enrolled in 1983, and there is every reason to believe that there will be a steady increase in LEP enrollments well into the next century—not only in California but in many other states as well. By definition these children speak a language other than, or in addition to, English in their homes. Since the non-English languages spoken by these children are often referred to as "heritage" (also called "home," "ancestral," or "native") languages, we will refer to students who speak them as Type H (for heritage) students.

A number of educators have observed that the competence that these students bring to our schools constitutes a potentially valuable national resource, one worthy of conservation. In response to the question

> In the spring of 1967, you testified at the U.S. Senate hearings that led to ESEA, Title VII. What did you tell the senators?

Joshua Fishman responded:

> I tried to convey the image of America that my research had helped me form—that is, a culturally pluralistic society in which our non-English cultures, whether immigrant or indigenous, deserved to be publicly recognized and fostered as contributing to the creativity, authenticity, and ethnic supportiveness of American democracy. *I emphasized the need to conserve the languages and cultures that make up the fabric of U.S. society. Today, America's non-English languages and cultures continue to represent resources of inestimable worth—resources that can contribute to the country's riches and to the cohesiveness of its communities.* (California Dept. of Education 1994:26; emphasis added)

Campbell and Schnell (1987) expressed similar views:

> Competencies in a large number of languages brought to our schools by representatives of linguistic minority groups are, through an unspoken policy of subtractive language education, irrevocably lost as national foreign language resources. This occurs in spite of repeated declarations of national leaders in commerce, defense, education, and international affairs that our foreign language resources are in a "scandalous" state. There are promising ways in which our schools can conserve the extraordinarily valuable language resources that are currently being squandered. (p. 177)

Many modern language educators have been quite conscious of Type H students, especially when they present themselves for enrollment into courses that are designed for Type T students. From the point of view of traditional language teachers, these students have, for very good reasons, been seen as problematic.

A brief, overly simplified, history of typical Type H students would include the following information. The primary language of communication in their homes and neighborhoods would be the language of their parents and ancestors; thus, the students' dominant and perhaps only language upon entering elementary school would be the home language. It is estimated that these children, by the age of five, would have acquired nearly 100 percent of the phonology of the heritage language, 80 to 85 percent of its morphology, an equal percentage of its syntactic rules, and many of the rules that govern conversational discourse. It is also the case that they would differentiate their speech according to the relative status of their interlocutors; that is, they would have usually acquired many of the sociolinguistic rules that govern choice of social register. Finally, by this age these children will have acquired the rather extensive vocabulary necessary to fulfill all the social functions associated with, and limited to, their brief life experiences in their homes and neighborhoods.

In a very limited number of American schools some of these children will have received early instruction in their home languages while, concurrently, studying English as a second language (ESL); however, even in these schools every effort is made to "mainstream" them, as soon as possible, into an all-English-medium curriculum. For these children, and certainly for children who do not even have the benefit of this transitional form of bilingual education, there will be no additional opportunities in our schools for them to build on the considerable language competence they exhibit when they begin their formal education.

In most cases, Saturday or after-school heritage language programs notwithstanding, these students change from being heritage-language-dominant to English-language-dominant during the intervening years between early elementary school and middle or secondary school. For most, not only will development in their home languages be aborted, but it is probable that there will be substantial loss or attrition of the oral skills they demonstrated when they were five or six years old and, of course, they will have no opportunity to attain literacy skills in their home languages.

It is argued, nevertheless, that these students retain a level of residual competence in their home languages that constitutes an extremely valuable national language resource. Most of them have retained most of the vocabulary, all or nearly all the phonology, and much of the ability to form words and sentences in agreement with the grammatical conventions acquired during their early childhood. These students also have considerable knowledge of the local community's cultural traditions and values and, by extension, of the larger international community that speaks varieties of their ancestral languages. In many ways, this body of retained competence is greater than what might be acquired or learned in traditional language courses by Type T students even after several years of instruction. It is also the case, however, that much of what Type T students are taught has not been available to Type H students; for example, Type T students are taught a so-called prestige dialect of the language, while Type H students, in most cases, have acquired a local dialect that exhibits some major differences in vocabulary and in grammatical categories. Type T students are taught to read and write in the target language while Type H students, as mentioned above, rarely receive instruction in these skills. Clearly these divergent characteristics suggest the apparent incompatibility for instruction of Type T and H students in the same classroom.

It has been argued (Campbell and Lindholm 1990) that the residual competence of Type H students can and should be considered a substantial basis on which to build instructional programs. The expectations are that such programs could economically produce a wealth of highly literate adult users of these heritage languages to the considerable benefit of the individuals and to the advantage of American educational, business, and diplomatic institutions. The considerable opportunities and challenges to the modern language teaching profession are, again, the design and implementation of language courses appropriate to help Type H students reach their potential.

Summary of Type H Students' Competence in Their Ancestral Languages

Clearly, the levels of linguistic competence and the depth of knowledge and appreciation of their community's culture that Type H students bring to our schools varies dramatically along a continuum from nearly no competence to that of an educated, literate native speaker of a prestige dialect. Nevertheless, it is possible to provide a profile that will capture the characteristics of a substantial sample of Type H students who are candidates for heritage language instruction in the middle or high school. Type H students will typically demonstrate

- Extremely good oral proficiency
- Command of nearly 100 percent of the phonological rules of a prestige dialect of the heritage language
- Extensive although restricted vocabulary
- Minor deviations from morphological, syntactic, and discoursal rules of a prestige dialect of the heritage language
- Functional illiteracy in the heritage language
- Knowledge and appreciation of, and sensitivity to, the heritage culture

Research on Type H Student Language Programs

Valdés (1995) has defined a number of fundamental questions that need to be addressed if we are to solve the many unanswered questions related to the design and implementation of appropriate courses for Type H students. Among these are

- What can be done in the classroom to create an environment in which the standard language can be acquired?
- How much access to the standard language is necessary before particular features are noticed and acquired?
- Does avoidance of stigmatized features and production of standard features depend on the development and use of an internal monitor? How does the monitor develop?
- What sets of activities promote language awareness?
- What kind of language exposure provides the most benefit?
- What kinds of exposure (e.g., reading, writing, viewing and analysis of videos, studying formal grammar) contribute *most* to the acquisition of an alternative set of rules?
- How is a prestige dialect acquired in natural settings?
- What is the order of acquisition of different features?
- How and why do such features become salient to the speaker of the nonprestige variety?

• How do personal interactions contribute to such language awareness? (p. 313)

Resolution of these and other questions will certainly provide teacher educators, curriculum designers, textbook writers, and language examiners vastly improved bases on which to build instructional programs for Type H students.

New Foreign Language Learners: Type HI Students

As described above, observers and evaluators of immersion programs, although pleased with the overall results obtained, recognize the shortcomings, especially insofar as production skills are concerned; therefore, they are constantly seeking ways to improve on the model through teacher education, quantitative and qualitative research, materials selection and production, and test development. Educators who deplore the predictable loss of the linguistic skills Type H students bring to our schools are, as exemplified by the questions cited above (Valdés 1995), also seeking opportunities to reverse the longstanding trend of subtractive bilingual education imposed on linguistic minority children.

During the mid 1970s, a group of educators in San Diego (San Diego City Schools 1982) posed one of the most important foreign-language-education-related questions of the past century; namely, what would be the consequences of enrolling Type H students, who were native speakers of the target language, in San Diego's Spanish immersion programs? This question led to the establishment of a two-way bilingual education (TWBE) curriculum model that promised an opportunity for anglophone children to acquire a second language and an opportunity for their Type H peers to maintain and develop their first language.

Champions of the immersion model saw the potential value for Type I children in TWBE in the fact that they would have input not only from the teacher but also from their Spanish-speaking peers, thus increasing manifold the acquisition data available to them. It was further assumed that the influence of peer evaluation might be as powerful as, if not more powerful than, teachers' reactions to deviant grammatical performance. (Even five- and six-year-old children can react derisively and embarrass a peer who joins a masculine definite article with a feminine noun, as in *el muchacha*.)

Educators and parents believed that a curriculum that taught 65 percent or more of the elementary school curriculum in the Type H students' home language might well provide them with the valuable opportunity not only to retain the skills they bring to the school site, but also to develop toward mature adult literate usage of that language. It was further understood that the original purpose of the *Lau vs. Nichols* (1974) supreme court decision would be served for the Type H students; namely, LEPs in the TWBE programs would be taught the basic, fundamental building blocks of scholastic development in a language they understood. Curriculum designers also expected that Type H students, along with their anglophone peers, would acquire one of the prestige dialects of the target language.

Finally, it was assumed that observation of their ancestral language employed by highly regarded teachers and school officials as the vehicle for a substantial part of the school's academic program had the potential for positive impact on Type H students' self-esteem and self-respect.

However, it must be noted, neither parents nor school officials would be satisfied with the single goal of heritage language development. They recognized the critical importance of concurrent development in English language skills and of acceptable scholastic achievement. It has been frequently observed that parents of Type H students would not tolerate a program that did not give top priority to these two goals.

Two-Way Bilingual Curriculum Design
for Heritage/Immersion Students

The question posed by those in San Diego concerned for both Type H and I students gave rise to a curriculum whose structural characteristics were almost identical to characteristics described for "one-way" immersion programs (that is, foreign language programs for anglophones). The most significant difference was that half the students in TWBE classes were Type H students and half were Type I students, thus an HI category of "new learner."

Christian (1994) establishes eight criteria for success in TWBE:

1. Programs should provide a minimum of four years of bilingual instruction to participating students.

2. The focus of instruction should be the same core academic curriculum that students in other programs experience.

3. Optimal language input (input that is comprehensible, interesting, and of sufficient quantity) as well as opportunities for output should be provided to students, including quality language arts instruction in both languages.

4. The target (non-English) language should be used for instruction a minimum of 50 percent of the time (to a maximum of 90 percent in the early grades), and English should be used at least 10 percent of the time.

5. The program should provide an additive bilingual environment where all students have the opportunity to learn a second language while continuing to develop their native language proficiency.

6. Classrooms should include a balance of students from the target language and English-speaking backgrounds who participate in instructional activities together.

7. Positive interactions among students should be facilitated with strategies such as cooperative learning.

8. Characteristics of effective schools should be incorporated into the programs, such as qualified personnel and home-school collaboration. (p. 2)

Goals

It was assumed by the designers of the TWBE model that a program that met Christian's eight criteria would attain the following goals:

• Students will develop high proficiency in their first language and in a second language.

• Students will perform at or above grade level in academic areas in both languages.

• Students will demonstrate positive cross-cultural attitudes and behaviors and great self-esteem. (Christian 1994)

Results

Although there are idiosyncratic variations, the basic TWBE model has now been adopted by 169 schools in 92 school districts in 17 states and the District of Columbia. Of these schools, 155 offer Spanish/English TWBE programs, 4 Cantonese/English, 3 Korean/English, 2 Navajo/English, 2 Japanese/English, and 1 each Russian/English, Portuguese/English, and French/English. A number of preliminary evaluations have been conducted to ascertain the success of the programs in meeting the defined goals. In synthesizing the evaluations, both Christian (1994) and Genesee (1987) find reason to be extremely optimistic about their efficacy. English-dominant students achieve about the same degree of linguistic proficiency in the target language as have students in one-way immersion programs and perform scholastically at the same highly satisfactory levels. The most substantial advantages for the anglophone population may well be in the social and psychological outcomes. For example, Lambert and Cazabon (1994) found a "clear preference for having friends from both (Anglo and Hispanic) groups" and for mixed ethnic/racial classrooms as opposed to ethnically segregated schooling.

The results for the Type H students in TWBE are equally positive. In research on non-native-English-speaking students in five urban districts, Collier (1994) shows that students in TWBE programs achieved greater educational gains than students in other bilingual and ESL programs. Although the Korean/ English TWBE programs cited above were inaugurated only four years ago, some extremely positive results have been recorded (Bae 1994). For example, tests of reading and writing in standard Korean orthography (*hangul*) were administered to three matched cohorts of students at the end of their first grade studies: cohort 1, native Korean children in an elementary school in Seoul, Korea; cohort 2, Korean-American children studying in an all-English-medium curriculum in the United States; and cohort 3, Korean-American children enrolled in Korean/English TWBE programs. The results clearly demonstrated the advantages that cohort 3 children had over cohort 2 students in that with rare exceptions the latter, not unexpectedly, demonstrated few literacy skills or none at all. When cohort 3 children were compared to their Korean peers (cohort 1), *no statistically significant difference* was found in their performance in either reading or writing.

The following transliterated (from *hangul*) and translated writing samples were produced under test conditions by typical representatives of cohorts 2 and 3. These samples reveal, even to those not familiar with the Korean language, the lamentable lack of writing skills of the Type H student in cohort 2 in contrast to the advanced, for first graders, literacy skills of the TWBE student from cohort 3. Both students were responding to the instructions: "Look at the picture and write a story in Korean."

The cohort 2 representative's entire response:

Nachinkupiey
I friend rain at

The cohort 3 representative's response:

Nayaka cipey kako issnuntay, etten ailul mannassta.
(When I was going home, I met a boy.)

Ku ainun wusani mangkacyese wulko issessta.
(The boy was crying because his umbrella was broken.)

Kulayse kathi wusanul ssessta.
(So I shared my umbrella with him.)

Kuainay cipkkaci taylta cwuessta
(I walked to his house)

Kuliko naycipey kassta.
(and went to my home.)

The cohort 3 sample demonstrates the student's ability to use advanced grammar rules of cohesion, reference, and tense and aspect markers.

Given the conditions and the demands of their bilingual education in the United States, there is little expectation that the H students will be able to maintain the rate and breadth of linguistic development in Korean of their peers in Korea. There is, however, strong evidence that the participants in the Korean/English program will avoid the linguistically impoverished fate of their Korean-American peers in the same schools who are not enrolled in the TWBE programs.

Characteristics of Type HI Students

There are two subgroups of students who emerge from TWBE programs— anglophones and "native speakers" of the target language.

The anglophones demonstrate essentially the same levels of achievement in the target language as do students emerging from one-way immersion programs. The native-speaker students demonstrate the following characteristics:

- Full capability of reading and comprehending grade-level textbooks written in the heritage language
- Adherence to semantic, grammatical, phonological, and sociolinguistic features of a prestige dialect of the heritage language
- Deficiency in academic writing skills (somewhat similar to English writing deficiencies often exhibited by anglophones after completing elementary school education)
- Great self-esteem and pride in the heritage culture

Of the four groups of students considered, Type T, I, H, and HI, clearly the native speakers who complete a TWBE program will be the most advanced, linguistically and culturally, of the students entering our middle and secondary schools. Designing and implementing courses appropriate for this population will be a formidable challenge. However, if the challenge is successfully met, the rewards could be immense in terms of the substantial increase in national foreign language and culture resources.

New Environments

The immersion and TWBE models of foreign language education are new environments in which American children—both anglophones and linguistic minority students—are provided outstanding opportunities to acquire competence in languages other than English. These programs are new only in the sense that they have been designed and developed largely without the involvement of traditional foreign language educators. One can imagine that if traditional educators had been involved, some of the shortcomings that immersion and TWBE students bring to middle and secondary school foreign language courses might be different in kind and in magnitude. It is expected that as applied linguists and language educators combine their efforts to resolve questions such as those defined by Lapkin, Shapson, and Swain (1990) and Valdés (1995), new environments, that is, new instructional strategies and formats, will emerge to accommodate Type I, H, and HI students.

It is probable that the new environments will include curricula that adhere to the principles and practices that define an approach to modern language education that is called content-based instruction (CBI). According to Brinton, Snow, and Wesche (1989), CBI principles are consistent with current second language acquisition theory and with historical positions held by language educators who claim that "a second language is learned most effectively when used as the medium to convey informational content of interest and relevance to the learner" (1989). Some of the positive learning conditions that are fulfilled by the CBI approach are

- The content-based language curriculum takes into account the interests and needs of the learners
- It incorporates the eventual uses the learner will make of the target language
- It builds on the students' previous learning experiences
- It allows a focus on use as well as on usage
- It offers learners the necessary conditions for second language learning by exposing them to meaningful language in use (Brinton, Snow, and Wesche 1989)

An extensive literature (e.g., Crandall 1987; Early, Thew, and Wakefield 1986; Wilkinson 1985) defines content-based instruction, reports on the results of its applications, and lays out future research and development activities. This same literature gives only sparse attention to the design and implementation of courses tailored to the strengths and deficiencies that Type I, H, and HI students bring to our schools. The foreign language teaching profession clearly has an opportunity to explore the apparent advantages of content-based instruction to serve these students.

It may well be that other new environments, ones that are increasingly being explored for Type T students, will be available to Type I, H, and HI students; namely, the expedient, flexible, individualized instruction that can come from computer-mediated learning, electronic networks, and multimedia systems. The contributions that emerging technology can make have just begun to be understood and exploited. Content-based models and electronic media tools should be developed with new learners in mind.

Conclusion

We began by noting that some 95 percent of our professional attention has traditionally been given to the foreign language and culture education of anglo-American young adults in our high schools and universities. While this is certainly deemed of great national importance and every effort should be made to increase the efficacy of our instructional programs for these Type T students, we are challenged to apply our experience, imagination, and energies to the instruction of Type I, H, and HI students, who have already acquired significant, valuable linguistic skills and cultural knowledge, so that they may be counted among those Americans who are truly mature, adult, literate users of English and at least one other language.

References

Bae, Jungok. 1994. "Preliminary Results of the Korean Literacy Development of Students in the Korean/English Two-Way Immersion Program (KETWIP)." Unpublished manuscript. UCLA.

Brinton, D. M., M. A. Snow, and M. B. Wesche. 1989. *Content-Based Second Language Instruction.* New York: Newbury House.

California State Department of Education, ed. 1984. *Studies on Immersion Education: A Collection for United States Educators.* Sacramento: California State Department of Education.

California State Department of Education. 1994. "BEOutreach Interviews Joshua Fishman." *BEOutreach* 5,2:26.

Campbell, Russell N. 1984. "The Immersion Education Approach to Foreign Language Teaching," pp. 114–43 in California State Department of Education, ed., *Studies on Immersion Education: A Collection for United States Educators.* Sacramento: California State Department of Education.

Campbell, Russell N., Tracy C. Gray, Nancy C. Rhodes, and Margaret-Ann A. Snow. 1985. "Foreign Language Learning in the Elementary Schools: A Comparison of Three Language Programs." *Modern Language Journal* 69,1:44–54.

Campbell, Russell N., and Kathryn J. Lindholm. 1990. "Conservation of Language Resources." *Second Language Acquisition/Foreign Language Learning* 226–39.

Campbell, Russell N., and Susan Schnell. 1987. "Language Conservation." *Annals of the American Academy of Political and Social Science* 490:177–85.

Center for Applied Linguistics. 1995. *Total and Partial Immersion Language Programs in U.S. Schools.* Washington, DC: Center for Applied Linguistics.

Christian, Donna. 1994. *Two-Way Bilingual Education: Students Learning through Two Languages.* Educational Practice Report No. 12. Washington, DC: The National Center for Research on Cultural Diversity and Second Language Learning.

Collier, Virginia. 1994. "Promising Practices in Public Schools." Paper presented at the annual meeting of Teachers of English to Speakers of Other Languages, Baltimore, MD.

Crandall, J., ed. 1987. *ESL through Content-Area Instruction: Mathematics, Science, Social Studies.* Englewood Cliffs, NJ: Prentice-Hall Regents.

Dolson, David P., and Kathryn Lindholm. 1995. "World Class Education for Children in California: A Comparison of the Bilingual/Immersion and European School Models," in Tove Skutnabb-Kangas, ed., *Multilingualism for All.* Netherlands: Swets & Zeitlinger.

Early, M., C. Thew, and P. Wakefield. 1986. *Integrating Language and Content Instruction K–12: An ESL Resource Book.* Victoria, B.C., Can.: Publications Service Branch, Ministry of Education.

Genesee, Fred. 1984. "Canadian French Immersion Education: Current Administrative and Instructional Practices," pp. 32–57 in California State Department of Education, ed., *Studies on Immersion Education: A Collection for United States Educators.* Sacramento: California State Department of Education.

———. 1987. *Learning through Two Languages: Studies of Immersion and Bilingual Education.* Cambridge, MA: Newbury House.

Greco, Jim. 1994. "LEP Student Enrollment Up 6.3 Percent in 1993." *BEOutreach* 5,1:18.

Krashen, Stephen D. 1984. "Immersion: Why It Works and What It Has Taught Us." *Language and Society* 22:61–64.

Lambert, Wallace E., and Maria Cazabon. 1994. *Student's View of the Amigos Program.* Research Report No. 11. Washington, DC: National Center for Research on Cultural Diversity and Second Language Learning.

Lapkin, Sharon, Stan Shapson, and Merrill Swain. 1990. "French Immersion Research Agenda for the 90s." *Canadian Modern Language Review/La Revue canadienne des langues vivantes* 46,4:638–74.

Lau vs. Nichols. 1974. United States Supreme Court. no. 72-6520.

National Standards in Foreign Language Education. 1995. *Standards for Foreign Language Learning: Preparing for the Twenty-first Century.* New York: National Standards in Foreign Language Education.

President's Commission on Foreign Languages and International Studies. 1980. "Strength through Wisdom: A Critique of U.S. Capability." *Modern Language Journal* 64:9–57.

San Diego City Schools. 1982. *Bilingual Demonstration Project.* San Diego, CA: San Diego Unified School District.

Valdés, Guadalupe. 1995. "The Teaching of Minority Languages as Academic Subjects: Pedagogical and Theoretical Challenges." *Modern Language Journal* 79,3:299–328.

Wilkinson, A. M. 1985. "A Freshman Writing Course in Parallel with a Science Class." *College Composition and Communication* 36,2:160–65.

6

Technology, Reform, and Foreign Language Standards: A Vision for Change

Mel Nielsen and Elizabeth Hoffman
Nebraska Department of Education

As the nation enters a second decade of sustained educational reform, the future of foreign language education appears bright. With much fanfare, the national K–12 student content standards in foreign language education made their official public debut in Anaheim, California, at the 1995 conference of the American Council on the Teaching of Foreign Languages (ACTFL). Although the national foreign language standards are a product of educational reform, the overall national reform movement, which has contributed so much to the advancement of foreign language education in the United States, is itself not in such a healthy state.

Melvin L. Nielsen (Ph.D., University of Nebraska, Lincoln) is director of Foreign Language Education for the Nebraska Department of Education and director of the Nebraska Foreign Language Standards and Frameworks Project. He is a frequent presenter, author, grant writer, curriculum consultant, and consultant in the pedagogy and technology of distance learning. He is a member of the board of reviewers for *Foreign Language Annals,* has served as president of the National Council of State Supervisors of Foreign Language (NCSSFL), and has taught literature and pedagogy in schools and colleges.

Elizabeth Hoffman (M.A., Creighton University) is the distance learning project coordinator at the Nebraska Department of Education for the Satellite Educational Resources Consortium (SERC) Japanese satellite distance learning language course. She was a German teacher for seventeen years. She has served as president of American Association of Teachers of German, National Federation of Modern Language Teachers Associations, and Nebraska Foreign Language Association. She is a member of the board of directors of the Joint National Committee for Languages/National Council for Languages and International Studies and has served on the board of directors of the Central States Conference on the Teaching of Foreign Languages. She has received many awards, including the Florence Steiner Award for Foreign Language Leadership K–12 in 1995, the Walt Disney Salute to the American Teacher Award, and the $10,000 Warren Buffett Outstanding Teacher Award.

National Reform

The year 2000 was to mark the time when issues cited in *A Nation at Risk* (National Commission on Excellence in Education 1983) would have been resolved, and the transformation of the nation's school system would be well under way. Unfortunately, the systemic reform that was to have resulted in the redesign of education and the restructuring of schools "from the bottom up and the top down" continues to be an elusive goal. Our nation's schools remain isolated in their efforts to effect significant and lasting change for all students. Few exemplary schools, for example, have led to significant and lasting improvements in learning for large numbers of young people, and by the year 2020, the number of at-risk students is expected to exceed 50 percent (Rossi and Stringfield 1995).

Sarason (1995:84) characterizes the current state of reform as "almost always working in the repair mode." This view is frequently reflected in the current professional education literature. No nation in the world has a larger store of knowledge and resources to draw upon than the United States. Why then has reform proceeded so slowly? Among the often-cited root causes are lack of coordinated effort in education policy, issues of control represented in the devolution of power to local schools, and failure to communicate a clear understanding of reform to a public already disenchanted with education. The reform movement has been characterized as either so ambitious and all-encompassing that it fails to take into account the extent and depth of what is required, or so confined within existing structures that it can operate "only in the repair mode."

Technology and Reform

Technology, which was to have been the agent of change in school reform, has failed to bring about the anticipated transformation of schools. Only a handful of schools currently have access to the technologies that were to have ushered in an era of equity and opportunity in learning. According to a recent report from the Office of Technology Assessment, even among the few schools fortunate enough to possess the equipment, most tend to use it in conventional applications (Brandt 1995).

Ironically, both technology and the knowledge to use it have been around for some time. Why then has technology not had the desired impact in the restructuring of schools? The answer may lie in the middle ground between the broad view of educational reform and the piecemeal efforts of local schools to address the multiple challenges of reform.

Why should schools remain isolated in their attempts at educational reform when technology can be used to overcome the obstacles of cost, distance, and time, all of which have brought previous attempts at reform to a halt? Rather than leave the overwhelming burdens of cost to schools, why not begin to think of technology as a way help schools move their reform agenda forward? How can this be done and who will do it? Perhaps an answer can be found by looking to the national standards.

National Standards

Although each discipline faced its own set of challenges in the writing of national standards, all were painstakingly developed with the input of thousands of teachers in schools throughout the United States. The process of creating the national goals and standards in foreign language education was both equitable and unprecedented. Some of the best minds in the field were brought together, not to decide what should be included in the national standards, but to create a document that reflected the views of an entire profession. There were no road maps to the national standards; a new approach was needed to create standards that were both visionary and democratic. The challenge was formidable, yet it was met. Eventually, state and national standards will guide but not direct local schools in their efforts to improve learning. As the individual states write their own goals and standards, they too must address a most important question: how can the standards be implemented so that all learners can benefit? Where does one begin?

The national goals may again offer an answer in terms of the process that was needed to bring them about. The national goals asked each discipline to review its mission and to construct a vision for systemic reform. Beginning with the end in mind, the vision for foreign language education must be of a world wherein all learners in all schools large, small, rural, and urban have equal opportunity to communicate in a language other than English. This is the very essence of systemic reform. And no discipline has more to gain or more to offer through a technology-based systemic initiative than foreign language education because (1) foreign languages belong in the restructured school, (2) the national standards are learner-centered, and (3) the national standards do not discriminate.

The Place of Foreign Languages in the Restructured School

The fact that foreign languages have not been part of the American core curriculum opens a unique window of opportunity to define a future free of many of the limitations that traditional systems impose. Realizing that it is far more difficult to change an existing structure than to create a new one, the foreign language profession can look to alternative delivery systems that are not rooted in the policies and practices of industrial-era schools. The factory model of education was compatible with the teaching of linguistic content but it does not support a communicative orientation, nor does it encourage using a foreign language to access new information. Rather than learning "about language," today's students must have access to the technologies that will connect them to the real world in which they will be living and working. The Internet, for example, is a foreign language teacher's dream come true and a magnet drawing new and relevant content into the school curriculum. Through the Internet and other distance transmission technologies, students can access full-color pictures of newly discovered French cave paintings and tour the Louvre or the Prado examining specific works of art. Through satellite and quick-time camera, they can communicate on site with archaeologists as they uncover new information about Mayan culture and civilization.

The Learner-Centered National Foreign Language Standards

The role and purpose of foreign language education in the United States have changed significantly to meet the "real world" language and cultural needs of today's students. Parents are demanding foreign language programs that go beyond a knowledge of language and culture; they want their children to learn to communicate in the languages they study. Traditional approaches do not work; a learner-centered environment is needed.

The fact that foreign languages are not ensconced in the core curriculum has also provided the opportunity to develop a model for pedagogy that puts the learners' needs first and does not depend on location. The national goals and standards in foreign language are not "educentric" or built around such limiting structures as self-contained classrooms, traditional schedules, and outdated pedagogies (Spady 1995). And the fact that foreign languages are not present as K–12 curriculum in most schools will make it easier to define what amounts to a "new" core curriculum within the context of a restructured school.

The changes that are taking place in foreign language pedagogy are also consistent with the current move toward accountability. As the demand for accountability increases, there is no discipline better prepared to lead in the area of assessment than foreign language education. When Goals 2000 and the national standards movement began to affect other subject areas, foreign language education was in the midst of a pedagogical transformation, one that was changing the primary focus from a grammar orientation to a proficiency one with specific performance criteria and performance assessments. Goals 2000 brought about a redefinition of the knowledge base upon which the foreign language discipline is built; in addition, the new national standards included a distinct communication focus that encourages performance assessment.

Fortunately, as the effort to describe performances takes other core disciplines into uncharted territory, the foreign language profession can revisit the area of performance while investigating new applications of technology to overcome the logistic and time barriers that have stood in the way of performance-based assessment.

Today, technology can be a vehicle for continuous authentic assessment not only in foreign language but in other curricular areas with a strong performance orientation, e.g., the performing arts and vocational education. Calling for a new philosophy and technology of assessment that is linked to the restructured school, Wiggins (1994:82) recognizes "the obstacles to lasting reform as more 'ecological' (political, structural and economical) and psychological than technical." It is time to consider how technology can be used to overcome the logistics of authentic performance assessment in foreign language education.

National Standards and Discrimination

The equity question, critical in all disciplines, poses a particular challenge in foreign language education. If foreign language education is for all students, then one must ask, For which generation of learners were the national goals written? The two-year language program is standard in school districts across the nation, and foreign languages are not present in any form in 80 percent of the nation's 67,000 elementary schools. Then there are the issues of requisite cost and time to train teachers and build programs in the thousands of schools that have the interest and commitment but lack the resources to develop a foreign language program. Where will schools find the necessary resources to offer what is, for all practical purposes, a new core discipline? Given the magnitude of the task, the answer is not to be found in conventional structures and systems. It will be necessary, therefore, to look to new approaches and new alternatives in the education delivery.

The Rural School Challenge

The effort can begin in the nations' rural schools where distance technologies are most needed. How many rural schools are there and where are they? According to Office of Educational Research and Improvement (OERI) data

(Nelson 1993), 47 percent of the nation's regular operating public school districts and 28 percent of the nation's 79,300 schools are rural. Every state has rural schools, ranging from Rhode Island (8 percent) to South Dakota (76 percent). An interesting fact is that although rural school populations are most often associated with western and midwestern states, New Jersey enrolls more rural students (66,000) than Montana (53,000).

Recognizing the potential of technology to overcome obstacles of distance, Seal and Harmon (1995:119) maintain "that schools in isolated rural areas can emerge as learning communities and as telecommuting villages. Technology will not only connect the school with the community but will also link the rural school with a global network of information and resources." Technology can also erase the physical boundaries separating rural and urban schools by linking them to each other while opening access to resources that the school system cannot provide. The equity issue is no less a quality issue, for learners deserve the opportunity not only to longer foreign language learning sequences but also to a pedagogy that provides both knowledge and skills to compete in a world that measures success in terms of performance.

Addressing the rural challenge through alternative delivery systems is an opportunity that the foreign language profession can either accept or continue to ignore. However, finding a way to assist local schools in their efforts to offer a foreign language will go a long way toward changing the way languages are valued in this country. The emerging revolution in global technologies is making it possible to open new opportunities in learning for all students, including in particular at-risk populations in urban and rural schools. Rural schools are the ideal place to begin because geography is a serious equity issue involving a large part of the school population in the United States. And if core curriculum is defined as essential curriculum, then students who are ill prepared to communicate in a foreign language are at risk.

Distance Learning

Fifteen years ago the term *distance learning* was unfamiliar to many educators. Today, nearly everyone has formed an opinion about distance learning and a perception about its strengths and its limitations. There is nearly always a comparison to the standard classroom and to television, since from its inception distance learning has been regarded as an alternative to the classroom.

In the early stages of distance learning, the image on the television set, however delivered, defined the limits of distance learning in the minds of its audience. Because there was no provision for active learner involvement, distance learning was to be used with caution and only when qualified teachers were not available, or to enrich programs, such as using television as a source of cultural information (Greer and Nielsen 1990). While the possibility of using distance learning to support listening and reading skill development was discussed, it was never taken seriously because it addressed only the receptive skills; there was little if any provision for language production.

Today distance learning has evolved far beyond the simple models of ten years ago, when such guidelines were written. Interactive satellite and the Internet are replacing the talking head of yesteryear and opening new avenues of communication. While interactive distance learning is offering new opportunities to rethink the whole teaching and learning process, the term *interactive* continues to have more to do with technology than with people.

The use of satellites to "deliver" instruction continues to be regarded as a poor substitute for the teacher-centered classroom while the possibilities in distance learning remain obscure. This reaction is predictable. The first applications of technology seem always to be employed as a time- and labor-saving device helping to do better and faster what has always been done. The phenomenon is hardly new. Marshal McLuhan's (Education SATLINK 1992:10) classic insight that each new medium begins in imitation of its predecessor (see Naiman 1992) is repeated today in Dede's warning against the danger of using technology "to automate traditional models of teaching and learning" (cited in O'Neil 1995a:4) This mentality, however, is not appropriate if distance learning or any technology is to be effective in school reform. Rather, it will be necessary to step outside familiar icons and seek new and creative applications of technology.

The Nebraska Model

Distance learning implies a learner-centered focus. However, critics of distance learning have often suggested that distance "teaching" would be a more accurate description. As two-way audio and two-way video are becoming increasingly commonplace, the term "traditional distance learning" is appearing with some regularity as a means of distinguishing systems that have little or no interactive capability from those that do.

Given that our interest in distance learning is more pedagogical than technical, we are looking for ways to use distance learning technologies to support learner outcomes. We are, therefore, developing a distance learning system that can be described as student-centered and performance-based. The locus of control in student-centered distance learning shifts from the studio to the learner; the interactive technology is at the service of the learner.

In lieu of duplicating traditional teaching and learning practices, Nebraska's distance learning model is an example of how telecommunications technologies can be utilized to support current language learning theory. The model was designed by the state director of foreign language education as a means of providing foreign language learning opportunities throughout the state to rural schools that expressed an interest in offering a foreign language but lacked the knowledge and the resources to start or maintain a program. The challenge and the incentive to create an alternative delivery system in Nebraska came from the customers: students, parents, teachers, and administrators in local schools who felt that foreign language was important to the state's economic future and to their children's education.

The development of an alternative delivery system began in 1982 when approximately only 60 percent of Nebraska's 325 secondary school districts offered a foreign language, and enrollments in those districts were near an all-time low. It was at that time that the state began to offer French, German, or Spanish to small rural districts through distance learning. It is interesting to note that once schools had the means to offer foreign language instruction, interest in doing so increased, and more districts requested delivery via distance learning. Interest in improving foreign language education eventually spread throughout the state, and foreign language enrollments increased from year to year.

Today, Nebraska requires that high schools offer at least two years of one foreign language. This has in turn made it possible to institute a foreign language entrance requirement in the state university system. In addition, once programs were established in the schools that use alternative delivery systems and enrollments became stable, many school districts hired certified foreign language teachers to take over the program.

Initially, the distance learning project was limited to French, German, and Spanish in Nebraska schools. Since then, thanks to a partnership between the Nebraska Department of Education, Nebraska Educational Telecommunications, and the Satellite Education Resources Consortium (SERC), the same model has been used on a national scale to offer Japanese to students in twenty-four states. It is interesting to note that, in applying a state distance learning model to the national level, the opportunity for learners to apply their language skills has not been compromised by demographics or program size.

The Japanese Distance Learning Program

The Japanese Distance Learning Program, produced in the studios of Nebraska Education Television, currently offers two levels of Japanese. The course is delivered via satellite using one-way video and two-way audio, an audio bridge, Japanese native speakers, a classroom facilitator, and print materials.

Program Design

Rather than allowing available technologies to determine the program design, the technologies that could best support the learning model were selected. The individuals responsible for developing this program were convinced that technology would be used to support rather than limit the pedagogical principles of the course. The model makes use of both satellite and telecommunications technologies in a program designed to incorporate sound foreign language acquisition and learning theories. It is not within the scope of this article to describe the model in detail. In summary, the telelinguist, the studio teacher-facilitator, and the local school facilitator coordinate their efforts to maximize learning through carefully selected input, focused feedback, and practice in language output production. The interrelationship and proper integration of key components and personnel in carrying out the underlying learning theory is important to the successful operation of the program.

Program Description

The program actually takes place at three locations: the local school, the teleconference center, and the studio or program source. The role and responsibilities of key personnel at each of the three sites is to provide optimal opportunities for students to acquire and use language. Presentation of material using *language input* is followed and closely tied to *language output*. The functions of the local school facilitator, the studio teacher, and the native telelinguist are interdependent and sequenced to help the learner acquire and use language skills.

Studio or Program Source. The most visible part of the program is the fifty-minute interactive satellite broadcast, which takes place in three fifty-minute sessions per week. During the live satellite telecast, students interact with the studio facilitator (television teacher) via telephone audio bridge. The studio teacher serves as the central host and learning facilitator for the course. This individual uses a variety of techniques and materials during the broadcasts to provide comprehensive language input and to support communication activities. Dramatized skits that focus on specific language skills and revolve around situations of interest to teens are produced in the studio. In addition, videos from Japan, home videos, pictures of students, and clothes and paraphernalia from featured schools are highlighted during each broadcast. The videos and realia serve as sources of themes and topics for communication activities. During the live broadcast, the studio teacher also interacts with students in several classrooms, modeling the communication strategies and activities that the telelinguists, who are native speakers, will utilize in ensuing teleconferences. This modeling activity is the bridge that permits the linking of language presentation to language production. Students react very positively to being "live" on television. The motivation and pride in seeing their school recognized and their students identified nationally is very important to them.

Teleconference Center. During this time, the three weekly broadcasts are supplemented by two twenty-minute interactive telephone sessions. The students are separated into groups of ten for meaningful use and practice of the language with a native Japanese speaker on the audio bridge. Since the students need to be motivated to use their language skills in a nonthreatening environment, it is vital to the development of communication skills that the thirty-six telelinguists build a strong rapport between the students and themselves. The telelinguists prepare themselves to conduct these teleconference by reviewing the entire studio program. However, their primary focus is on the modeling activities that have taken place between the studio teacher and the participating students.

While there is no particular element that is not essential to the whole program's operation, the importance of the native speaker or telelinguist in this distance learning program cannot be overstated. In fact, it should be noted that the paraprofessional native speaker is a powerful and greatly underutilized resource in foreign language education (Hammelmann and Nielsen 1974). Distance technologies can be used to tap this valuable human resource to provide for authentic communication skill development.

The Local School. The success or failure of a distance learning program is also in the hands of the local school facilitator. The facilitator's role is vital in that this individual must be both a colearner and an on-site manager of learning activities. The local school facilitator provides for the use of materials and equipment at the local site and manages classroom activities when satellite transmission or telephone interaction is not taking place. Materials and exercises are designed for independent on-site use by the students and school facilitators. The pedagogical benefits of having a facilitator who must, in fact, facilitate learning is one of the positive outcomes inherent in the design of this distance learning course. The following letter describes the Japanese program through the eyes of a local facilitator. Dr. Mara Anderson teaches German at Ephrata High School in Ephrata, Pennsylvania, and also acts as the local facilitator for the Japanese program.

The program is without a doubt one of the most exciting teaching/learning experiences that I have been involved with during my 25 years of teaching. . . . The work of Krashen, Terrell, Asher among others, and the proficiency movement have given teachers many practical guidelines based on sound theory as to what strategies and methodologies work best and why. I was pleased to see much of this research reflected in practice in the presentation of the Japanese materials. Quite frankly I had some reservations about a TV class and whether the results could match those I can achieve in my proficiency-oriented classroom. . . . [T]he ones that I have seen do not do the job that needs to be done. It is quite clear that this Japanese staff has put and continues to put much thought, time, and very careful planning into each TV episode, the accompanying textbook material, the tests, the design of the telephone sessions, and the grading procedures and standards. There is clear evidence of an awareness of the ACTFL proficiency guidelines in the sequencing of the materials and the activities. The TV classes do an excellent job of providing comprehensive input. Comprehension is then reinforced through many of the textbook and workbook materials. Communication is completed through the emphasis on the productive skill. Language production has also been carefully sequenced. Students have sufficient opportunities to practice speaking and writing in a nonthreatening environment before they are tested orally or in writing. Success is ensured if students follow the suggested program and sequence of activities.

Because this program is based on sound foreign language methodology it produces students who can actually do something with the language. I have had several Japanese visitors in the classroom who have presented themselves as speaking no English. It has been rewarding to watch and listen to the students create with Japanese under such circumstances. They have managed to understand and make themselves understood in a variety of situations.

. . . Today, when oral proficiency is stressed as one of the goals of foreign language teaching, most classroom teachers don't test it—SERC counts it as 35% of the grade. . . . [M]y students are also developing a cultural awareness of Japan that is lacking in our country today. They are learning about working together for the good of the group—they know they must each work hard for themselves but also for the group and for the school. I find that my students, who are among our best, are meeting a challenge in this course that is rarely presented to them.

It is obvious that Dr. Anderson finds that students in the Japanese distance language program are not disadvantaged in their ability to acquire and use language. She uses video segments from this program in her college methods class to demonstrate how efficiently languages can be acquired in a non-English-speaking environment. Dr. Anderson also notes that demonstrating sound theories of foreign language learning on the larger scale provided by distance learning can be a means of influencing the best practice in schools and preservice and post-service teacher education.

Commonly Held Assumptions about Distance Learning

Learning to see a new venture's possibilities and limitations is necessary if progress is to be made. However, as products of traditional classrooms, we often tend to overlook deficiencies in familiar structures while seeing difficulties, real and imagined, in what is new and untried. In our experience with distance learning, the obstacles that seemed insurmountable were often readily overcome, while other concerns, either unanticipated or lightly taken, became major challenges. It is important to note, however, that venturing into a new area can also be a serendipitous experience, as unforeseen benefits and new possibilities emerge along the way. We submit that our efforts to design and produce a distance learning program that is both cost-effective and pedagogically sound have led us to a position on the potential of distance learning that is very different from that of some professional colleagues. We have chosen to present our position in a series of responses to what we frequently hear from colleagues both inside and outside the foreign language profession. Table 6-1 contrasts what we consider to be "commonly held assumptions" about distance learning with the positions we have taken as a result of our recent experience. Each of the nine points is then discussed separately.

1. Distance learning has led to the employment of foreign language teachers. As a consequence of alternative delivery, all Nebraska secondary schools now offer foreign language, up from about 60 percent in 1982. The number of students enrolled in foreign languages has grown by over 400 percent since the mid 1970s, increasing the demand for endorsed teachers.

2. The most distinctive feature of the Nebraska model is its provision for the development of communications skills. Students interact with each other and with native speakers over a telebridge (two-way audio). Communication activities follow and are based on comprehensible input originating from the television studio, audiotapes, videotapes, and other sources. (See the program description earlier in this article.)

3. The national standards, focusing on what the learner should know and be able to do, reflect a remarkable consensus on content; however, they do not prescribe specific content. Content decisions remain within the purview of states and local schools. The movement away from a purely linguistic orientation to one of language performance has also led to some uniformity of thought, not only about what should be learned but about how it can best be learned. The language

Table 6-1. Distance Learning Viewpoints

	Commonly Held Assumption	Our Position
1.	Distance learning will replace foreign language teachers.	Distance learning can increase employment opportunities for foreign language teachers.
2.	Distance learning cannot be used to develop language proficiency.	Distance learning is compatible with second language acquisition.
3.	Distance learning is a "one size fits all" approach to education.	Distance learning can accommodate a wide variety of needs and interests.
4.	Distance learning programs should be developed only with a solid base in published research.	Distance learning opens exciting new avenues for action research.
5.	Distance learning bypasses the classroom teacher.	Distance learning can empower classroom teachers.
6.	Students in distance learning programs are less involved and less committed to learning.	Distance learning can increase students' motivation to learn.
7.	Distance learning costs too much.	Distance learning can be cost-effective.
8.	Distance learning bypasses teacher-education programs.	Distance learning has a significant role in teacher education and staff development.
9.	Let George do it. Failing to plan equals a plan to fail.	A plan incorporating distance learning will have a significant influence on the teaching and learning of foreign languages.

functions included in current syllabi are fairly constant. So, while curriculum content decisions will be made at the local level, state and national foreign language standards should encourage schools to make use of the new learning models and the numerous resources available through distance education.

It is also possible for much of the content in a distance learning program to be learner-centered and even learner-directed through appropriate use of telecommunications technologies. A current experimental project, involving eleven Nebraska elementary schools, is making use of distance technologies to support content-related learning. The distance component in this project is designed around extant themes in the school curriculum. The locus of control remains in the local school with the regular classroom teacher in charge of both the curriculum and the technology.

4. There is a scarcity of research that establishes a connection between distance education and current models of pedagogy. While the number of articles proclaiming the marvels of interactive satellite delivery is on the rise, few new ideas about how to realize this potential are forthcoming. There is, therefore, a need for distance learning research that is not rooted in familiar structures and outmoded beliefs about teaching and learning. Distance learning can open a new arena for language acquisition research and subsequent language learning theory because it is not bound by traditional schedules, classrooms of thirty students, and outdated technologies. The widening gap between research and practice can be closed through distance learning programs that connect technology to quality learning.

5. Distance learning programs can empower the classroom teacher. An overload of daily preparations and the lack of time for interactivity, for portfolio assessments, or for collaborative learning are but a few of the conflicts that weigh heavily on teachers. It is a reasonable assumption that no professional in any field is asked to do more with less than the classroom teacher.

Envision instead a school where teachers have access to the latest technologies and the knowledge to use them, not simply for the purpose of handling routine tasks, but rather for providing an interactive, high-performance learning environment where students use their foreign language skills to accomplish the goals proposed in the national standards document such as gaining knowledge and understanding of other cultures and connecting with other disciplines. In this school, teachers would, for example, engage their students in cooperative and constructivist learning activities, provide for continuous authentic assessment, open new channels for communication and research through the Internet, CD-ROM, and e-mail. Technology would serve as an instrument to improve learning.

Unfortunately, financially overburdened schools do not have the resources to purchase or maintain the technology and the knowledge base required to provide new learning environments. The few teachers who do have access to a computer tend to use it as a labor-saving device, e.g., in testing and grading applications. The simple act of purchasing additional computers will not improve learning. Distance learning technologies, on the other hand, can be used to provide continuous access to new information and new technologies that will enable teachers to work productively and fulfill their role as professional educators. In one distance learning program involving the teaching of a less commonly taught language, it was suggested that the local classroom facilitator, a teacher certified in a commonly taught language, pursue an endorsement in Japanese. Her response: "Why? There is no way that I could replicate the quality of the distance learning program, given the time and resources available to me in our school district."

6. Students in performance-based distance learning programs are motivated by the opportunity to apply their language skills in meaningful use and practice activities with each other and in authentic communications with native or near-native speakers of the language. Fortunately we can refer to a recent study of efficacy measures targeting the SERC/NE Japanese language program conducted by Dr. Roger Bruning (in press), professor of education psychology at the University of Nebraska, Lincoln. The study included a questionnaire anonymously administered to students in both distance learning and traditional Japanese classrooms in several states. The questionnaire was designed to evaluate self-efficacy, or the individual student's confidence level in completing certain tasks in the target country of Japan: finding one's way, ordering food in a restaurant, making a purchase, and traveling by train or subway. The instrument also measured interest in continued study of Japanese and interest in learning another foreign language. The results of the questionnaire were significant. The self-efficacy study revealed that the confidence level of students in the distance learning class was significantly higher than that of students in the traditional Japanese classroom. Even average and below-average students expressed greater confidence in accomplishing the tasks. Yet another revealing finding was the fact that students in the traditional Japanese classes were less interested in continuing their study of Japanese or in visiting Japan.

7. Distance learning is responsive to economies of scale. Utilizing satellite and telebridge as core technologies, distance learning can, under efficient management, become financially self-sustaining in a relatively short period of time. Why then has distance learning not been more widely used by schools? One reason may be that its

potential has not been realized because its primary use has been to fulfill certain didactic and administrative functions associated with the transmission of content and information, or as a substitute for traditional approaches to learning. School districts might begin to place a higher value on distance learning when it is used to facilitate new models of teaching and learning and to train teachers in the use of technology. In addition, distance learning technologies could themselves be a conduit through which knowledge about their own impact on learning can flow to schools. In return, this might relieve the huge cost and endless duplication of resources and equipment that occurs from school district to school district. At the same time, telecommunication technologies can magnify and give visibility to the creative ideas of students, teachers, and administrators, which, all too often, do not go beyond classroom doors or school district boundaries.

It should be noted here that the hardware in distance learning will change, but until a large number of learners and teachers can benefit, satellite and telebridge appear to be the most cost-effective distance technologies; they may continue to have a role to play even as the number of Internet connections to schools increases.

8. Distance learning can narrow the gap between preparation and practice while meeting the "real time" needs of the classroom teacher. In two NEH-funded institutes at Kansas State University, a telebridge was used to connect local school foreign language teachers to each other and to KSU foreign language and methods specialists. The telebridge made the year-long project possible because it provided a way for the participants to "meet" at regular intervals from their homes and from their work places, thereby overcoming the very real obstacles of time, distance, and expense that isolate teachers from each other and limit access to the resources and technical support system they want and need in their local schools. Although language proficiency was not the focus of the institute, entry and exit evaluations of language proficiency revealed substantial gains in listening, speaking, reading, and writing skills. These gains were a consequence of using the target language in the telebridge session to discuss content and pedagogical issues. The use of language in context, based on relevant subjects and themes, was a model that teachers soon began to apply in their classrooms.

The institute also produced some benefits that were as much a consequence of the new structure as the planning that went into it.

Pedagogical gains were implicit in the learning experience as the interactive learning model used in the institute found its way into the classrooms of the participating teachers. During the institute, both university and local school personnel gained an in-depth understanding and appreciation for each other and their respective work that would likely not have been achieved in any other way.

9. Failing to plan for alternative delivery systems in foreign language education will, in effect, be a plan to fail. The incentives for distance learning program development by interests outside the profession are more financial than educational. While economics has seldom been paramount in the minds of educators, the economic benefits of alternative delivery systems are well known in the private sector. Bringing sound foreign language acquisition theory into practice may be the goal of the foreign language profession but it is not the primary concern of commercial distance learning providers.

The Vision and the National Standards

Technology is not about tools, it deals with how humans work. (Peter Drucker)

The national goals and standards are visionary; they define foreign language education not in terms of its present status but in terms of what it can become. Visions energize and excite as they open the door to new challenges and new opportunities. And visions must be built by those who share a common purpose.

Some Recommendations

The future of foreign language education and foreign language program development lies not in following the path of education and technology reform, but in leading and building upon the vision established by national standards. It is fortuitous that the emerging global revolution in technologies is taking place at a time when educational reform has provided the opportunity for foreign language to enter the mainstream curriculum. The following are some ideas, not in any particular order, about how to build on the vision created by the national foreign language standards so that all learners can benefit:

• Continue to build on the approach that produced the national standards by capitalizing on the autonomy and power inherent in a truly democratic process

- Create an electronic network with on-line service to connect local teachers, resource centers, policymakers, and foreign language specialists (Examples already in place are the Getty Center's ArtsEdNet and PBS Mathline.)
- Seek funding for a nationwide systemic initiative based on the national goals and standards to assist local schools in their efforts to initiate and expand foreign language programs (There are likely more funding sources seeking creative solutions to problems of educational reform than the reverse.)
- Look to cost-effective technologies, e.g., satellite and telephone, that can reach a large number of teachers and do not require a large investment on the part of local schools
- Capitalize on the autonomy inherent in professional organizations by working independently of the control of bureaucracies, businesses, and other outside interests
- Integrate policy and action (There is little to risk and everything to gain by taking a commonsense approach to reform based on what is already known about foreign language teaching and learning.)
- Tap into the power of technology and educational reform by using new models of learning and teaching that do not depend on location and are not encumbered by cost, distance, and time

Some Potential Outcomes

It is difficult to predict the power of change, especially to determine when it will happen and how widespread its impact will be. Nevertheless, we conclude this essay by conjecturing what this vision might foresee should technology, reform, and national foreign language standards achieve their desired goals:

- A support system that enables schools to initiate and expand foreign language programs
- Teachers empowered by new technologies and the knowledge to use them
- A systemic initiative based on technology and educational reform that recognizes local autonomy and overcomes barriers of cost, distance, and time
- Schools where current foreign language learning theory is part of daily practice

- Foreign language learning practices and procedures that are compatible with the restructured school

Had it not been for educational reform and Goals 2000, not only would there be no national goals and standards in foreign language education, but also the foreign language profession would not have been given the opportunity to stake its claim to be part of the core curriculum. While national standards will not drive educational reform, they can be a catalyst for change. Technology at the service of educational reform can be used to fulfill the promise of national standards.

References

Brandt, Ron. 1995. "Overview." *Educational Leadership* 53,2:5.

Bruning, R. In press. "Examining the Utility of Efficacy Measures in Distance Education Research." Proceedings of the Third Distance Education Research Symposium. University Park, PA: American Center for Distance Education.

Grier, Susan M., and Mel Nielsen. 1990. "Position Statement on Distance Learning in Foreign Languages." National Council of State Supervisors of Foreign Languages.

Hammelmann, William M. R., and Melvin L. Nielsen. 1974. "The Native Paraprofessional: Identifying His Role in the Foreign Language Program." *Foreign Language Annals* 7:346–52.

Naiman, Adeline. 1992. "The Death of the Talking Head: Interactive Satellite Learning." Part I. *Education SATLINK*: 10–11.

National Commission on Excellence in Education. 1983. *A Nation at Risk.* Washington, DC: National Commission on Excellence in Education.

Nelson, Steve. 1993. "Exemplary Program: The SMART Project." *Dwight D. Eisenhower Mathematics and Science Education* 3,1:6–7.

O'Neil, John. 1995a. "On Technology and Schools: A Conversation with Chris Dede." *Educational Leadership* 53,2:6–9.

———. 1995b. "On Using Standards: A Conversation with Ramsey Selden." *Educational Leadership* 52,6:12–14.

Rossi, Robert J., and Samuel C. Stringfield. 1995. "What We Must Do for Students Placed at Risk." *Phi Delta Kappan* 77,1:73–76.

Sarason, Seymour B. 1995. "Some Reactions to What We Have Learned." *Phi Delta Kappan* 77,1:84–85.

Seal, K., and H. Harmon. 1995. "Realities of Rural School Reform." *Phi Delta Kappan* 77,2:119–25.

Spady, William G. 1995. "Response: We Need More Than 'Educentric' Standards." *Educational Leadership* 53,1:82–83.

Wiggins, Grant. 1994. "Toward More Authentic Assessment of Language Performances," pp. 69–85 in Charles R. Hancock, ed., *Teaching, Testing, and Assessment: Making the Connection.* Report of the Northeast Conference on the Teaching of Foreign Languages. Lincolnwood, IL: National Textbook.

7

The Programmatic Implications of Foreign Language Standards

Walter H. Bartz

Indiana Department of Education

Margaret Keefe Singer

Louisiana Department of Education

Current practices in education have not been systematically adapted to accommodate societal changes since the 1950s. Among the reasons for this state of affairs are the system's piecemeal approach, the failure to integrate suggested solutions, the discipline-by-discipline study of education, and overconcern for the boundaries of the existing system (Banathy 1991). "Public education's overwhelming success as a pattern maintenance institution is at the heart of its failure to match changing societal expectations" (Betts 1992:38). In reaction to the above obstacles, a new paradigm has emerged in education that incorporates systems thinking, part of management theory's Total Quality Management, into education. When implementing systemic change in education, practitioners emphasize new models, and they include elements such

Walter H. Bartz (Ph.D., The Ohio State University, Columbus) is consultant in foreign language education for the Indiana Department of Education. He is a frequent presenter at workshops in Indiana and professional meetings around the country. He has been author for various professional publications, including coauthorship (with Schulz) of a chapter in the *ACTFL Review of Foreign Language Education.* He was a member of the board of reviewers for the National Foreign Language Standards and currently is a reviewer for *Foreign Language Annals* and the *Modern Language Journal.* He has served as president of the National Council of State Supervisors of Foreign Languages (NCSSFL) and on the board of directors of the Central States Conference on the Teaching of Foreign Languages. He has been a teacher of German in both schools and colleges.

Margaret Keefe Singer (M.A., Louisiana State University) is foreign language program manager for the elementary-level foreign language program (4–8) at the Louisiana Department of Education. She is a regular presenter at state, regional, and national foreign language meetings. She has taught in elementary, middle, and high schools and is currently director of Louisiana's foreign language assessment project and a member of its Content Standards Development Task Force. She is project director for a two-year Foreign Language Assistance Program grant from the U.S. Department of Education.

as outcome-related standards, benchmarks for standards, self-assessment, and assessment on performance related to benchmarks rather than the performance of other students. The creation of national standards as part of systemic change is intended to positively affect student learning in a society with evolving needs.

The standards movement has been encouraged by Goals 2000 funding. Mathematics educators took the lead in developing the first standards documents, which appeared in 1989. The other subject areas, including foreign languages, have followed and developed standards, thus taking part in major educational reform partially encouraged by federal funding.

As the changes reflected in the National Standards for Foreign Language Education trickle down to the states, the profession has many questions about their possible effect on the teaching and learning of foreign languages. What is the role of standards in the reform movement? Will their very existence be enough to affect teaching and learning? to what extent? This article will explore whether standards will affect school systems and the nature of the effect.

Goals 2000 and National Standards

The intent of Goals 2000 was to provide a broad-based structure of goals upon which states and local school systems might rethink and redesign curriculum and education strategies in a manner appropriate to their local situations. State frameworks narrow down national standards and benchmark tasks, and then local school systems write curriculum specific to their areas and their needs. The relationships between the national, state, and local systems are further clarified in figure 7-1, included in the final draft of the foreign language standards document.

The boxes in figure 7-1 represent the goals, standards, and progress indicators at the national, state, district, and individual teacher levels. What is "standards" at the national level evolves to "frameworks" at the state level, to "district curricula" at the district level, and finally to "lesson/unit plans" at the classroom level. The tendency of movement from very general guidelines at the national level toward very specific guidelines at the local level is further observed through the progression of the three major category headings at the national level: goals, standards, and sample progress indicators. As the reader's eye moves from the national to the individual classroom level, a marked transformation is noted in the category headings. "Goals" become "specific objectives for learning," "standards" become "content lesson

Figure 7-1. The Relationship between National, State, and Local Standards-Related Documents

National Standards		State Framework		District Curricula		Lesson/ Unit Plan
Goals	↔	Goals for instruction	↔	Local goals for instruction	↔	Specific objectives for learning
Standards	↔	Content unit types; structure of content; scope and sequence	↔	Content unit specifics; suggested units and sequence; methods; resources	↔	Content lesson specifics; unit topics and lessons procedures; teaching/ learning resources for unit lessons
Sample progress indicators	↔	Recommended assessment procedures	↔	Specific assessment techniques	↔	Specific objectives and assessments

Adapted with permission from the *Visual Arts Education Reform Handbook: Suggested Policy Perspectives on Art Content and Student Learning in Art Education.* National Art Education Association, 1995.

specifics," and "sample progress indicators" become "specific objectives and assessments." This evolution from general to specific emphasizes the responsibility placed on the local school systems and the breadth of their more prescriptive roles in attaining local, state, and national objectives.

Several of the content areas have already developed their national standards in either draft or final form, including math, science, social studies, English/language arts, the arts, and foreign languages. The final draft of *Standards for Foreign Language Learning: Preparing for the Twenty-first Century* was released at the annual conference of the American Council on the Teaching of Foreign Languages (ACTFL) in November of 1995. These standards have been in development for three years, but the most important and most difficult work is still ahead: the implementation of the standards in actual classrooms.

The mathematics profession, the first to actually complete its standards, has found it difficult to provide evidence of improved student learning, even though the National Council of Teachers of Mathematics (NCTM) published its standards in 1989. For seven years now NCTM has spent a good deal of its own money to develop and implement standards. Yet it remains to be seen to what extent actual classroom practice reflects the standards. O'Neil (1993a) states that

> The math experience suggests that proponents of National Standards should be cautious in their hope that the standards can help spur widespread improvement in teaching and learning. Many changes are necessary, such as better textbooks, improved staff development, etc. (p. 8)

Alexander (1993), deputy assistant in the U.S. Department of Education, agrees with O'Neil that textbooks and tests have a significant influence on what is taught and learned but emphasizes that higher standards are also important as replacements for the current low standards in texts and tests. She contends that, in addition to better textbooks and tests, revitalized classroom experiences represent yet another consequence of higher standards. She goes on to say that "students who used to sit in math classrooms and watch the teacher demonstrate one way to get the right answer now manipulate objects to reason through new math concepts" (p. 10).

In an interview with Lauren Resnick, director of the New Standards Project, and Warren Simmons, director of equity initiatives for the New Standards Project, O'Neil (1993b) shows how these leaders support the idea that teacher involvement is most essential to the implementation of national standards because the teacher is the one who must prepare the student for the assessment. Resnick and Simmons believe that the teacher must be involved in the development of tasks, the scoring procedures, and the decision to determine what is "good enough." For example, the New Standards Project directed by Resnick involves teachers working to develop performance-based assessments in math, English, and science for grades 4, 8, and 10, in order to provide the groundwork for a voluntary student examination system.

An additional obstacle to determining the direct impact of the mathematics standards on classroom teaching and student learning is the scarcity of research, which is due to the relatively short time that the standards have been in existence. Among various efforts, the NCTM has initiated a project called Recognizing and Recording Reform in Mathematics Education, whose purpose is to monitor their own and other activities designed to implement the standards and to monitor a broader program of research and development. Ferrini-Mundy and Johnson (1994) tell us that several sites of reform have been identified and studied in order to learn about the change process and the interpretation of the ideas contained in the standards documents. A preliminary finding shows that the process followed in some schools is characterized as interpretation rather than implementation of the standards.

In another study, Garret and Mills (1995) found that some aspects of practice, especially technology, appear to be changing more rapidly than others, but "the use of new forms of assessment, although increasing, remains relatively limited" (p. 386). A subsequent finding in the data dealt with variation in practice across schools. This variation was explained in terms of organizational features and departmental resources that support change, such as a department chair who guides and supports change in his or her school. Wiske and Levinson (1993) interviewed more than forty pioneering math teachers whose classrooms reflected the mathematics standards. In their conclusion they state that

> progress toward the desired reforms is possible but that there are no short-cuts. Accomplishing deep changes in mathematics curriculum, teaching, and assessment requires linked leadership across levels of the education system, comprehensive attention to the key components of classroom life, and sustained support for teachers as they and their students forge new directions in mathematics teaching and learning. (p. 12)

Sample National Foreign Language Programs Designed to Affect School Systems

Even before national standards were finalized there was a growing national concern for improving education among those who are most closely involved. In response to this concern, several national programs have emerged in several content areas, including foreign language. Programs that we will consider are the Pacesetter Project, funded by the College Board; the New England–based Articulation and Achievement Project; and the Columbus, Ohio, area Collaborative Articulation and Assessment Project.

The Pacesetter Project

The Pacesetter Project was designed by the College Board to integrate standards, teaching, and assessment for educational reform at the secondary school level. Along with standards, a coordinated package of course curricula, student assessment, and professional development opportunities in the subjects of mathematics, English, and Spanish are being prepared and piloted in designated schools. According to the *Pacesetter Letter* ("College Board's Strategy" 1993), this initiative is designed to "raise expectations and improve performance of all American students." All elements of the mathematics, English, and Spanish packages are being developed in cooperation with members of the leading national subject-matter associations. As outlined by Charles Stansfield (1994),

> the Pacesetter program is based on five premises: (a) higher educational goals can be met only if teachers and subject-matter experts are actively involved in

the development of these goals, (b) educational reform must begin with definitions of specific student outcomes necessary to compete in the workplace, (c) student outcomes must be defined before it is decided how to measure progress, (d) teachers must be prepared to assist students in developing the skills specified in the student outcomes, and (e) assessment should be conducted by a variety of methods, including performance based tasks. (p. 53)

The *Pacesetter Letter* ("Pacesetter Mathematics" 1994) reports that the mathematics program includes 6,000 students, 137 teachers in 60 high schools, and 39 rural, urban, and suburban school districts in 20 states, while the English course is being piloted by 85 teachers and 3,000 students in 54 secondary schools in 15 states. The Spanish program has been extended to 6 states and 34 teachers. The course is designed as the third year of high school Spanish, with "learning outcomes specifying levels of performance well beyond those most students achieve in high school today" (p. 3). It treats language as a tool for understanding the cultures of the Spanish-speaking world, and language proficiency is regarded as but a vehicle for communication. Teachers' reactions to this project seem to be positive at all levels. In December 1995 they met to compare their students' work samples and to get help in mastering the Pacesetter courses in scoring performance assessments and in using rubrics.

The Articulation and Achievement Project

The Articulation and Achievement Project, funded by the Fund for the Improvement of Post-Secondary Education (FIPSE), represents a programmatic reaction to national concerns for the improvement of foreign language education and is being developed jointly by the College Board, ACTFL, and the New England Network of Academic Alliances in Foreign Languages. The project's Learning Outcomes Framework is already in draft form and attempts to provide a model articulation framework that clearly defines learning outcomes for each level and includes expectations for cultural and literary competence. The work has focused on the student transition levels between middle school and high school and between high school and postsecondary education. The articulation framework clearly defines learning outcomes for five levels or "stages." In addition to these learning outcomes, teachers are developing matching assessment strategies (LaBouve 1993).

The Collaborative Articulation and Assessment Project (CAAP)

Another important project, also funded by FIPSE, began in 1993 in Columbus, Ohio, when twenty-six language instructors from local high schools, a community college, and a university began collaborating to devise recommendations for articulation and assessment plans and for the eventual implementation and testing of these plans. In a special issue of the *CAAP Update* (1995), the project's two goals are described as follows:

1. The formulation of a workable articulation plan to facilitate the often difficult transition from secondary to postsecondary levels

2. The creation of an early assessment program that evaluates the language skills of high school juniors in order to give them a projection of their possible university placement and to provide diagnostic feedback where necessary

The above projects describe national efforts to bring about systemic change. However, the key attempt at applying national standards will come with the efforts of individual states to develop their own standards and to apply them.

The Relationship between State Foreign Language Curriculum Frameworks and Local Curricular Development

The Need for and Use of State Frameworks

Throughout American education, individual states have played diverse roles in designing and developing curriculum for the schools. In many cases today, states are developing frameworks that are intended to assist districts and schools in several domains, including curriculum development, staff development, and textbook selection. Ravitch (1993) suggests the purpose of a state curriculum framework:

> It is a declaration of the state's standards for its children—a description of what it expects children to know and be able to do. State frameworks are usually more detailed than statements of national standards, and they usually serve as a basis for textbook adoptions and state assessments. A state framework should also be a strategic plan for education, starting with what children know and using that as the basis for reforming teacher education, teacher certification, staff development, textbooks assessments and so on. (p. 767)

Whether all states develop frameworks for exactly these purposes has not been investigated. However, in many cases it appears they are created to assist school districts and schools in developing and designing a curriculum that reflects current professional thought as well as the needs of students in an ever-changing society. In a study by LaBouve (1993) of four state foreign language frameworks, it was found that in all cases, the frameworks had a direct impact on local curriculum and staff development. In three of the states the frameworks also influenced textbook adoption, and in two other states they encouraged change in school accreditation and teacher certification.

Since the early 1980s, the change from an emphasis on grammar-oriented curricular goals to one on communicative proficiency goals may explain why state foreign language curriculum frameworks have had a significant influence on the local process of design and implementation. LaBouve (1993) states

> The changes in language education in the nation's elementary and secondary schools . . . have been dramatic over the last ten years. Significant movement exists away from a curriculum that emphasized knowledge about a language toward one in which communicative competence or proficiency in a language is the goal. (p. 32)

The impact of the so-called proficiency movement on curricular design at both the state and local levels became even stronger with the development of the *ACTFL Proficiency Guidelines*. The shift from grammar-oriented goals to goals that addressed student performance (outcomes) in real-life contexts became an overriding principle in the development of most state curriculum frameworks. However, many teachers were neither ready nor willing to accept the premises on which the proficiency movement was based.

A great number of foreign language teachers had not been trained in their preservice education to address these changes. They had to rely on state frameworks, textbooks, and professional publications for support in designing curricula that address these issues. For example, in Indiana (LaBouve 1993), the process of disseminating the state framework included workshops throughout the state. The workshops were designed to help teachers develop curriculum and select instructional materials that would be appropriate to meet the outcomes defined in the state framework.

In states such as New York, where statewide assessments are based on the state framework, it becomes even more crucial that the outcomes (benchmarks, indicators) defined in the framework play an important role in the classroom. In states where framework and assessment go hand in hand, one can usually expect a significant impact on both local curriculum development and instruction.

Other examples of strong influence at the state level exist in Louisiana and in North Carolina, where state mandates to include foreign language instruction in the elementary school curriculum have been put in place. If a state has such a mandate, it requires school districts not merely to consider strongly, but rather to comply with, the state-designed framework for local implementation of a program. Although there are many impediments to implementing statewide mandates, mandates create a solid foundation for local curriculum development based on state frameworks.

Planning and Designing Local Curriculum and Instruction

Since foreign languages have traditionally been offered as elective subjects, and since their existence in school programs vary from district to district, the implementation of national standards may present complex challenges to local curriculum planners and teachers. Programs differ from state to state and from school district to school district, ranging from fully mandated elementary through high school programs to high-school-only programs. An extension of this scenario is the problem of multiple entry points for foreign language students. Even though the majority of programs begin in ninth grade, an increasing number of school districts have initiated middle school foreign language programs, but many of them are optional. The problem is complicated even more when one considers the ever-increasing number of elementary school programs. Louisiana and North Carolina, for example, have state mandates with very solid elementary school programs, yet each has a different entry level, fourth grade and kindergarten respectively. Due to the fact that many school districts cannot maintain separate tracks for students beginning at different entry points, teachers are forced to deal with students of varied foreign language backgrounds in the same classroom setting. These programmatic differences will have to be taken into consideration when designing local curriculum based on national standards. It is therefore obvious that local teachers will have to be fully involved in adapting state frameworks to local classroom needs.

As was identified in the mathematics standards projects, the importance of involving classroom-based teachers and educators who think in innovative ways when writing state frameworks and determining benchmarks or indicators is essential for ensuring the successful implementation of standards in the classroom. The foreign language profession began its standards project with this idea in mind when it decided that the task force charged with writing the standards should be composed of mostly classroom practitioners. In fact, a member of the Foreign Language Standards Task Force maintains that it will be the teachers who ultimately take the "big steps" to convince school systems to write curriculum guides and to move toward implementation of national, state, and local standards.

The Role of Assessment in Implementing Standards

In order to determine whether the standards have been met, local curriculum-writing teams will need to take into account the appropriate use of testing and assessment strategies. The importance of utilizing assessment practices that mirror and feed into the learning process becomes clearer when one realizes that students in American schools learn what they know they will be tested on (Marzano, Pickering, and McTighe 1993). Without assessment and accountability, any content area is considered unimportant to American students, their parents, and the community. Teachers must know appropriate assessment strategies and apply this knowledge if their students are to succeed and to compete within and beyond the local arena.[1]

Local input into standards and performance indicators along with ongoing staff development for and by teachers at all levels is essential to full commitment from the clients, that is, the school systems, the teachers, and the students who themselves are the very focus of the standards. In an effort to prime teachers for this commitment, and recognizing that testing cannot be isolated from teaching, the mathematics task force included along with their standards document a statement of assessment principles adopted by the profession. The foreign language profession would do well to imitate this action so that the message of assessment philosophy as it pertains to standards will be clear at the outset.

An implication of national standards is the development and administration of district and statewide assessments. While such assessments might be more easily accepted at the middle and high school levels of instruction because of existing grading practices, elementary programs will be greatly affected by required assessments. In recent years, elementary school foreign language programs have grown by leaps and bounds, but most have not been accompanied by a program of assessment. In anticipation of future concerns about the lack of assessment, the Center for Applied Linguistics has created the Foreign Language Performance Assessment Initiative as part of the National K–12 Foreign Language Resource Center. The goal of this initiative is to improve the ability of foreign language teachers to assess their own students. The assessment project also aims to facilitate collaboration among foreign language teachers and educational researchers and to help teachers conform assessment practices with the national foreign language standards. In 1995 the project established a K–8 assessment bibliography, conducted a workshop to find out how teachers currently use assessment, and brainstormed with researchers about innovative research strategies. Goals for the future are to develop, pilot, and disseminate to the public draft assessment guidelines for K–8 (Rhodes 1995).

An example of the impact of assessment on existing programs can be found in Louisiana, a state that has had an elementary school program in place for more than twenty years. In some school districts a program traditionally seen as one of "enrichment" was transformed to one of "academics" when the state began a testing project for students enrolled in elementary and middle school language classes. The goals of the testing project were to provide information needed for proper articulation between elementary and middle school and between middle and high school, to influence teaching methodology and classroom testing practices, and to provide information about student performance statewide.

The Foreign Language Standards Pilot Project

The only actual application of the foreign language standards to date has taken place in six school sites that were selected to pilot them. Several factors determined their selection, such as city size, school size, school population, and languages offered. At the June 1995 meeting of the ACTFL Standards Task Force in Salt Lake City, Utah, the pilot teachers made short presentations of their observations as they experimented with implementing the ACTFL standards in draft form in either their own or other teachers' classrooms. What was interesting about their comments was the fact that these teachers, who were from all over the country, had similar observations about the standards. Their observations, quoted below, fell in the following categories: the personal development of the teacher; the standards as realistic, achievable goals; elements necessary to meet national standards, the impact of standards on school districts, and student reactions to standards.

Personal Development

- The standards provided the impetus to foster communication among the teachers.
- The standards made all three of us teachers sit together and talk. They made us think bigger.
- The standards really helped me and my fellow teachers reflect on our own practice. We became thinkers of our work, not just doers.
- Some teachers who were thought to be very traditional turned out to be very creative and turned on by the standards.

Standards as Realistic Goals

- In my opinion, all students can attain all five goals.

- Goal 3, connecting with other disciplines, gave the teachers the most difficulty because of a lack of cooperation from teachers in the content areas.
- We were able to come up with a chart that correlated our lessons with the standards.
- I found it rather easy to generate additional learning scenarios.
- I've been doing these national standards for a long time and never realized it.
- The standards are definitely doable.

Elements Necessary to Meet Standards

- I think that the communicative approach is best for bringing the students up to "standard."
- What you need to bring the students up to "standard" are the following:

  A clear roadmap of terminology

  A buy-in by the teachers

  Interactive T.V. programs K–7

  Smaller class sizes

  Language labs

  Coordination among teachers

- In trying to apply the standards, I didn't finish my book and I didn't care!
- I like a variety of assessment tools in the classroom, but I'm not sure that I support national assessment.
- In my opinion, high school textbooks and materials presently on the market are adequate to help bring students up to "standard."
- I'm in favor of national assessments for foreign language.
- The communicative approach is ideal to bring students up to "standard."

Impact of Standards on Districts

- As a result of the standards project, the school board adopted a resolution stating that all students must pass the equivalent of one year of FL to graduate from high school.

- The school board passed a mandate that every entering freshman this September will graduate with a minimum of one year of foreign language.
- If standards are going to work, university methods professors are going to have to teach them in their preservice classes.
- In my school district where 70 percent of the students are eligible for school lunch, the standards were responsible for our planning to assess foreign languages in 1999.

Reactions to Standards

- Students liked the practical application of Spanish.
- Parents have been really supportive.
- [Student] Wow, this is great stuff!
- [Student] No way, leave me alone!
- Students had positive reactions to the standards.

Reactions of State Foreign Language Supervisors to the National Standards

To sample how state education agency foreign language specialists, school administrators, and foreign language teachers perceive the role of national and state standards, three surveys were conducted. One survey was sent to all state education agency foreign language supervisors. A similar survey was sent to a 5 percent random sample of district and school administrators in Indiana and a 10 percent random sample of K–12 Indiana foreign language teachers.

It should be noted that because development and implementation of the Standards for Foreign Language Learning were in their early stages at the time the surveys were conducted (spring 1995), most respondents had little or no experience with actually using the standards for state or local curricular development. Thus, they had to rely on their best judgment in predicting the impact that the national standards might have once they are used for state or local purposes.

Potential Influence of the National Standards on State Frameworks

The question of whether national standards will have an effect or influence on state frameworks is one that must be considered in light of the role that state frameworks play on curriculum, instruction, and materials development.

In the survey of SEA foreign language supervisors, three statements were posed that requested a yes/no/not applicable response (items 11, 12, and 13; see table 7-1). The other items (4–10) used a 1–5 Likert scale, with 1 being strongly disagree and 5 being strongly agree. On items 9 and 10, it was possible to answer not applicable (NA).

A great number of those states responding to the survey (27) either plan to use national standards to develop frameworks or feel that their current state frameworks correlate highly with the national standards. From this information the following questions come to mind:

- Do state foreign language supervisors view the national standards as a model and vision for the development of state frameworks?
- Do they feel that national standards and state frameworks will have a significant impact on the development of local curricula and on classroom instruction?

Responses to the five segments of survey item 4, corresponding to the five major goals of the national standards document, will shed light on these questions. The five goals are communication (Goal 1), culture (Goal 2), connections (Goal 3), comparisons (Goal 4), and communities (Goal 5).

The state foreign language supervisors reacted positively to all five goals (items 4–8). It is interesting to note that more than 80 percent of the respondents gave Goals 1 and 2 a rating of 5. The other three goals received the highest rating from 63 percent, 63 percent, and 67 percent of respondents, respectively, with 22 percent of the respondents giving Goal 3 a rating of 3. This points to the fact that the first two goals are probably still being perceived as the traditional and most important reasons for foreign language learning.

In a later survey, foreign language teachers responded in a similar manner to the five major goals (see table 7-2), but superintendents, principals, and district curriculum coordinators (table 7-3) showed a less enthusiastic rating for all five goals.

Responses to item 5 by the state supervisors showed some doubt that "the standards sufficiently define the content necessary to achieve each goal." This item received an average rating of 3.9 with only 30 percent rating it a 5. Foreign language teachers responded to this item in a similar fashion, but somewhat more positively (see table 7-2). This, of course, raises the question of the relevance and practical use of the national standards. The perception seems to be that they are not nearly comprehensive enough to be meaningful or useful for curriculum planning or for implementing instruction.

Table 7-1. National Standards Survey: State Foreign Language Supervisor Responses

	Rating										AV
	1		**2**		**3**		**4**		**5**		
	F	%	F	%	F	%	F	%	F	%	
Item 4: The 5 goals define a desirable and attainable vision for foreign language education in America.											
Goal 1: Communication	0	0	1	4	0	0	3	11	23	85	4.7
Item 4 **Goal 2: Cultures**	0	0	2	7	0	0	3	11	22	81	4.7
Item 4 **Goal 3: Connections**	0	0	0	0	6	22	4	15	17	63	4.4
Item 4 **Goal 4: Comparisons**	0	0	1	4	2	7	7	26	17	63	4.5
Item 4 **Goal 5: Communities**	0	0	1	4	5	18	3	11	18	67	4.4
Item 5: The standards sufficiently define the content necessary to achieve each goal.	0	0	3	11	4	15	11	40	8	30	3.9
Item 6: The sample benchmarks are appropriate for the grade levels indicated.	1	4	0	0	4	15	11	40	10	37	4.1
Item 7: I feel that local school districts will be able to develop curriculum based on the national standards.	2	7	3	11	7	26	6	22	7	26	3.5
Item 8: I feel that national standards are important and should be used as a basis for curriculum development.	1	4	0	0	2	7	3	11	20	74	4.6

(Continued)

Table 7-1. National Standards Survey: State Foreign Language Supervisor Responses (continued)

	Rating										AV
	1		**2**		**3**		**4**		**5**		
	F	**%**	**F**	**%**	**F**	**%**	**F**	**%**	**F**	**%**	
Item 9: In our state, the state curriculum framework has a strong impact on the development and design of local standards.	0	0	2	7	3	11	7	26	NA 5 / 10	NA 18 / 37	4.1
Item 10: In our state, the state curriculum framework has a strong impact on classroom instruction and assessment	1	4	3	11	9	33	7	26	NA 5 / 2	NA 18 / 7	3.2

Y=Yes, N=No, NA=Not Applicable	Y		N		NA	
Item	**F**	**%**	**F**	**%**	**F**	**%**
Item 11: Our state will use the national standards as the basis for its development of a state curriculum framework.	15	56	4	15	6	22
Item 12: Our state has recently completed a curriculum framework, but will revise it in the near future in order to base it on the national standards.	3	11	7	26	14	52
Item 13: Our current state curriculum framework correlates highly with the proposed national standards.	14	52	9	33	3	11

F: Frequency of response. AV: Average rating. NA: Respondents indicating item not applicable.

The grade-level appropriateness of the benchmarks (item 6: referred to as "sample progress indicators" in the final standards document) was viewed quite positively, with 37 percent of supervisors rating the item a 5 and 40 percent rating it a 4. Teachers and administrators gave the item a slightly lower rating.

It was most interesting to note that although 88 percent of the state supervisors felt that national standards are important and should be used for curriculum development (item 8), approximately half of them were less positive about local school districts being able to develop curriculum based on the national standards (item 7).

Responses to items 8 and 9 make it appear that the state supervisors feel quite strongly that the national standards should be used as a basis for curriculum development, but it was unclear whether their impact will be felt in the local schools both for curriculum and classroom instruction. The low rating for item 7 of the survey, on whether districts can develop curriculum from the standards, is an indication that some supervisors view the national standards as less useful than desirable for developing curricula.

Influence of State Frameworks on Local Curriculum and Instruction

Most states have neither a statewide foreign languages assessment nor a mandate requiring languages in the curriculum. In the survey of state foreign language specialists, two of the items (items 9 and 10) addressed the impact of state frameworks on local curriculum design, instruction, and assessment. The items were rated from 1 (strongly disagree) to 5 (strongly agree).

Although the survey is not comprehensive, it does appear that state education agency foreign language supervisors perceive a stronger influence of state frameworks on local curricular development than on instruction and classroom assessment. In many cases the supervisors were uncertain whether a state framework really affects what happens in the classroom (for item 10, 48 percent responded with a 3 or below on the scale). School districts appear to use the state framework for local curriculum development, but the framework's impact on daily instruction is somewhat questionable. One might further question then whether the district curriculum, itself patterned on the state framework, has any impact on instruction. Such doubts point to the need to address two curriculum development issues, whether they be at the national, state, or local level:

1. Teacher involvement in the curricular development process
2. Staff development for all other personnel

Educational literature is replete with testimonials that teacher involvement and especially staff development are most important if curricular goals and standards are to make a difference in the classroom (Darling-Hammond 1990; David 1993; Murray 1992). Smith, Fuhrman, and O'Day (1994) also point out

> Though it would be important that new instructional materials based on the new standards be developed and that schools have the other material resources necessary to teach the content standards, none of this will help unless there is a dramatic effort to prepare teachers to teach the new content. . . . The content expectations would also call for new ways of teaching, for strategies that actively engage students. Most teachers are not used to teaching in such ways. They have few opportunities and little time to learn on the job. Nor does preservice professional development meet these challenges. (p. 21)

Influence of State Frameworks on Instructional Materials

Traditionally in foreign language education, the textbook has had a greater impact on daily instruction than state frameworks or local curricular guides. In many states, especially where there is statewide textbook adoption, publishers attempt to align their materials with the state framework. This does not necessarily happen in states where adoption is strictly a local option. In Indiana, a textbook adoption state, textbook publishers are required to show a correlation between the textbooks and the state framework. Even though this is an "after-the-fact" exercise (in that most textbooks have already been published by the time the correlations are done), it is a requirement that influences publishers to look into the future as they develop materials and to make an attempt to align their materials with state curriculum documents.

Most teachers still agree that the textbook has the greatest influence on daily instruction. Although local textbook selection should be based on some form of curriculum guide, in reality, the opposite is often true. Teachers tend to base their curricular goals and instruction on the textbook they have selected. The state of Indiana has attempted to address this phenomenon by conducting statewide workshops as part of the dissemination of the state framework. At these sessions teachers are not only introduced to the framework but are also asked to develop "sample local curricula" on which to base their textbook selection. The Indiana framework (Bartz 1995) states

> In the past, it was common practice to allow textbooks to dictate specific classroom content. This often resulted in a piecemeal approach to teaching and learning. It came as a result of having a vast amount of information, little time, and no system for deciding what content to teach or what resources to use. (p. 7)

Foreign Language Teachers' Reactions to the Potential Influence of State Frameworks on Local Curriculum, Instruction, and Assessment

"Perhaps the most important question being raised regarding the standards movement is: will it make any difference?" (O'Neil 1993a:8) This question is ultimately the most important, in that the answer will determine whether the effort, time, and resources that are being spent in the development of national standards will improve student achievement. If teachers do not perceive national standards as something that will affect their instruction and ultimately student achievement, then the "national standards movement" will not achieve the desired results.

Since there has been no opportunity to apply the standards on local curricula and in the classroom, an attempt was made to obtain initial feedback from teachers on the impact of national standards on local curriculum. A questionnaire and the April 1995 draft copy of the national standards were sent to a 10 percent random sample of Indiana foreign language teachers (140). Forty-four teachers (31 percent) responded. Table 7-2 indicates the responses of Indiana teachers to the survey.

Three items (7, 10, and 11) dealt with how teachers perceived the influence of the national standards on local curriculum development. The overall teacher reaction was positive to all three statements; however, it is worth noting that neutral or negative responses were at 30 percent on item 7. This demonstrates a strong but not overwhelming consensus that the national standards are usable for local curriculum development.

Item 12 from the survey indicates how teachers imagined the impact of national standards on their own classrooms. In general they agreed that the standards would have an impact on classroom instruction. A closer examination of the responses to this statement, however, shows that 23 percent were not in strong agreement, rating the statement a 3 or below.

A look at information obtained from a survey sent to mathematics teachers by the National Council of Teachers of Mathematics in March 1992 may provide further insight about teacher perceptions of the potential influence of national standards on curriculum development and classroom instruction. O'Neil (1993a:8) states that "only about 22 percent of teachers in grades K–4, 31 percent of teachers of grades 5–8, and 48 percent of teachers of grades 9–12 say they are 'well aware' of the NCTM standards." In the survey of Indiana foreign language teachers, 43 of the 44 respondents indicated they are aware that national standards are being developed for foreign language education. This nearly 100 percent affirmative response is probably due to the fact that most foreign language teachers in Indiana are secondary teachers,

Table 7-2. National Standards Survey: Teacher Responses

	Rating										AV
	1		**2**		**3**		**4**		**5**		
	F	%	F	%	F	%	F	%	F	%	
Item 4: The 5 goals define a desirable and attainable vision for foreign language education in America. **Goal 1: Communication**	0	0	1	2	1	2	6	14	36	82	4.8
Item 4 **Goal 2: Cultures**	0	0	0	0	3	7	5	11	36	82	4.8
Item 4 **Goal 3: Connections**	0	0	0	0	4	9	14	32	26	59	4.5
Item 4 **Goal 4: Comparisons**	0	0	0	0	2	5	11	25	31	70	4.7
Item 4 **Goal 5: Communities**	0	0	0	0	7	16	11	25	24	55	4.4
Item 5: The standards sufficiently define the content necessary to achieve each goal.	0	0	0	0	7	16	20	45	17	39	4.2
Item 6: The sample benchmarks are appropriate for the grade levels indicated.	0	0	4	9	8	18	18	41	14	32	3.9
Item 7: I feel that local school districts will be able to develop curriculum based on the national standards.	0	0	4	9	9	20	17	39	14	32	3.9
Item 8: The sample benchmarks and learning scenarios will be useful for me in planning instruction and assessment.	1	2	2	5	8	18	15	34	18	41	4.1
Item 9: I am already including in instruction many of the activities suggested in the sample benchmarks and the learning scenarios.	1	2	2	5	12	27	14	32	15	34	3.9

(Continued)

Table 7-2. National Standards Survey: Teacher Responses *(continued)*

	Rating										AV
	1		2		3		4		5		
	F	%	F	%	F	%	F	%	F	%	
Item 10: I feel that national standards are important and should be used as a basis for curriculum development.	1	2	0	0	4	9	12	27	26	59	4.4
Item 11: Our school/school district will pay attention to the national standards for its curriculum development and planning.	3	7	0	0	4	9	20	45	13	30	4.0
Item 12: I feel that the national standards will have an impact on my classroom.	2	5	0	0	8	18	17	39	15	34	4.0

F: Frequency of response. AV: Average rating.

that is, they are foreign language subject specialists as opposed to elementary generalists. Moreover, information on the development of foreign language national standards has been widely publicized and respondents to a survey such as this tend to be those that are generally more informed on trends and recent developments in the profession.

The crucial question, however, is not whether one is aware of the standards but rather whether one agrees with the vision, philosophy, content, and pedagogical implications that national standards set forth, and ultimately whether they will cause the students' acquisition of skills and proficiency to improve:

> success or failure of the NCTM standards will depend not on whether they work in theory, but on whether they can produce higher levels of learning in the nation's classrooms. If . . . there is no way to demonstrate the superiority of the new standards and the new methods, they will be subject to the same criticism that derailed the new math. (Ravitch 1995:129)

In the survey of Indiana teachers, five items (items 4, 5, 6, 8, and 9 in table 7-2) attempt to address not only awareness of the standards, but degree of agreement with issues of content, philosophy, and methodology.

Item 4 deals with the ability of each of the five goals (communication, culture, connections, comparisons, communities) to define a desirable and attainable vision for foreign language education in America. Results show a generally positive agreement that all five goals do indeed define a desirable and attainable vision, but Goals 3 (connections) and 5 (communities) received somewhat weaker support. The connection and integration of foreign language study with the study of other disciplines in American schools has been almost nonexistent, especially on the secondary level. It is more likely that such integration takes place on the elementary level. The Indiana survey respondents were all middle or high school teachers, the majority being high school teachers. Goal 5 (communities) describes an outcome that represents the ultimate achievement of foreign language education in any country. However, it may be the perception that attainment of this goal is beyond the capability of many students, given the limited resources and relatively short sequences of study in Indiana schools. In addition, students from most communities in Indiana would seldom have the opportunity to participate in multilingual communities and global society. This attitude was reflected in some of the comments on the surveys:

> attainable only after long-term study, i.e., 6–8 years.

> only after teachers are given time to redesign the curriculum, after they are taught how to attain the goals, (i.e., developing activities), after textbook companies focus on these goals and teachers and administrators change their mind-set, i.e., that foreign language learning is a *long* process.

> the goals are unrealistic, especially at the upper level(s).

> Without language experiences well beyond the classroom (i.e., study abroad) most of the upper level goals are *not* attainable by the average student.

It could be that it did not occur to many of the respondents that participation in multilingual communities could be accomplished in the future and even today via telecommunication and that language proficiency need not be at an exceptionally high level to accomplish this.

The teachers' response to item 5 on the survey, on whether content was defined appropriately, indicates general agreement, with an average score of 4.2; however, 16 percent of the teachers gave the item a neutral response.

Item 6 investigated whether the benchmarks were appropriate for the grade levels, and item 9 measured the extent to which teachers included the suggested activities in their instruction. Although these two items received positive responses (3.9), they were the least positive of all items dealing with issues of content, philosophy, and methodology. Item 8, which measures the usefulness of the benchmarks and learning scenarios in planning instruction and assessment, received a slightly more positive average rating of 4.1.

Local Administrators' Reactions to the Potential Influence of State Frameworks on Local Curriculum, Instruction, and Assessment

The survey and a draft copy of the national standards (ACTFL 1995) were sent to a 5 percent random sample (152) of Indiana school principals and district superintendents. Response to this survey was 29 percent, or 44 administrators. Table 7-3 indicates their responses.

Using the same approach taken with the supervisor and teacher surveys, we will first study items 7, 10, 11, and 12, which address the potential impact of national standards on the local curriculum. The means for these four items were similar to those of the teachers, but there were more administrators who gave them a neutral or negative rating.

Items 4, 5, 6, 8, and 9 of the survey address the issues of vision, philosophy, content, and pedagogical implications as revealed in the goals, standards, benchmarks, and learning scenarios. The administrators tended generally to agree that the five major goals of the standards define a desirable and attainable vision. It is interesting to note that the average response among administrators for Goal 1 (communication) was 4.3 versus 4.8 for teachers. In fact, only 45 percent of the administrators rated Goal 1 a 5 whereas 82 percent of the teachers gave it the highest rating. This may be a reflection of a lack of awareness among administrators of the profession's recent emphasis on proficiency and communicative competence.

On the other hand, the average rating (4.6) of Goal 2 (cultures) indicates that the administrators view the knowledge and understanding of culture as slightly more important in foreign language education than the ability to communicate in another language (Goal 1).

Administrators gave Goal 3 (connections) the same ranking as Goal 1 (communication), implying that in their view connections is just as important as communication.

Goal 4 (comparisons), like Goal 1 (communication), received a slightly weaker rating from administrators than from teachers. Seventy percent of the teachers and only 43 percent of the administrators gave it a 5 rating. Over the years, the study of foreign languages has been encouraged because such study would help students to understand better their own language and culture. However, reality suggests that foreign language curricula and teaching materials have seldom made an overt attempt to achieve this goal and teachers

Table 7-3. National Standards Survey: Administrator Responses

	Rating										AV
	1		**2**		**3**		**4**		**5**		
	F	**%**	**F**	**%**	**F**	**%**	**F**	**%**	**F**	**%**	
Item 4: The 5 goals define a desirable and attainable vision for foreign language education in America.											
Goal 1: Communication	1	2	1	2	0	0	22	50	20	45	4.3
Item 4 **Goal 2: Cultures**	0	0	1	2	1	2	13	30	28	64	4.6
Item 4 **Goal 3: Connections**	0	0	1	2	4	9	21	48	17	39	4.3
Item 4 **Goal 4: Comparisons**	0	0	1	2	0	0	23	52	19	43	4.4
Item 4 **Goal 5: Communities**	1	2	1	2	8	18	13	30	20	45	4.2
Item 5: The standards sufficiently define the content necessary to achieve each goal.	0	0	1	2	8	18	29	66	5	11	3.9
Item 6: The sample benchmarks are appropriate for the grade levels indicated.	1	2	2	5	9	20	25	57	5	11	3.7
Item 7: I feel that local school districts will be able to develop curriculum based on the national standards.	0	0	1	2	13	30	21	48	9	20	3.9
Item 8: The sample benchmarks and learning scenarios will be useful for teachers in planning instruction and assessment.	0	0	1	2	2	5	24	55	17	39	4.3

(Continued)

Table 7-3. National Standards Survey: Administrator Responses *(continued)*

	Rating										AV
	1		**2**		**3**		**4**		**5**		
	F	%	F	%	F	%	F	%	F	%	
Item 9: Teachers are already including in their instruction many of the activities suggested in the sample benchmarks and the learning scenarios.	3	7	4	9	7	16	24	55	5	11	3.6
Item 10: I feel that national standards are important and should be used as a basis for curriculum development.	1	2	0	0	8	18	19	43	13	30	4.0
Item 11: Our school/school district will pay attention to the national standards for its curriculum development and planning.	0	0	3	7	8	18	19	43	13	30	4.0
Item 12: I feel that the national standards will have an impact on foreign language classrooms in my school/district.	0	0	3	7	11	25	21	48	8	18	3.8

F: Frequency of response. AV: Average rating.

have seldom incorporated specific instruction addressing the issue. Nevertheless, teachers gave this goal their second-highest rating, indicating that they feel the goal is important. Administrators, on the other hand, seemed less convinced of its importance.

The goal that received the lowest rating by both administrators and Indiana teachers was Goal 5 (communities) where only 45 percent of the administrators and 55 percent of the teachers rated it a 5, and 30 percent and 25 percent respectively rated it a 4. These results again suggest the perception that few opportunities exist in Indiana for students to participate in multilingual communities.

On item 5 of the survey, on whether content is well defined, administrators were not as strong in their agreement as were the teachers. However, even the teachers' responses indicate that they felt that the standards are not as comprehensive and helpful in determining content as they could be. The differences between these two groups are probably best explained by the fact that the teachers are by profession familiar with the content of foreign language teaching and learning.

Only 11 percent of the administrators rated item 6 a 5, on grade-level appropriateness. Teachers agreed more strongly, with 32 percent of them rating it a 5. The item did not show a strong average rating by either group and there was a substantial "spread" of responses. In both groups a fairly high percentage rated the item either a 3 or a 2. As pointed out in research conducted by Rosenbusch (1995:10), "the benchmarks are not stated narrowly and precisely. Respondents may interpret the benchmarks in varied ways. Typically, the benchmark includes descriptors that help to clarify its meaning. There is no way of knowing, however, whether teachers were responding to all descriptors provided, to several, or to just one."

Administrators' agreement on the usefulness of the benchmarks and learning scenarios (item 8) is stronger than the teachers', with 94 percent showing an agreement (rating of 4 or 5) with the item, whereas 75 percent of the teachers rated the item a 4 or above. The teachers' responses were somewhat spread out over the scale, which may indicate the uncertainty of whether the benchmark can really be translated into daily classroom instruction.

A fairly large number of administrators did not feel that "teachers were already including in their instruction many of the activities suggested in the sample benchmarks and the learning scenarios" (item 9): 32 percent rated it a 3 or below. This item received the lowest average rating by administrators of any of the items.

In general, administrators tended to give a less positive rating than the foreign language teachers to most of the items on the survey. It could be speculated that this indicates that administrators are less enthusiastic about the potential effectiveness of national standards on foreign language instruction. Item 10 of the survey, on the general importance of the standards, seems to further confirm this lack of enthusiasm, with only 30 percent of the administrators rating this item a 5 as opposed to 59 percent of the teachers.

As an initial effort to gauge the reaction of three populations to the national standards (state foreign language supervisors, foreign language teachers, and district and school administrators), these surveys have shown that, in general, the reaction is positive. This positive attitude is similarly reflected in the reactions of elementary school foreign language teachers. The National Network for Early Language Learning (NNELL) was asked to critique the K–4 benchmarks (progress indicators) of a draft version of the national standards document. The results of a questionnaire completed by 25 FLES teachers showed that the implementation of two-thirds of the benchmarks or proficiency indicators was rated as feasible. As concerns the remaining indicators, the FLES teachers felt that these might be "feasible," but that their implementation would take "major changes in teaching methodologies, training, and/or program administration."

Summary and Recommendations

It is obvious from the discussion that the impact of national standards on foreign language curriculum development and classroom instruction is still too early to assess. When this publication appears, the official version of the standards will only recently have made its debut and its actual application in the classroom will not have gone much beyond the work of the six pilot sites. Nevertheless, foreign language teachers have responded positively to the collaboration among the various segments of the profession required by the standards process, and foreign language leaders are of the opinion that the national standards can be implemented in foreign language classrooms. Because three of the five major goals (connections, comparisons, and communities) had never before been explicitly expressed as goals, one might have predicted opposition. However, preliminary survey results indicate an open-mindedness of the foreign language profession toward potential change. It is also interesting to note that several states began their work of defining state frameworks even before the completion of the national standards. This, too, shows a willingness on the part of state and local officials to assume leadership responsibilities in fostering systemic change to improve foreign language education.

Even though there is evidence of willingness among the profession, local implementation of the standards will be a complex process, because of the many facets of systemic change. For meaningful change to occur, consideration will have to be given to a wide spectrum of variables. We conclude our remarks by offering the following recommendations, which should be considered in the process of implementing national standards locally.

- State leadership is vital. Because leadership supervisory positions tend to be limited to large and affluent districts, most foreign language programs must rely on state supervisors for direction. The state automatically inherits the responsibility not only to disseminate information about the very existence of foreign language standards, but also to promote and foster their use.

- A comprehensive professional development program must be established. If teachers are to be involved in the change from writing standards to implementing them, they must have the up-to-date information to do so. Professional development programs will have a greater chance for success if they are established in cooperation with state education agencies, institutions of higher learning, and other school districts.

- Textbooks must be rewritten and updated. It is an established fact that textbooks often define local curriculum. Therefore, publishers have a responsibility to produce basal materials that lead students to attain the national standards.

- Assessment instruments that reflect the standards must be developed. Without assessment, there is no evidence of achievement nor much motivation to achieve.

- Preservice teacher-education programs must pave the way. It is imperative that teacher-education programs throughout the country include the national standards as a vital part of their course of study. The new generation of teachers entering the profession will be better prepared to affect their classrooms with positive change.

- Time and patience are key factors in implementing the national standards. The NCTM, for example, published their standards in 1989, yet today less than half the teaching profession has been affected. Similarly, individuals at all levels of the foreign language profession will need to exercise patience with each other, and the profession itself will need to allow the time for change to occur.

Note

1. A discussion of the ongoing changes in the field of assessment, including authentic and performance testing, is found in chapter 8 of this volume.

References

ACTFL. 1995. "Standards for Foreign Language Learning." (Draft.)

Alexander, Francie. 1993. "National Standards: A New Conventional Wisdom." *Educational Leadership* 50:9–10.

Banathy, Bela H. 1991. "New Horizons through Systems Design." *Educational Horizons* 69 (Winter):83–89.

Bartz, Walter H. 1995. *The Indiana Foreign Language Proficiency Guide.* Indianapolis: Indiana Department of Education.

Betts, Frank. 1992. "How Systems Thinking Applies to Education." *Educational Leadership* 50,3:38–41.

CAAP Update. 1995. Special Issue 3,1:1.

"College Board's Strategy for Education Reform." 1993. *Pacesetter Letter.*

Darling-Hammond, Linda. 1990. "Instructional Policy into Practice: The Power of the Bottom over the Top." *Educational Evaluation and Policy Analysis* 12,3:339–48.

David, Jane L. 1993. "Systemic Reform: Creating the Capacity for Change." Unpublished manuscript. New Brunswick, N.J.: Consortium for Policy Research in Education.

Ferrini-Mundy, Joan, and Loren Johnson. 1994. "Recognizing and Recording Reform in Mathematics: New Questions, Many Answers." *Mathematics Teacher* 87,3:190–93.

Garret, Michael S., and Virginia L. Mills. 1995. "Changes in Teaching Practices: The Effects of the Curriculum and Evaluation Standards." *Mathematics Teacher* 88:380–88.

LaBouve, Robert. 1993. "Proficiency as an Element in Curricula for World Languages in Elementary and Secondary Schools," pp. 31–54 in June K. Phillips, ed., *Reflecting on Proficiency from the Classroom Perspective.* Lincolnwood, IL: National Textbook Company.

Marzano, Robert J., Debra Pickering, and Jay McTighe. 1993. *Assessing Student Outcomes: Performance Assessment Using the Dimension of Learning Model.* Alexandria, VA: Association for Supervision and Curriculum Development.

Murray, Christine E. 1992. "Rochester's Reforms: The Teacher's Perspective." *Educational Policy* 6,1:55–71.

O'Neil, John. 1993a. "Can National Standards Make a Difference?" *Educational Leadership* 50,5:4–8.

———. 1993b. "On the New Standards Project: A Conversation with Lauren Resnick and Warren Simmons." *Educational Leadership* 50:17–21.

"Pacesetter Mathematics Still Growing; English and Spanish Start to Flourish." 1994. *The Pacesetter Letter.*

Ravitch, Diane. 1993. "Launching a Revolution in Standards and Assessments." *Phi Delta Kappan* 74:767–72.

———. 1995. *National Standards in American Education: A Citizen's Guide.* Washington, DC: The Brookings Institution.

Rhodes, Nancy. 1995. Personal communication.

Rosenbusch, Marcia. 1995. "Elementary Teachers Critique K–4 Benchmarks of the National Standards." *FLES News,* spring, pp. 10–13.

Smith, Marshall S., Susan H. Fuhrman, and Jennifer O'Day. 1994. "National Curriculum Standards: Are They Desirable and Feasible?" pp. 12–29 in Richard F. Elmore and Susan H. Fuhrman, eds., *The Governance of Curriculum.* Alexandria, VA: Association for Supervision and Curriculum Development.

Stansfield, Charles W. 1994. "Developments in Testing and Instruction," pp. 43–67 in Charles R. Hancock, ed., *Teaching, Testing, and Assessment: Making the Connection. Report of the Northeast Conference on the Teaching of Foreign Languages.* Lincolnwood, IL: National Textbook.

Wiske, Martha Stone, and Cynthia Y. Levinson. 1993. "How Teachers Are Implementing the NCTM Standards." *Educational Leadership* 50:8–13.

8

Assessment: From Content Standards to Student Performance

Judith Liskin-Gasparro

University of Iowa

> Standards will be meaningless if students continue to be tested without regard to them. Unless current tests change, the standards will wither and die. (Ravitch 1993:772)

When foreign languages were added to Goal 3 of the America 2000 education initiative, the foreign language profession accepted responsibility not only for producing national standards for foreign language learning K–12, but also for bridging the gap between these national content standards and the assessment of students' knowledge and skills in light of them. "Content standards" in the America 2000 context are understood as "what students should know and be able to do . . . the knowledge, skills, and understanding that students should have in order to attain high levels of competency in challenging subject matter" (U.S. Department of Education 1994:2).

The notion of establishing a single set of content standards for all foreign language students implies major educational reform; indeed, the debate about national standards in general has been described as "one of the most powerful and provocative to emerge from the nearly 10-year-old school reform movement" ("By All Measures" 1992). The paradigm shift in assessment that must accompany the implementation of the content standards is no less staggering.

Judith E. Liskin-Gasparro (Ph.D., University of Texas, Austin) is assistant professor of Spanish and director of the Lower-Division Language Program in the Department of Spanish and Portuguese at the University of Iowa. She is the author of textbooks, articles, and manuals on oral proficiency testing, listening comprehension, and proficiency-oriented teaching and curriculum development. She is a frequent presenter at conferences and workshops and has directed numerous projects related to professional development of teachers and oral proficiency assessment. She has served on the boards of directors of the Northeast Conference on the Teaching of Foreign Languages and the Vermont Foreign Language Association and has chaired the Northeast Conference.

Far from the tradition of large-scale standardized tests developed by psychometricians, administered by teachers, and scored by machines, the new assessment models are characterized by teacher engagement in the development and scoring of tasks, the application of results to instructional improvement (O'Neil 1993) and, overall, a complex web of connections among curriculum, instruction, and assessment.

This article defines the terms of the discussion about authentic, or alternative assessments, places the new assessments in a historical context, and outlines some of the thorny issues that the new assessment paradigm must confront. It concludes with case studies of schools and school districts that are currently experimenting with alternative assessments.

New Assessment Models: Defining the Terms of the Discussion

The new assessment models, which have been called "authentic assessment," "alternative assessment," and sometimes "performance assessment," have in common the goal of guiding instruction so that all students can achieve high levels of mastery (Hiebert and Calfee 1992). Absent from the new assessments are norms, large-scale administrations, right-or-wrong responses, and machine scoring. The new assessments are designed to include observation and evaluation of the thinking processes students use in arriving at a response or a demonstration of knowledge and skills. Information about the processes that students use to complete tasks is valued as highly as the products the students create (Schwager and Carlson 1994).

Old Tests and New Assessments

Grant Wiggins has written extensively on authentic assessment and on the differences between traditional tests and the new assessment models. His discussion on the etymologies of the words *test* and *assessment* (Wiggins 1994) provides some insights in this regard. The original testum was an earthenware pot that was used as a colander, to separate gold from the surrounding ore. The term was later extended to the notion of determining the worth of a product or of a person's effort. The key notion here is that a test measures knowledge or ability *a posteriori*.

The root of *assessment* is *assidere,* which is also the root of the French *asseoir.* It was first used in the sense of setting the value of property to apportion a tax. Assessors traditionally make a site visit—they inspect the property or the situation and its documents, they categorize its functions, they hear from the owner of the property, they evaluate it by setting it against already existing standards, and so forth. The assessment requires time, as well as interaction between the assessor and person or property being assessed, so that the congruence of perception with reality or, in our case, the congruence between underlying mental processes and surface observation, can be verified.

The discussions of the new assessment models in the educational reform literature are admittedly quite polemic, with authentic assessment cast as the hero and standardized, paper-and-pencil tests as the villain. Some of the more salient distinctions drawn are the following (Haney and Madaus 1989; Wiggins 1990; among others):

- Authentic assessments are viewed as "direct" measures of student performance, since tasks are designed to incorporate the contexts, problems, and solution strategies that students would use in real life. Traditional standardized tests, in contrast, are seen as "indirect" measures, since test items are designed to "represent competence" by extracting knowledge and skills out of their real-life contexts.

- Items on standardized instruments tend to test one domain of knowledge or skill only to avoid ambiguity for the test taker. Authentic assessment tasks are by design "ill-structured challenges" (Fredericksen 1984), since their goal is to help students prepare for the complex ambiguities of the adult world.

- Traditional tests focus instructional time, energy, and attention on the simpler skills that are most easily tested and away from creative endeavors and higher-order thinking skills. Authentic assessments, in contrast, create positive links between testing and instruction (Flood and Lapp 1993), encouraging teachers to sit down together to hammer out ways to improve curriculum and teaching (O'Neil 1993).

- Authentic assessments focus on processes and rationales. There is no single correct answer; instead, students are led to craft polished, thorough, and justifiable responses, performances, and products. Traditional tests, on the other hand, are one-time measures that rely on a single correct response to each item; they offer no opportunity for demonstration of thought processes, revision, or interaction with the teacher.

- In the new assessment models, the teacher is an important collaborator in creating tasks, as well as in developing guidelines for scoring and interpretation. Standardized tests, which are externally developed, promote greater distance between teachers and assessment.

- The new assessment models involve long-range projects, exhibits, and performances that are tied to the curriculum. Students are aware of how and on what knowledge and skills they are to be assessed. Traditional tests, in contrast, must be kept under lock and key so students do not have knowledge about or access to them ahead of time.

Validity and Reliability

The tension between authentic assessment and standardized testing in large part stems from the competing demands of test validity and test reliability. Validity, the faithfulness of a test to the constructs it purports to measure, pulls the test developer in the direction of multifaceted, complex assessments that resemble the problems and situations of the real world. Reliability, which refers to the consistency and precision of test scores, pulls the test developer in the opposite direction, toward assessments that can be evaluated without ambiguity or fear of shifting standards. Well-constructed multiple-choice items that test facts in the absence of their "messy" contexts result in highly reliable scores but, unfortunately, often at the cost of their resemblance to real-life tasks and problems, i.e., their validity.

Test designers have to strike a balance between validity and reliability. Perhaps in reaction to what he perceives as an excessive emphasis on reliability, Wiggins (1993) argues forcefully for new tests that respond to the demands for validity:

> Forms of testing [that are designed to minimize the ambiguity of tasks and answers] simply do not tell us what we need to know: namely, whether students have the capacity to use wisely what knowledge they have. This is a judgment that we can make only through tasks that require students to "perform" in highly contextualized situations that are as faithful as possible to criterion situations. (p. 202)

Historical Antecedents

In the history of U.S. education in the twentieth century, the pendulum has swung repeatedly from periods of expanded educational opportunities to demands for new and increased assessment (Resnick 1987). At the turn of the century, formal education was a scarce and selective resource; assessment consisted of direct performance of academic tasks, for which students had to show their work and explain their thinking (Calfee 1994). The waves of immigration during this period resulted in greater size and heterogeneity of public school populations. The "school efficiency movement" (1911–1916), a reform movement that sought to redesign schools in accordance with factory productivity models (Callahan 1962, cited in Wiggins 1989a), resulted in the creation of the century's first standardized tests, whose purpose was to classify students according to levels of academic achievement.

Both World War I and World War II were followed by periods of educational expansion. From the 1950s well into the 1970s, for example, as waves of post–World War II baby boomers entered the public schools, federal legislation, specifically the National Defense Education Act of 1958 and the Secondary Education Act of 1965, led to the creation of large-scale, discrete-point standardized testing programs. The predominant educational paradigm was behaviorism, which, according to Calfee (1994), was the ideal conceptualization for handling the greater number and greater diversity of school populations. The focus on specific objectives that could be realized through practice and reinforcement made for a natural fit with standardized tests that measured mastery of those objectives via discrete-point items. Indeed, standardization of curriculum and assessment was seen as a positive force for the elimination of the teacher subjectivity that had worked against the newer populations of students because of gender, race, and poverty (Calfee 1994:343).

In the 1980s the pendulum swung from expansion and equality of opportunity to demands for excellence. Thirteen educational policy reports were published between 1982 and 1991; most of them called for tougher standards, more demanding courses, more rigorous testing and grading, and more stringent high school graduation and college entrance requirements (Ornstein 1992). Nearly all the reports either mandated a new form of testing or expanded the uses of existing assessment instruments (Pipho 1985, cited in Haney and Madaus 1989:684).

A number of states responded to these reports by devising new assessments whose main goal was increased accountability. Marcoulides and Heck (1994) cite California as one state that dramatically increased its use of assessment instruments. A typical district that used one standardized test in the 1970s was giving several tests a decade later, including a district minimum standards test for graduation, the California Test of Basic Skills (CTBS) or the California Achievement Test (CAT), the California Assessment Program, the Golden State Exams in math and history, and the Preliminary Scholastic Aptitude Test (Heck 1987).

The push for more testing extended into the current decade as well. In response to the urging of Lamar Alexander, newly appointed secretary of education in the Bush administration, Congress voted in 1991 to establish the National Council on Educational Standards and Testing (NCEST). The thirty-two-member bipartisan body issued a report a year later that called for the establishment of voluntary national standards in key subject areas and a national system of achievement tests based on these national standards. The original plan called for an assessment system with two components: large-scale sampling assessments, which would be provided by the National Assessment of Educational Progress (NAEP) and other assessments intended to show results for individual students, rather than groups. The tests themselves would be developed by states or local districts but would be linked to the national standards.

Controversy over the NCEST report was immediate, particularly as it related to the role of assessment in the current reform initiatives. Proponents argued that the deleterious effects associated with standardized, multiple-choice tests would be overcome by replacing them with performance-based assessments more closely linked to curriculum frameworks (Brown 1993, cited by Marcoulides and Heck 1994). Opponents argued that talking about assessments and higher standards without first addressing the basic inequities among schools would be a recipe for failure, that the profession would "end up proving once again that poor kids don't score as well as rich kids" (Sizer, quoted by O'Neil 1995:6). The arguments reflected the ongoing polemic between expansion of educational opportunities and the need for more stringent standards of excellence. This question and other equally complex ones are raised in the "Issues" section below.

The Promise of the New Assessments: Empowerment of Teachers, Excellence for Students

The proposed models of authentic assessment (Calfee 1994; Schwager and Carlson 1994; Wiggins 1989a, 1989b, 1993, 1994) encourage test designers and teachers to move toward testing and teaching that are project-oriented, in which students are drawn into a process of self-assessment as they continuously challenge themselves to meet standards of excellence. The new assessments also call for a level of teacher involvement that is unparalleled in previous proassessment periods. More than the introduction of measurement tools, assessments reform is seen as springing from contemporary cognitive theories of learning that emphasize how the learner structures knowledge. Of more central importance are long-term memory and the ways it categorizes knowledge, the interplay of language and thought, the interaction between "knowing" and "doing," and an appreciation of the concept and role of metacognition (Calfee 1994).

The New Assessments: Teacher-Centered

According to Calfee (1994) and Wiggins (1993), perhaps the most vocal proponents of the new assessments, authentic tests of intellectual performance represent a fundamental change in the goals of education. Several features distinguish this movement:

- *Engaging and worthy problems or questions of importance.* Problems in which students must use knowledge to fashion their performance effectively and creatively are the centerpieces of authentic assessments. The tasks are either replicas or analogs of the problems faced by adult citizens and consumers or professionals in the field (Wiggins 1993:206).

- *Emphasis on high-level competence in complex tasks.* "Project" rather than "item" is the typical assessment unit. The approach to assessment is integrative, since a complex project will show evidence of reading, writing, and research skills, understanding of concepts, awareness of audience, etc. Differences in student competency are addressed by "scaffolding up" (creating at graduated levels of difficulty) the assessment tasks (Hart 1994:11), rather than simplifying them for the less able students.

- *Frequent interactions between student and teacher/assessor while assessment activities are underway.* The tasks ask students to "show their work" and explain their reasoning; the "right answer" in isolation is not sufficient. Teachers have the opportunity to respond to students, ask probing questions, and listen to students' justification of their responses. Students, in turn, "pose questions, make judgments, reconsider problems, and investigate possibilities" (Hart 1994:12). For Wiggins (1994), the interactive element is at the heart of the new assessments:

  > Does a correct answer hide thoughtless recall? Does a wrong answer hide thoughtful understanding? We can only know by responding with further questions, seeking more explanation or substantiation, requesting a self-assessment, or by soliciting the student's response to the assessment. (p. 70)

- *Transparent or demystified criteria and standards.* The standards by which assessment information is interpreted and judgments are made are known to all in advance. Indeed, in a collaborative assessment model (Sperling 1993; see discussion below), the teacher and students work together to set standards for future assessments and identify samples of student work that exemplify the various levels of performance. In addition to sharing evaluation standards widely, proponents of authentic assessment encourage students to discuss and clarify assessment tasks with peers and the teacher and to develop habits of self-assessment.

- *Trained teacher/assessor judgment.* Trained judgment, in reference to clear and appropriate criteria that have been developed by groups of teachers, guarantees the link between assessment and curriculum.

- *Assessment that is guided by development standards.* Teachers search for patterns of responses in diverse settings. No single piece of an assessment is considered to represent the student. Rather, the emphasis is on the consistency of a student's work, which, over time, becomes the assessment of "*habits* of mind in performance" (Wiggins 1993:207). Welsh (1992) and Meier (Lockwood 1993) have also recommended that work habits and effort be stressed as key ingredients of success for all students. Teachers' notes about each student will refer to the growth of the student over time, as well as to patterns of strength and weakness.

- *Assessment that is both summative and formative and is geared toward the reflection on, and improvement of, instruction.* At the summative level, the goal of the new assessments is for all students to produce final products of high quality. At the formative level, student performances on a given task are not so much signs of mastery, or of failure, but rather stimuli to the teacher to reflect on larger curricular goals and to modify the teaching situation as needed. For Calfee (1994:346), it is this continual reflection on students' performance that is the key to cognitive assessment.

Instruments and Procedures: Student Empowerment

Assessment activities that are consonant with the descriptions outlined here are already being used in foreign language classrooms at all age and instructional levels. Their use tends to be sporadic rather than systematic, and as of this writing there are no full-scale authentic assessment programs in place. The instruments and activities described below are among those that readers will find most familiar. Portfolios, oral proficiency measures, and performance assessments are presented first, followed by additional strategies that support and complement the first three major assessment types.

Portfolios. A portfolio is, simply speaking, "a container that holds evidence of an individual's skills, ideas, interests, and accomplishments" (Hart 1994:23). The most basic portfolio is the scrapbook type, in which students' work is collected over time in a folder. Best-work portfolios are those whose contents are selected by the student. Portfolios often have a reflective component, in which students write about each piece they select, explaining the reason for its inclusion in the portfolio, the circumstances surrounding its creation, and any changes in perceptions about the piece that the author may have experienced over time. Portfolio artifacts, as they are called, can be creative or analytical, written or oral, visual or manipulable.

Portfolios allow for longitudinal assessment, since they document the learning that takes place over a period of time. When a team of teachers looks at a group of student portfolios together, the contents of portfolios can serve as a starting point for discussions about what is happening in classrooms (Evans 1993). Even the types of work in a scrapbook portfolio can be instructive: the ratio of work sheets to artifacts initiated by the student; the presence or absence of artifacts that involved several drafts or sections crafted over a period of time; the ratio of creative to analytical artifacts.

According to Hart (1994), a well-designed assessment portfolio can serve four distinct purposes: assessment of the growth and progress of individual students; communication between teachers and parents about a student's work; evaluation of instructional programs by teachers and supervisors; and active participation by students in the assessment process. The student-initiated component is central to the whole enterprise: students must develop personal standards to evaluate their own work and then apply those standards to select pieces for their portfolio. The self-assessment process is further expanded and refined in the reflections they write about each piece they have selected.

Teachers who have worked with portfolio assessment find the student self-evaluation and self-reflection component to be both the most challenging and most valuable aspect of portfolio work. Wolf (1989), who worked on Harvard Project Zero, an arts education project, addressed the challenge:

> Portfolios are messy. They demand intimate and often frighteningly subjective talk with students. Portfolios are work. Teachers who ask students to read their own progress in the "footprints" of their works have to coax and bicker with individuals who are used to being assessed. Halfway through the semester, at least half a dozen recalcitrants will lose every paper or sketch or tape they have ever owned. (p. 37)

Donato and McCormick (1994), who used portfolio assessment in a fifth-semester college French conversation course, discovered that students' ability to reflect on their work grew significantly over the course of the semester. This is hardly surprising, given—as Wolf also commented—their familiarity with being the objects of assessment rather than the assessors. Donato (1995) commented that they grew in self-reflection from initial unfocused and banal comments (e.g., "I really liked this essay") to well-focused, insightful commentary that was anchored in evidence.

What students put into a portfolio depends on the purpose of the portfolio, as well as the students' own choice. How they are evaluated also depends on the teacher's purpose in incorporating a portfolio into the instructional program. Portfolios used within a single classroom are ideal for developing students' habits of self-evaluation (Hart 1994); if portfolio assessment is used more widely within a school, district, or state to evaluate instructional programs, then formal standards would have to be developed.

Oral Proficiency Measures. Teachers have been using oral proficiency interviews (OPIs) for well over a decade to measure their students' speaking ability. Given the expense of the formal testing procedure and the relatively small number of ACTFL-certified testers, a number of teachers have learned how to conduct OPIs over a restricted range of proficiency for internal purposes. Tschirner (1992), for example, routinely trains his graduate teaching assistants in German to conduct OPIs at the Novice and Intermediate levels with first- and second-year college students. Cole and Miller (1985) conducted OPIs with high school French students who had completed a three- or four-year course sequence. In these cases, among many others, the purpose of the OPIs was both to give students a sense of their own accomplishment and to measure the effectiveness of the language programs in developing students' oral skills.

Large-scale oral proficiency testing, as well as testing in the less commonly taught languages (LCTs), for which there are very few certified testers, have been undertaken with tape-mediated instruments known as SOPIs (Simulated Oral Proficiency Interview). The SOPIs are designed to elicit language that is similar to language that would be elicited during the level check and probe phases of an OPI. Correlation studies in five languages have indicated that the SOPI can be used with confidence in place of the OPI (Stansfield 1990). The SOPI can be administered to groups of students and does not require a trained interviewer.

The Center for Applied Linguistics (CAL) is currently in the last phase of a project to develop SOPIs in Spanish, French, and German. Intended for students at high school and postsecondary levels, these SOPIs measure oral proficiency through a series of prompts that include such tasks as giving directions, describing pictures, recounting a story, comparing and contrasting, arguing in favor of a proposal, and considering hypothetical situations. Students have a booklet with pictures to describe, issues to address, and situations to respond to. Instructions and time limits are given on a master tape and students record their speech samples on individual response tapes. CAL has designed the SOPIs for institutional use and has included the master tape, a test booklet, administration instructions, and rater training materials in the packets that it distributes. As of this writing, CAL is making these SOPI materials available to teachers in rater training workshops.

Performance Assessment. Oral proficiency measures are one example of the types of tasks that might be included under the rubric of performance assessment. In general, performance assessments are designed to measure the ability of students to bring their accumulated knowledge and skills to bear on tasks that students carry out individually or collaboratively. The tasks can be relatively short, such as writing a letter, describing a picture, telling a story, or carrying out a discussion or debate. Extended performance tasks are long-term multigoal projects, such as the news broadcast written and produced by Spanish students in Williamston, Michigan, which is described in the case study that concludes this article.

Short assessment tasks are more likely to focus on one or two of the five national standards goals. The letter-writing task below assesses communication in languages other than English (Goal 1) and knowledge and understanding of other cultures (Goal 2). Note that scaffolding is provided in the form of guidelines about topics to address in their letters.

Because they are long and complex, extended tasks can assess several of the five goals. Students might work together for a month to produce a newspaper in the target language. The research, writing, production, and distribution of a newspaper might well touch on all five goals.

Self-Assessment. Self-assessments are meant to complement, rather than replace, teacher assessments of student work. In the spirit of communication about assessment that characterizes the new models, students know the criteria for evaluation and can use them to assess their own work in midstream, upon completion, or even after it is assessed by the teacher. Students can also work with a partner, using the criteria to assess both pieces of work (Sperling 1993).

Figure 8-1: Short Performance Assessment Task

Task. Your school is going to host an exchange student from Hamburg, Germany. The student's name is Hans Schmitter. Write Hans a letter in German welcoming him to your school and your community. In your letter, write about:

- Your town or city: location, size, special features
- Your school and typical daily activities
- Your interests and hobbies
- Two or three things that you expect Hans will find strange or different, given what you know about German high schools and how they are different from your school.

Collaborative Assessment. With this strategy, teachers and students work together to create an assessment scale that is then used for self-assessments, peer assessments, and teacher assessments. Sperling (1993) reported on the use of collaborative assessment for writing in the native language in a fourth-grade class. The teacher began by selecting sample papers and writing criteria for each level of performance on a task that involved having the entire class participate in interviewing one student; each student then wrote a composition about the interviewee. The teacher then gave the criteria and the papers (unclassified) to the class. Students worked in pairs to grade the papers using the criteria and to explain why they thought one paper was better than another. After group discussion, the teacher incorporated students' rationales into the criteria.

The criteria plus a sample of writing at each level were made available to the students as they wrote, and students assessed their own papers before handing them in. According to Sperling (1993), the availability of samples of writing across the whole grading scale shows students what it would take to make their writing better.

Learning Logs. A combination of project planner and project journal, this assessment strategy is typically used to document and support students' learning process while they are undertaking a major project. The planner component, in which students think about the stages of the project and how they will undertake them, what resources they will need and how to find them, and the like. The journal component documents the steps the learners are taking as the project progresses, in addition to providing a forum for reflecting on the project as it takes shape.

Learning logs can also be used as a tool to encourage students to reflect on their progress in a course in a more general way. Valette (1994) reported on the use of learning logs by elementary college French students. The students recorded their daily contact with the French language outside formal classroom instruction—time spent on written homework, activities in the language lab, viewing a film, etc. The goal of the logs in that project was to help students focus on and develop habits of regular preparation and practice with the language.

Journals. Journals are reflective diaries that students keep not only to record some of their learning activities, but to reflect on their progress. Like the learning log, a journal is typically a vehicle for self-awareness and self-assessment. Villalobos (1995), for example, asked students in his college-level third-semester Spanish class to keep journals about their growth as writers. Because the journals were in the target language, the students spent far more time writing in Spanish than they would have otherwise. Villalobos reported that students used their journals to ask him questions about grammar that came up for them while writing their entries, to reflect on the formal writing assignments in the course, and to comment on their readings and other class activities. In addition, they used the journals as a forum to express their feelings about the course, as well as about events in their personal lives. The students reported great satisfaction with the journal project on several fronts: extra communication with and attention from their instructor; the chance to ask questions about course content at the very moment the questions arose; and the additional practice with their writing in the target language that the journal afforded them.

Difficult Issues: Is Authentic Assessment Possible?

In spite of the promise of the new assessment models for raising standards for student achievement, increasing professional collaboration among teachers, and forging stronger links between teaching and assessment, numerous thorny issues must be addressed at the local and national levels before authentic assessment programs can be implemented in states, districts, schools, or even classrooms within a school. The difficult issues are discussed in this section, and an example of a major authentic assessment activity in one school district is described in the section that follows.

Technical Issues: Validity and Reliability

The tension between validity and reliability that underlies all test development efforts was discussed briefly in an earlier section. For the new assessments, the test developer's balancing act becomes all the more difficult. Tasks that are designed to "help students rehearse for the complex ambiguities of . . . adult and professional life" (Wiggins 1990:4) will be high in face validity, or credibility, since they will have the appearance of assessing what they claim to assess. The more difficult question is to assure the construct validity of an assessment activity. Construct validation involves going beneath the surface appearance of the activity to determine whether the underlying concepts and constructs that are being assessed are the same as those in the curriculum (Calfee 1994; Messick 1989). If the validity of an assessment is called into question, then fairness to students is also at issue.

The other side of the coin is reliability. If the nature of the new assessments gives the new models an edge in validity, it is also true that reliability is far more difficult to achieve than for standardized tests. Wiggins (1989a, 1993) rather cavalierly relegates to a secondary position the practical problems inherent in the implementation of large-scale individualized assessments. The problems he spells out can be summarized under the rubric of reliability:

> If we wish to design an authentic test, we must first decide what are the actual performances that we want students to be good at. We must design those performances first and worry about a fair and thorough method of grading them later. Do we judge our students to be deficient in writing, speaking, listening, artistic creation, finding and citing evidence, and problem solving? Then let the tests ask them to write, speak, listen, create, do original research, and solve problems. Only then need we worry about scoring the performances, training the judges, and adapting the school calendar to insure thorough analysis and useful feedback to students about results. (1989a:705)

Other writers on educational policy link the reliability issue more directly to the success of new assessment models in the long run. Calfee (1994) acknowledges that very few proponents of authentic assessment have addressed the issue of consistency in evaluating student work over judges and tasks, although he asserts that it can be done. Winfield and Woodard (1994), on the other hand, doubt that the local entities can design assessments linked to national standards. In a nutshell, for alternative assessments to be successful, i.e., both valid and reliable, they must be designed in light of common standards across classrooms, schools, and districts; teachers must work together to develop standards of performance for assessment tasks; and experts must be available to supply ongoing training to teacher-assessors to refine the criteria, apply them to samples of student work, and interpret the results (Marcoulides and Heck 1994).

Schwager and Carlson (1994) warn that partial adoption of alternative assessment strategies, without an "underlying paradigm shift" in one's view of teaching and learning, may jeopardize both the validity and reliability of the assessments. The new assessment formats—designing and evaluating portfolios, multistage projects, global measurement of language skills in a performance context—are time-consuming to learn, require continuous attention and refinement, and must be undertaken by groups of teachers working cooperatively. As Schwager and Carlson (1994:391) remark, "classroom testing has rarely been subjected to such scrutiny and psychometric rigor."

In addition to the difficulty of achieving consistency among judges in evaluating student work in terms of a common standard, there is the even more difficult task of compiling a pool of comparable tasks. When the nature of the assessment context is such that variability in tasks is expected, e.g., portfolios, then the issue of comparability is complicated even further.

Professional Issues: Teacher Involvement

As the discussion of reliability issues implies, providing appropriate technical support to teachers is essential to implementing alternative assessment models. The evidence from studies of assessment reform in other subject areas suggests that a combination of personal beliefs about teaching and assessment, administrative leadership, and the availability of technical support interact to create optimal conditions for new assessments to take hold (Schwager and Carlson 1994). Studies of portfolio assessment programs, for example, have shown that the distinction between learning activities and assessment activities can be easily blurred in the absence of a strong professional development component (Aschbacher 1992). A study of an assessment initiative untaken in conjunction with the national standards in mathematics found that teachers seemed to have greatest difficulty adapting to notions of student-generated learning (Guthrie 1990, cited by Schwager and Carlson 1994). In a study of the relationship between school environment and teachers' attitudes toward alternative assessments (Schwager and Carlson 1994), it was found that administrative leaders who encouraged experimentation and innovation enabled a much smaller group of innovation-minded teachers to act as leavening for the others than in schools in which the administration did not explicitly provide encouragement in this area.

Extending Authentic Assessment Models to Urban Schools

The third and final issue to be addressed in this section is the feasibility of extending new assessment models to schools that are already strapped for human, fiscal, and material resources (Massell and Kirst 1994). The implementation issues are both conceptual and practical.

At the practical level, some researchers (Calfee 1994; McGill-Franzen 1993) question whether urban schools, in which behavioral objectives paradigms are still entrenched, can come up with the critical mass of innovation-minded teachers that will be needed to start the process of experimentation with alternative assessments, collegial involvement, and consensus-building. Complicating the picture are federal and state regulations governing the use of Chapter 1 and special-education monies that require monitoring by means of standardized tests (Calfee 1994).

At a deeper level, the standards movement has stimulated debates that have particular salience for urban schools. Advocates suggest that higher standards will be especially beneficial to urban students, who have suffered for years under the "help" of low expectations (Massell and Kirst 1994). Cautionary notes are sounded by critics who fear that national standards will not reflect the culture of students from other than white, middle-class backgrounds (Massell and Kirst 1994). Also expressed is the fear that eliminating standardized tests will mean reintroducing bias and subjectivity (Calfee 1994).

Winfield and Woodard (1994) reject the assumption that student-centered alternative assessments would prevent unfairness or reduce the achievement differences between racial or ethnic groups. They cited several studies that found that gaps between the scores of white and nonwhite students on various kinds of test items remained wide. Along the same lines, LeMahieu (1992) found that African Americans received lower scores on their portfolio evaluations than whites regardless of the race of the rater. Cultural differences seemed to account for at least part of the phenomenon, in that the African American students' selection of their "best writing" did not match the selection that the raters would have made. The implication is that the construct of "best writing" is, at least to some extent, culturally determined.

Other educators argue flatly that the new debates about standards and alternative assessments do not address the needs of urban schools. Darling-Hammond (Lockwood 1993) claimed that school funding is the central issue, and until the allocation of resources is equalized, urban schools will lag behind their wealthier suburban counterparts. With some irony, she commented that "the new standards are [not] likely to convince people to correct resource disparities any more quickly than the old standards have done" (p. 3). Meier, who has worked for more than twenty years to build change models in urban schools, believes that high standards can raise student performance levels, but that the focus of attention should be placed on infusing school culture with what she calls "habits of mind" and "habits of work," not with assessments tied to national standards (Lockwood 1993). She advocates modeling by adults of high-level performances, as well as demonstrations of intellectual curiosity, flexibility, and good work habits:

> If I am going to teach a kid tennis, the first thing I want is to make sure that he has seen tennis played well. And then I want to engage him in a tennis game, with more opportunities to practice tennis, and more opportunities to practice it with people who are slightly better than he is. (p. 8)

The "habits of mind" that Meier and her staff agreed to model for students as much as possible are posted all over the school in the form of questions, such as: How do you know what you know? Can you think of another way to look at the same thing? Can you see connections between that and other things? The "habits of work," which teachers also consciously model for students, include initiating activities, meeting deadlines, revising one's work, and reflecting on one's work to see how it might have been done differently (Lockwood 1993).

In spite of Meier's mistrust of assessment in general, her approach of having teachers at a single school work together to decide on an educational philosophy and to work actively to establish and nurture a school culture that fosters excellence is precisely the process that needs to be undertaken by groups of teachers to design appropriate assessments for their students.

Implementation: Can the Standards Be Assessed?

Authentic assessment in first-language instructional areas is a relatively new undertaking, and in foreign languages even more so. Can we design assessment tasks that are performance-based and that engage students in complex and intellectually challenging tasks? Can we learn how to evaluate student performance on these tasks consistently and reliably, in ways that reflect well the best that all students are capable of? Finally, can we find ways to attach the standards to the new assessment models? This section addresses these questions by outlining some possible assessment strategies for the five goals of the standards. It concludes with a case study of an extended performance assessment task designed by the Spanish teachers in the Williamston, Michigan, public schools.

Goal 1 is familiar assessment ground for most language teachers. For a number of years we have been devising tasks that assess students' language skills in a performance context. One such task, appropriate for students at all levels, is described in figure 8-2. It assesses the speaking skill, Standard 1.3.

Assessment tasks that focus on the other four goals will naturally include evaluation by and through the language skills that underlie Goal 1. Indeed, perhaps the most interesting and challenging assessments will be those that include several goals. The task in figure 8-3, which draws on both knowledge and skills, is adapted from the guest speaker learning scenario in the national standards document.

Figure 8-3 shows a task that assesses standards that belong to several goals. Students' preparation and posing of questions, comprehension of the presentation, and follow-up summaries involve language skills that belong to Goal 1. The acquisition of cultural information falls under Goal 2. The use of French to learn about Togo addresses Goal 3. Finally, the collaboration with an individual from a Francophone country relates to Goal 5.

It is interesting enough to imagine that Goals 2, 3, and 5—which directly address the learning of content, particularly cultural content, through the target language—may be the goals that inspire teachers to incorporate culture more fully into instruction and assessment. Moore (1994) reported on a project in two rural high schools in New York that used a portfolio approach to culture

Figure 8-2: Assessment Task for Goal 1: Leave Your Teacher a Telephone Message

Task. Call your teacher on the phone and leave a message on his/her answering machine. (Administrative note: Have students call a number dedicated to this purpose or, if feasible, the teacher's or another person's number at a time when nobody will be there to answer the phone.) Your message should include the following information: your name, the day and time of your call, and your message, which can be anything that you wish to communicate to your teacher. Leave your message just as you would in English—do not write your message and then read or recite it from memory. Note that you will lose points if your message does not sound spontaneous.

Evaluation. Your performance will be evaluated on the basis of comprehensibility, inclusion of the three pieces of information requested, and spontaneity. See the evaluation scale below.

Descriptor	Points
Message is totally comprehensible and has all three elements.	10
Message is too brief or not complete and/or it is not completely comprehensible.	5
Message sounds as though it is being read or recited from memory.	3
Student did not leave a message.	0

learning. From the topics in the syllabus, students working individually or in small groups selected one or two topics per semester to develop into artifacts for their portfolios. The artifacts could be research studies, case studies, oral histories, or various kinds of group projects, including video production, pictorial displays, clay models, and collages. Teachers helped students design their projects, develop an activity plan, locate relevant resources, and decide on the format of the products that would go into the portfolio. Students were also supplied with self-evaluation forms to encourage

Figure 8-3: Sample Assessment Task That Includes Several Goals and Standards

Guest Speaker

Task. Monsieur Mensah, a native of Togo, visits a French class to talk to the class about Togo—geographical, historical, and cultural information, as well as personal stories about growing up there. Students have tasks to accomplish before, during, and after the presentation.

Preparation. Students accessed printed and electronic information about Togo. Most of the information they found was in English, but some of it was in French. Each student prepared two questions in French on a topic of personal interest to ask during the presentation. Groups of students worked together to edit their questions to avoid repetition. Each student was responsible for asking one question during the presentation.

Presentation. (Administrative note: M. Mensah was briefed about students' linguistic level and prepared his presentation accordingly, using visuals to illustrate his points and facilitate comprehension.) M. Mensah distributed a brief outline of his presentation. Students looked it over and noted places where their questions might be most appropriate. During the presentation students jotted down notes about the most interesting points and asked their questions. Each student was responsible for remembering the answer to his or her question.

Follow-up. After the visit, students prepared a summary of the information in M. Mensah's presentation in either cassette or written form. Each student included his or her question and the answer M. Mensah had given. Students then met in groups to read each other's summaries and decide on a topic about Togo to research in greater depth. That research would then become the subject of a future assessment.

them to reflect on their work. Moore described the project undertaken by Chaz, a seventh-grade student originally from Quebec, for his culture portfolio.

A complex, multistage project such as the one described in figure 8-4 will almost by necessity relate to more than one area of the standards. Indeed, this project serves both to develop and to assess knowledge and skills related to all five goals. Writing questions and interviewing informants relates to Goal 1. Learning about greetings and leave-takings in several Francophone cultures assesses progress in Goal 2. Acquiring skill with the camcorder and video editing equipment falls under Goal 3. Discovering similarities and differences between greeting and leave-taking patterns in French and North American English relates to Goal 4. Finally, meeting and working with French speakers in the community touches on Goal 5.

From these few examples, it appears that the development of interesting and integrated tasks can flow naturally from a curriculum that integrates language skill development with cultural content. More difficult will be the technical issues of devising evaluation criteria for these open-ended, multi-stage tasks and applying them consistently.

Since foreign languages were the last subject area to be included in the America 2000 initiative, we are able to draw on the experience of the subject areas that have been part of America 2000 from the beginning and, therefore, are considerably more advanced in the process of developing assessment programs in consonance with their content standards. The results of a study of six sites attempting to implement alternative assessments in math and social studies (Aschbacher 1992) are summarized here to provide a context for the case study that follows.

Although the six districts that Aschbacher studied were quite different from each other, she found similarities in both the barriers to implementing alternative assessments and factors that facilitated implementation. The major

---

Figure 8-4: Portfolio Approach to the Assessment of Culture Learning

> **Greetings and Leave-Takings in French**
>
> **Preparation.** Chaz and his teacher worked together to identify eight French speakers in the community: two students from Haiti, two teachers from France, two students from Quebec, and two adults from the Ivory Coast. With the help of his teacher, Chaz prepared five questions to ask each informant related to greetings, leave-takings, and accompanying gestures.
>
> **Implementation.** Chaz interviewed his informants and filmed them greeting and taking leave of each other. He analyzed the clips, edited them, and wrote a reflective piece for his portfolio to accompany the tape and the results of his analysis of the scenarios and his informants' responses to his questions.
>
> Source: Zena T. Moore, "The Portfolio and Testing Culture," pp. 173–74 in Charles Hancock, ed., *Teaching, Testing, and Assessment: Making the Connection.* Northeast Conference Reports. Lincolnwood, IL: National Textbook, 1994.

barriers included teachers' use of assessments primarily as learning activities rather than as a means to assess student performance; teachers' difficulty in specifying criteria for judging student work; teachers' fear and anxiety over assessment; teachers' lack of time to learn, plan, practice, use, and reflect; and the lack of a long-range implementation plan. The factors that appeared to facilitate the implementation of new assessments were purposeful commitment by teachers to innovative assessment and instruction; professional development and specific training provided to teams of teachers; administrative support; and, most of all, sustained technical assistance. Aschbacher found the professional development, training, and technical assistance component of alternative assessments to be both the most serious stumbling block and the most effective facilitator:

> The kind of instruction that should support performance assessments is sorely lacking. We have observed great reluctance on the part of teachers to articulate desired student outcomes and to embrace the development of criteria and standards for assessment. Successful development and use of alternative assessments by teachers, therefore, requires a significant paradigm shift that cannot be sustained with just a few in-service meetings. (p. 27)

The case study below is drawn from the group of six sites selected by the National Standards Project to "live with the standards" for the academic year 1994–95. Along with exploring teaching and learning in light of the standards, the districts experimented with new forms of assessment.

Case Study:
Williamston High School, Williamston, Michigan[1]

Williamston is a rural district that teaches Spanish as its only foreign language in its one high school and one middle school. The two teachers at the high school share responsibility for four levels, although the third- and fourth-year courses are often combined. The fourth-year course is taught in conjunction with the local community college. The third teacher conducts a six-week rotational exploratory program at the middle school.

Among the assessment tasks that the teachers developed was a 15- to 20-minute newscast that was designed, written, and produced entirely by teams of students in Spanish II. Originally developed as a learning activity, the newscast also served as the final exam for the course. The full text of the task is included in the Appendix.

The task is multidisciplinary, in that it includes video production; world, national, and local current events; advertising and marketing; and linguistic knowledge and skills. Underlying cultural frames inherent in U.S. television and news broadcasting are made explicit, which could serve as the foundation for a study of news broadcasts in the target cultures.

Evaluation of the task consists of multiple measures that are formative and summative and provided by the students themselves, by peers, and by the teacher. The task has numerous stages, with ample opportunity to consult, practice, rewrite, and polish one's performance. Collaboration among members of the broadcast team is of utmost importance, as is members' taking responsibility for the tasks that they agree to undertake.

In the postbroadcast evaluation, students are asked to rate the project direction skills of their producer, to assess their own level of involvement on each of the tasks, and to assign ratings to the various facets of their team's final product. Finally, they are asked to evaluate the assessment task overall and to make comments that the teachers might take into consideration in future iterations of the task. According to Kendall (1995), the project was evaluated in the most enthusiastic terms by every student in the spring 1995 administration.

It is interesting that Kendall (1995) also reported that the opportunity for the three Spanish teachers in the district to meet together regularly was perhaps the greatest impetus for change. Given the special task and a modest amount of technical assistance from the National Standards Project, the teachers worked through the draft standards document, figured out ways to relate the standards to their curriculum and their curriculum and learning activities to the standards. Assessment tasks emerged naturally from the learning activities.

Conclusion

As authentic assessment projects increase in number and are undertaken by larger and more diverse school districts, the administrative and technical issues discussed above will have to be addressed. Districtwide and statewide assessment programs will have to incorporate a significant research component to meet the challenges posed by technical standards of validity, reliability, and fairness. In addition, research will be needed on ways in which schools can make the most productive use of assessment information to improve instruction (Kean 1992).

Not the least of questions to be addressed is the role of current testing models. Can traditional tests complement the new assessments? Will open-ended, multistage assessments be reserved for summative evaluation, or can they be incorporated into the daily life of the classroom? What are the cost implications? Can the results of the new assessments provide information that will aid in placement of individual students and program articulation? In the months ahead, as teachers study the standards and begin to explore their implications for instruction and assessment, we will begin to see responses to some of these questions.

Note

1. The materials for this case study were provided by Cindy Kendall of Williamston High School, Williamston, Michigan.

References

Aschbacher, Pamela R. 1992. *Issues in Innovative Assessment for Classroom Practice: Barriers and Facilitators.* CSE Technical Report No. 359. Los Angeles: University of California, National Center for Research on Evaluation, Standards, and Student Testing.

Brown, Dianne C. 1993. "America 2000 and Policy Implications for the Country." *Measurement and Evaluation in Counseling and Development* 26:48–53.

"By All Measures: The Debate over Standards and Assessments." 1992. *Education Week,* 17 June.

Calfee, Robert C. 1994. "Cognitive Assessment of Classroom Learning." *Education and Urban Society* 26:340–51.

Callahan, Raymond. 1962. *Education and the Cult of Efficiency.* Chicago: University of Chicago Press.

Cole, Charlotte, and Floy Miller. 1985. "Developing a Proficiency-Based Curriculum at the Secondary Level." *Foreign Language Annals* 18:463–68.

Donato, Richard. 1995. Personal communication, October.

Donato, Richard, and Dawn McCormick. 1994. "A Sociocultural Perspective on Language Learning Strategies: The Role of Mediation." *Modern Language Journal* 78:453–64.

Evans, Christine Sobray. 1993. "When Teachers Look at Student Work." *Educational Leadership* 50:71–72.

Flood, James, and Diane Lapp. 1993. "Clearing the Confusion: A Closer Look at National Goals and Standards." *The Reading Teacher* 47:58–61.

Frederiksen, Norman. 1984. "The Real Test Bias: Influences of Testing on Teaching and Learning." *American Psychologist* 39,3:193–202.

Guthrie, James W., ed. 1990. "The California Mathematics Study." *Educational Evaluation and Policy Analysis* 12,3. (Special issue).

Haney, Walter, and George Madaus. 1989. "Searching for Alternatives to Standardized Tests: Why, Whats, and Whithers." *Phi Delta Kappan* 70,9:683–87.

Hart, Diane. 1994. *Authentic Assessment: A Handbook for Educators.* Menlo Park, CA: Addison-Wesley.

Heck, Ronald H. 1987. "Designing District Minimum-Standards Tests." *THRUST for Educational Leadership* 17,3:34–35.

Hiebert, F., and Calfee, Robert C. 1992. "Assessment of Literacy: From Standardized Tests to Performances and Portfolios," pp. 70–100 in Alan E. Farstrup and S. Jay Samuels, eds., *What Research Has to Say about Reading Instruction.* 2d ed. Newark, DE: International Reading Association.

Kean, Michael H. 1992. "Targeting Education and Missing the Schools: A Consideration of National Standards." *NASSP Bulletin* 76:17–22.

Kendall, Cindy. 1995. "Report on Implementing the National Standards in Foreign Language Education in Williamston, Michigan." Salt Lake City, UT: National Standards in Foreign Language Education.

LeMahieu, Paul G. 1992. "Defining, Developing a Well-Crafted Assessment Program." *NASSP Bulletin* 76:50–56.

Lockwood, Anne Turnbaugh. 1993. "National Standards: Who Benefits?" *Focus in Change*. No. 11. Madison, WI: National Center for Effective Schools.

Marcoulides, George A., and Ronald H. Heck. 1994. "The Changing Role of Educational Assessment in the 1990s." *Education and Urban Society* 26:332–39.

Massell, Diane, and Michael Kirst. 1994. "Determining National Content Standards: An Introduction." *Education and Urban Society* 26:107–17.

McGill-Franzen, Anne M. 1993. *Shaping the Preschool Agenda: Early Literacy, Public Policy and Professional Beliefs.* Albany: State University of New York Press.

Messick, Samuel. 1989. "Validity," pp. 13–104 in Robert L. Linn, ed., *Educational Measurement.* 3d ed. New York: Macmillan.

Moore, Zena T. 1994. "The Portfolio and Testing Culture," pp. 163–82 in Charles Hancock, ed., *Teaching, Testing, and Assessment: Making the Connection.* Northeast Conference Reports. Lincolnwood, IL: National Textbook.

O'Neil, John. 1993. "On the New Standards Project: A Conversation with Lauren Resnick and Warren Simmons." *Educational Leadership* 50:17–21.

———. 1995. "On Lasting School Reform: A Conversation with Ted Sizer." *Educational Leadership* 52:4–9.

Ornstein, Allan C. 1992. "The National Reform of Education: Overview and Outlook." *NASSP Bulletin* 76:89–101.

Pipho, Chris. 1985. "Tracking the Reforms, Part 5: Testing—Can It Measure the Success of the Reform Movement?" *Education Week,* 22 May.

Ravitch, Diane. 1993. "Launching a Revolution in Standards and Assessments." *Phi Delta Kappan* 74:767–72.

Resnick, Daniel P. 1987. "Expansion, Quality, and Testing in American Education," pp. 5–14 in Dorothy Bray and Marcia J. Belcher, eds., *Issues in Student Assessment.* New Directions for Community Colleges 59. San Francisco: Jossey-Bass.

Schwager, Mahna T., and Jerry S. Carlson. 1994. "Building Assessment Cultures: Teacher Perceptions and School Environments." *Education and Urban Society* 26:390–403.

Sperling, Doris. 1993. "What's Worth an 'A'? Setting Standards Together." *Educational Leadership* 50:73–75.

Stansfield, Charles W. 1990. "A Comparative Analysis of Simulated and Direct Oral Proficiency Interviews." Paper presented at the Annual Meeting of the Regional Language Centre Conference, Singapore, April.

Tschirner, Erwin. 1992. "Oral Proficiency Base Lines for First- and Second-Year College German." *Unterrichtspraxis* 25:10–14.

U.S. Department of Education. 1994. *High Standards for All: Putting Excellence in Education.* Washington, DC: U.S. Department of Education.

Valette, Rebecca. 1994. "Teaching, Testing, and Assessment: Conceptualizing the Relationship," in Charles Hancock, ed., *Teaching, Testing, and Assessment: Making the Connection.* Northeast Conference Reports. Lincolnwood, IL: National Textbook.

Villalobos, José. 1995. "El uso del 'diario interactivo' para promover el desarrollo de la escritura en español como lengua extranjera: Una experiencia de enseñanza/aprendizaje." Paper presented at the Segundo Congreso de las Américas de Lectoescritura, San José, Costa Rica, August.

Welsh, Patrick. 1992. "It Takes Two to Tango." *American Educator* 16:18–23.

Wiggins, Grant. 1989a. "A True Test: Toward More Authentic and Equitable Assessment." *Phi Delta Kappan* 70,9:703–13.

————. 1989b. "Teaching to the (Authentic) Test." *Educational Leadership* 46,7:41–47.

————. 1990. "The Case for Authentic Assessment." *ERIC Digest.* Washington, DC: ERIC Clearinghouse on Tests, Measurement, and Evaluation.

————. 1993. "Assessment: Authenticity, Context, and Validity." *Phi Delta Kappan* 75,3:200–214.

————. 1994. "Toward More Authentic Assessment of Language Performances," pp. 69–85 in Charles Hancock, ed., *Teaching, Testing, and Assessment: Making the Connection.* Northeast Conference Reports. Lincolnwood, IL: National Textbook.

Winfield, Linda F., and Michael D. Woodard. 1994. "Assessment, Equity, and Diversity in Reforming America's Schools." *Educational Policy* 8:3–27.

Wolf, Dennie Palmer. 1989. "Portfolio Assessment: Sampling Student Work." *Educational Leadership* 46,7:35–39.

Appendix: Alternative Assessment: Newscast by Spanish II Students

Williamston High School, Williamston, Michigan

Overview. In cooperative groups students will write, produce, and videotape a news show that will include news events (past, present, and upcoming), a "live on the scene" report, weather, sports, and commercials.

Instructions to Students

Description. Your team will create, produce, and edit a newscast. Your newscast will have the following components:

- Introduction with theme music

- Two anchors (stories to include one news event in each of the following categories: a news event from the Spanish-speaking world, a news event from the U.S., a news event from Michigan, and a news event from Williamston)

- A "live, on-the-scene" report on a topic of your choice. You may want to tie it into one of your news stories

- Four commercials (You must incorporate *tú, usted,* and *ustedes* commands.)

- Weather: yesterday's weather as well as your forecast

- Sports
- Upcoming events calendar
- Closing with credits and theme music

Any modifications of the above must be preapproved by the teacher.

Grammatical Structures. You should be sure to include the present, preterite, imperfect, formal, and informal commands.

Length. Your taped broadcast should be 15–20 minutes in length.

Technological Assistance. Miss Vant is available for taping and editing. Schedule appointments with her in advance! Plan on spending a considerable amount of time (4–5 hours) on these tasks. It will probably take you more than one session. Film and edit in 8 and high 8, and transfer to VHS at the end. The school has a camera. You need to schedule its use through Miss Vant and agree to the conditions she sets forth.

Other. The teacher will proofread your script, and you will rewrite and correct it in accordance with her suggestions. You will also practice your pronunciation with the teacher before filming.

You are not allowed to read from your script (except for anchors, who should just glance at their scripts, but not read them). Behind-the-scenes cue cards are acceptable; make sure that it is not obvious to the viewer that you are reading. Pronunciation and intonation practice is of utmost importance!

On the due date your team will turn in to the teacher a copy of each script, typed and double-spaced, along with a videotape in VHS format. Indicated on the script will be the participants in each segment, as well as a detailed description of what each person did to contribute to the production of the segment.

Grade. Your entire newscast is worth 210 points, which will be distributed as follows:

Grammar 50: accurate use of moods, tenses, vocabulary

Visuals 30: accurately reflect content, help in presentation of information

Pronunciation 30: accent, vowels, syllables, consonants, intonation, fluency

Use of technology 30: flow of newscast, smooth transitions, effort, flexibility in working with Miss Vant, Miss Vant's evaluation

Teamwork 30: each member contributes to the production, completing tasks in a timely fashion

Props and costumes 30: to help you convey your information and make your newscast realistic

Evaluation by self and peers 10: evaluation to be completed during final exam period

Implementation. Your team will turn in a weekly report (see below) that details what tasks each group member has completed. The teacher has the authority, upon consultation with the group, to dock points (amount to be determined by the teacher) from any group member who has not fulfilled his or her tasks for the week. Each group will designate a producer who will be responsible for making sure each group member knows what his or her responsibility is for the successful completion of the newscast. The producer will check on the progress of each segment and help keep the project moving forward. Your team will also complete a postproject evaluation of your own performance. If there is blatant noncollaboration by any group member, that member will be removed from the group and will receive zero points for the entire project. **WARNING: A zero on this project will more than likely result in a zero for the semester and no credit for this class.**

Before beginning this project, your team will determine who will be responsible for what facets of the newscast. Divide your team so that members are responsible for only one or two facets of your broadcast. Each member must participate orally in at least one segment. Each member must also participate in the writing of the script for at least one segment. Your team will develop a timeline that indicates deadlines, with your producer working as facilitator. Your timeline will be posted on the wall of the classroom. As tasks are completed, the person responsible and date it was completed will be noted on the timeline. Any adjustments to the timeline will be indicated. This will allow you to keep your deadlines and responsibilities in mind and also allow you to see the contributions of the team, since there is a lot of behind-the-scenes work to be done in a project as big as this one.

Timeline.

May 8–17: Preparation

You will have in-class time on May 8, 19, 12, 15, and 16 to write, rewrite, proofread, practice, plan, and film (if possible).

May 18–24: Filming

Filming will be done on your own time and in class if you are able to arrange for use of the equipment. If you are not filming, you will use the time to write, plan, and practice for the newscast.

May 25–June 9: Editing

Schedule appointments with Miss Vant. You may schedule up to three hours of editing time during first period.

Weekly Report

Producer: _____ Date: _____

These tasks have been assigned to the following group members:

Adjustments to timeline (also indicated on wall):

The following people did a great job this week on the task indicated!

The following tasks were not completed:

Comments:

9

Reactions to the Catalyst: Implications for Our New Professional Structure

June K. Phillips
Weber State University
Robert C. Lafayette
Louisiana State University

"National Standards Are Ready" proclaimed a front-page headline in the January 1996 *Cardinal,* the newsletter of the Ohio Foreign Language Association. The headline of course referred to the release of the national standards for foreign language education, *Standards for Foreign Language Learning: Preparation for the 21st Century,* during the annual meeting of the American Council on the Teaching of Foreign Languages (ACTFL) on November 18, 1995, in Anaheim, California. The event marked the culmination of a joint three-year effort by ACTFL, the American Association of Teachers of French (AATF), the American Association of Teachers of German (AATG), and the American Association of Teachers of Spanish and Portuguese (AATSP).

This volume, partially titled "Catalyst for Reform," has dedicated eight articles to the discussion of national standards and their impact on a variety of fields closely related to foreign language learning and teaching. Jennings set the stage by discussing the standards movement in general, Zimmer-Loew investigated the efforts of the profession to develop professional policy in language teaching, Heining-Boynton addressed the potential impact of the standards on preservice teacher development programs, and Glisan provided guidelines for the successful continuing education of teachers. Campbell described the new and different populations that we as a profession must

June K. Phillips (Ph.D., the Ohio State University) is dean of Arts and Humanities at Weber State University in Utah. She served as director of the national standards project for K–12 foreign languages under the auspices of ACTFL, AATF, AATG, and AATSP.

Robert C. Lafayette (Ph.D., the Ohio State University) is professor of curriculum and instruction and professor of French at Louisiana State University, where he currently serves as chair of the Department of Curriculum and Instruction and as director of the French Eduction Projects.

address. Nielsen and Hoffman claimed that we will have to implement distance learning instruction to reach many rural areas. Bartz and Keefe Singer called for the involvement of classroom practitioners throughout the curriculum development process and suggested the addition of an assessment component to the standards. Finally, Liskin-Gasparro proposed different models of authentic assessment and demonstrated how the new national foreign language standards can indeed be assessed. In this final article we propose to discuss the impact that the standards have had even prior to their official release; to evaluate the foreign language standards using the "Criteria for High Quality Standards" developed by Shanker (1994) and a committee from the American Federation of Teachers; and to examine the various implications of the standards to the profession in general.

The power that the foreign language standards exert for educational change depends upon the effect generated within the profession and the integration of the discipline into core studies in schools. The very act of drafting standards for language learning entailed greater interactions across disciplines than has been the norm when paradigms shifted within the field. The constant sharing of issues and information enabled the foreign language standards to reflect, and also to be judged by, criteria of a generic nature.

A cursory examination of the programs of national, regional, and state conferences makes it abundantly clear that national and state standards and their subsequent implications are paramount in the minds of foreign language leaders organizing these conferences. The 1995 ACTFL annual meeting, during which the national standards were presented to the profession and the public, bore the name "Standards and Assessment: Implementing the Vision." It featured more than thirty sessions on standards. Standards were also very prominent at all the 1996 regional conferences. The Northeast Conference, for example, devoted three major workshops to the topic. In Louisiana, three fall 1995 regional conferences that attracted more than 800 teachers were entirely consecrated to SAM, a statewide project linking state and federal funds whose goal is to develop standards, assessment instruments, and materials aimed at an articulated 4–12 program. Finally, in Ohio, the 1996 spring conference had as its theme "National Standards—Local Realities."

Textbooks and the National Standards
for Foreign Language Learning

In their article in this volume titled "Programmatic Implications of Foreign Language Standards," Bartz and Keefe Singer conclude with a series of recommendations to be considered in the process of transplanting national standards to the local level. Among them is the following:

> Textbooks must be rewritten and updated. It is an established fact that textbooks often define local curriculum. Therefore, publishers have a responsibility to produce basal materials that lead students to attain the national standards.

Publishers are well aware of this responsibility. They are also aware that keeping up with such an important development in the profession will make their products much more attractive to teachers and to states that have state-wide textbook adoption, which often requires publishers to align their materials with the state framework or guidelines.

The latest additions to the textbook market do indeed demonstrate that publishers have kept up with the work of the foreign language national standards task force since it began its work in 1993. For example, the teacher's editions of the new Holt, Rinehart and Winston series in French, German, and Spanish include an article by Labouve (1996) titled "Standards for Foreign Language Education," which features a draft version of the standards highlighting the five major goals of communication, cultures, connections, comparisons, and communities. The new Scott, Foresman Spanish textbook, *Paso a paso* (Met et al. 1997), had the recently released national standards printed on the inside cover of teacher's editions sent to a local school district for examination in early 1996.

During the past few years, demographic pressures have convinced publishers to pay greater attention to heritage language users in schools. The national standards document, as well as the Campbell article in this volume, have emphasized this inclusion in strong terms and extended recognition to languages other than Spanish. For example, the new *¡Ven conmigo!* (1996) includes a Native Speaker Activity Book as well as an article by Rodríguez-Pino (1996). She suggests that a task-based, whole language approach be used in Spanish for Native Speakers (SNS) programs. She recommends that receptive and productive skills be developed through culturally meaningful activities whose contexts are community, school, home, and self. Included among the suggestions for improving production skills are oral history projects, ethnographic interviews, sociolinguistic surveys, dialog journals, letter writing, and other activities that focus on interactions among students, teacher, and community. The ancillary program of this same textbook offers a Native Speaker Activity Book with a diagnostic instrument and, chapter by chapter, additional reading practice based on authentic literature that addresses topics of interest to native speakers.

Paso a paso (Met et al. 1997) also deals with the SNS phenomenon but does so in a more generic context. Its teacher's edition includes as a component "Strategies for Reaching All Students." A regular feature of this component is suggestions on working with Spanish-speaking students, students needing extra help, and gifted students. The most frequent suggestions deal with teaching Spanish to Spanish-speaking students.

¡Dime! (Samaniego et al. 1994) a slightly older publication, also has in its extended teacher's edition a rather thorough discussion of "working with native speakers of Spanish" (T24–25). It takes each of the lesson components and explains how to use them with native speakers of Spanish.

Paso a paso (Met et al. 1997), the latest of the new publications and the one with the greatest opportunity to reflect the national standards, has a section in each chapter that reflects Goal 3 and is called *"Conexiones."* There, students are offered an opportunity to apply the chapter content to other subject-matter areas. In addition, in the individual chapter-planning segment of the teacher's edition, there is a segment called "cross-curricular connections." Connections are made to social studies, mathematics, geography, language arts, physical education, science, and art.

Liskin-Gasparro in this volume mentions that there are currently no full-scale authentic assessment programs in place, but assessment activities are found in many foreign language classrooms. Among the latest foreign language textbooks on the high school market, most pay considerable attention not only to testing, but to assessment as well. There is an attempt especially to promote the use of portfolios as an important tool in communicative, whole-language approaches to foreign language learning. The teacher's edition of the three Holt, Rinehart and Winston textbooks, for example, include an article by Wilson (1996) on using portfolios in the foreign language classroom and one by Heining-Boynton (1996) on higher-order thinking skills.

Finally, the last of the five major goals (communities) that encompass the eleven national standards is especially reflected in the latest wave of textbooks. French textbooks have chapters set in Francophone Louisiana and units in Spanish textbooks take place in El Paso, Miami, Los Angeles, and San Antonio as well as in many of the Central American countries. *Paso a paso* (Met et al. 1996) also includes in the planning segment of each chapter of the teacher's edition a paragraph titled "Spanish in Your Community" in which are included numerous suggestions for making use of and learning about the local Spanish-speaking community.

Teacher Development and the National Standards for Foreign Language Learning

Phillips (1994) maintains that instructional change such as the implementation of national and state standards requires a totally new dimension of professional development as well as a revamping of teacher-education programs. The day of "methods" and prescriptions and "cookbooks" of neat ideas has passed. When dealing with the spectrum of human communication, it no longer suffices to exert tight instructional control that carefully dispenses prescribed structures and vocabulary and formulaic messages. Learners must also be prepared to confront unique utterances and text. They must become adept at processes and not just products (p. 4). Zéphir (1995) provides similar advice. She claims that "it is incumbent on foreign language education programs to provide teachers with decision-making, reflective, and evaluative skills necessary to respond to the needs of the learners of the ever-changing classrooms of the twenty-first century" (p. 54). The bottom line is empowerment.

According to Moeller (1995:10), teacher development and content standards are inexorably linked: "In order for students to achieve the content standards found in the national standards, their teachers must have the language and pedagogy skills to facilitate the learning process." The content standards serve as a frame, a map, to the range of alternative pedagogical strategies used by the teacher to optimize foreign language learning. In an interview by O'Neil (1993), Darling-Hammond maintains that tougher achievement standards will not lead to better schools unless delivery standards and standards for practice receive equal attention.

Smith (1995) looks forward to the methodologies of the future and suggests that "some of the new pressures to be placed upon second language instructors will entail developing methodologies to

- Maximize class time use
- Provide more authentic input (cultural as well as linguistic) in the classroom
- Provide opportunities to develop intracultural and intercultural awareness
- Foster more output
- Assess objectively performance levels according to widely recognized standards
- Equip the learners with marketable skills

Although the standards do not advocate any specific instructional approach, the definition of communication in Goal 1 and its subsequent division into three related standards (interpersonal, interpretive, and presentational) suggest that teacher-development programs will need to offer at least a basic understanding of the principles of whole language. Met (1994) claims that foreign language learning today bears little resemblance to that of twenty years ago. She says that it has undergone a paradigmatic shift, and that today

> effective foreign language instruction is holistic, performance-oriented, and based on constructivist views of learning. It requires collaborative learning and practice, connects to other areas of the curriculum, and is enhanced through explicit instruction in metacognitive and cognitive learning strategies. (p. 87)

Fox (1995) also maintains that since Goal 1 (communication) of the standards is central to all subsequent goals, it is imperative that teachers clearly understand how an individual develops communicative competence. He suggests that the best approach to developing communication among learners is not only whole language instruction, but whole language instruction that uses storytelling as its primary tool.

AFT's Criteria for High Quality Standards and the National Standards for Foreign Language Learning

The *Standards for Foreign Language Learning* (1996) will reverberate throughout the profession: at national, regional, and state conferences; in state departments of education; in local school districts; in schools and colleges of education; in meetings of boards of directors of policy-making organizations; in television studios and on the World Wide Web; and most important, in actual classrooms. The standards will be studied, discussed, judged, criticized, and defended in all these venues, and rightly so because they belong to the profession as a whole. Nevertheless, since all of the above activity will take place within the profession, it might be important to see how well the standards measure up to outside criteria established for all content-area standards.

Albert Shanker, president of the American Federation of Teachers, has written numerous thoughtful articles about *Goals 2000* and the standards that characterize so much of the force of the legislation. Shanker recognizes that success or failure of national disciplinary standards, such as we now have in foreign languages, will rise or fall on state and local efforts. In fact, he states that "Goals 2000 is not really a single reform plan, but a strategy for catalyzing more than 50 separate reform movements. It has the potential to succeed or fail in 50 places, depending on the quality of states' plans and their ability to carry them out" (1994:15).

In the same article, Shanker posits ten criteria for high quality standards. While intended for states, there is value in judging the newly issued national standards for foreign languages against these criteria. Granted, the national standards have refrained intentionally from venturing into curriculum; at the same time, their viability as a useful gauge and as a provocative prompt for states resides in a catalytic power that should be responsive to Shanker's points. Consequently, at this early time in the life of national standards for foreign language learning, one might examine the standards against Shanker's criteria (enumerated below) and repeat the process as states assume their role.

1. *Standards must focus on academics.* The foreign language standards have attempted to move from a narrower definition of skills to include broader curricular content. Specificity of content has been left to curriculum development, but the designation of goal areas and standards has firm academic roots. Shanker's concern with this criterion was a reaction to outcomes-based education, in which process tended to exclude product. The national standards identify the content areas as part of the "weave of curricular elements" (*Standards* 1996:29). The academic underpinnings include among content not only the language system, but also cultural knowledge, subject matter from related disciplines (e.g., art, history, science), and strategies that specifically pertain to the learning of second languages. The standards task force intended that the academic base of the standards be robust; it remains to be seen how states translate that to curriculum. If they opt for less specific content than exists in the national progress indicators, they may err toward nonacademic outcomes. On the other hand, if they take the next step toward designated content, they will move the academic nature of the standards forward.

2. *Standards must be grounded in the core disciplines.* Shanker's concern here is that the movement toward "interdisciplinary expectations" might cause students to abandon the "knowledge and skills that arise from the disciplines" (p. 22). Foreign language education is, perhaps, in the unique position of being able to connect more deliberately with other disciplines without losing its core. The connections standards strengthen our attachment to the rest of the curriculum and prevent our being isolated in the schools or allowed to remain at the fringe. In the past, many foreign language

teachers opted for interdisciplinary units that supplemented lessons; the new standards call for assessing these interdisciplinary ventures, thereby rendering them more central to the mission.

3. *Standards must be specific enough to ensure the development of a common core curriculum.* The draft of the national foreign language standards probably does not reach the level of specificity that Shanker would propose, but we need to see the efforts of the first states that have built upon them to ascertain the fit with state frameworks. However, the national document does meet his criteria of a common core that would not "limit students who chose to go beyond it to advanced-level high school courses" (p. 22). In fact, the standards were written to address what *all* students should know and be able to do as they exit high school, but the advocacy of a longer sequence should permit students to attain the standards before the twelfth grade; those with special interests or talents in second languages should be able to pursue further studies.

   The "common curriculum" can become more of a reality as states coalesce around the five goal areas of the standards and ensure that all students develop skills and abilities in communication, cultures, connections, comparisons, and communities. Were that to happen, we would articulate curriculum more effectively across state boundaries and be able to assess performances in these areas more informatively.

4. *Standards must be manageable given the constraints of time.* Certainly as foreign language study seeks to extend into elementary and middle school, the question of time in the curriculum comes to the fore. The strong acknowledgment in the foreign language standards of the whole school should encourage a more integrated curriculum for students, one in which the study of another language reinforces common learning. Second, the approach taken to the design of standards for communication and culture reflects the approaches in the language arts and social sciences to a greater degree than before. Therefore, foreign language study becomes less different and more adaptable to school restructuring.

5. *Standards must be rigorous and world-class.* A great deal of effort has been expended in other subject areas to compare units of study as well as results of national tests, to ensure that disciplinary standards make U.S. students internationally competitive. Unfortunately, so little time has been given in the United States to the study of the world's languages that comparison is nigh to

impossible. The fact that American students gain any kind of competency with only the typical two-year high school program is remarkable. Virtually every other nation, whether a competitor nation or a developing country, begins instruction in a second language by the age of ten or eleven. Having developed standards for K–12 in the United States is in itself a giant step toward rigor and world-class standards.

6. *Standards must include "performance standards."* The charge to the national task force and to other disciplines funded through *Goals 2000* was to develop content standards, i.e., *what students should know and be able to do.* Development of performance standards, i.e., *how good is good enough?* was to be the task of states and local districts. Shanker, of course, is correct in his view that the "how well" is the key to the rigor and the challenge. Within the design of content standards, the task force constantly kept in mind that their product must be capable of assessment at the state, and perhaps someday at the national, level. To see how the standards measure up, one would have to modify the criterion above to the ability of the content standards to engender performance standards. Checking assessability in the sample progress indicators in *Standards for Foreign Language Learning: Preparing for the 21st Century* provides insights into the standards themselves. A key question for states will be not only how good is good enough for their purposes but how wide a range of sampling constitutes performance of the larger sample.

The profession will need to explore whole new types of assessments (see Liskin-Gasparro in this volume) to capture the performances proposed in the new standards. Again, foreign languages will not stand alone, for all disciplines are having to embrace new kinds of assessment strategies. Discussion has already determined that the current standards lend themselves to assessments that determine achievement and proficiency while serving as valuable feedback to learner and to teacher. The final standard, 5.2 ("students show evidence of becoming life-long learners by using the language for personal enjoyment and enrichment"), has rightly been criticized (Mitchell 1996) because "enjoyment is not to be mandated." In its defense, what that standard does is emphasize that achievement at a level where independent learning can take over is a goal, a standard worth pursuing.

7. *Standards must include multiple performance levels.* Again, particularities will evolve at the level of states, but preliminary information from places beginning to look at performance indicates that this is exactly what is occurring. Nebraska, for example, has adopted the first ten of the eleven national standards and set progress indicators at three levels: beginning, developing, and expanding (1996 draft version).

8. *Standards must combine knowledge and skills, not pursue one at the expense of the other.* With this criterion, Shanker seeks to ensure balance between process and product. He points out the absurdity of trends that promote, for example, teaching critical thinking in the abstract. The five goal areas for foreign language education are supported by curricular elements that underlie all the standards. That curricular weave includes communication strategies, critical thinking skills, and learning strategies but also language system, cultural knowledge, and subject matter from other disciplines. The very purpose of this part of the standards document (*Standards* 1996:28–32) was to emphasize adherence to the balance delineated in the criterion above.

9. *Standards should not dictate how the material should be taught.* In a profession where paradigms for language learning have a history of accompanying prescribed methods, a standards-focused curriculum should be liberating. From the outset the task force has explained that "Current research and classroom practice indicate that a variety of approaches can successfully lead learners to the standards. The evolving research base in second-language acquisition is identifying effective practices, but all the answers are not yet in" (*Standards* 1996:20). The national document and state publications in draft are rich in examples in which the intent to illustrate rather than dictate dominates. While great flexibility in institutional approach is promoted, the case for uniformity will be made for performances that meet the standard.

10. *Standards must be written clearly enough for all stakeholders to understand.* Certainly for a field used to talking to itself, advancement toward meeting this criterion was a challenge for the task force. The advisory board to the standards project served as a valuable sounding board for ridding the document of unnecessarily obtuse jargon while allowing for some key phrases to enter the public dialog, e.g., heritage languages. States, too, are doing clean-up work in this area and each iteration helps make a more cogent case for foreign language study to the public.

This initial assessment of the national foreign language standards against criteria posited by a knowledgeable educator-at-large represents only a first experiment. It will have to be replicated by others at the state level and certainly by those further removed from the drafting of the standards. Laboratory scientists do not stop after experimentation with a process identifies a catalyst or observes its reaction. They persevere to develop more powerful reactions, to create additional uses for products, to keep pushing the frontiers.

Conclusion

Anderson (1995) conducted nine case studies in middle schools and high schools across the country in order to better understand the dilemmas facing practitioners who seek to implement standards. He found that the reforms are complex and of major proportions, and that putting them into practice is a difficult and demanding task. The major dilemmas uncovered were (1) the fact that for many, coverage of content was more important than depth of understanding, (2) not all parents and students wanted these changes, especially those who had a high socioeconomic level and greater college aspirations, and (3) that there is never enough time. Among the successful cases, there was much importance accorded the national and state frameworks and standards, local teachers assumed leadership roles, and collaboration was paramount among the individuals working on the project.

By far the most important element in the three-year process of arriving at national foreign language standards was the collaboration among all elements and individuals involved: first and foremost, members of the task force; professional organizations; various advisory groups; teachers at the pilot sites; state and local leaders; and the more than 1500 teachers who reacted to various drafts of the standards. It was a whole-profession effort, and collaboration is what made it possible.

In her article on professional development in this volume, Glisan discusses the existing "collaboratives" within the profession and includes a table that illustrates a collaborative approach to professional development. In the words of Anderson (1995),

> When given an opportunity to develop materials together, to plan together, to share teaching ideas with one another, and to help one another make new connections with content, teachers did reform their teaching. (p.35)

Glisan correctly points out that perhaps one of the most important outcomes of the standards effort will be the creation of a collaborative, supportive, and collegial process of sharing and experimenting in the context of mutual respect and reflection.

Anderson (1995) suggests that reformers (1) think systemically, (2) focus on matters of student learning, (3) make teacher collaboration the foundation of their work, and (4) provide the support that teachers need. Efforts to improve education should focus on changing the role of students, on the nature of the work they do, and on the means by which their learning is assessed.

Standards setting is a first venture for this profession. It will cause reactions in many venues, at many levels of instruction; it will foment change, trigger reactions to change, and in the best of all worlds, promote new knowledge in the teaching and learning of foreign languages.

References

Anderson, Ronald D. 1995. "Curriculum Reform: Dilemmas and Promise." *Phi Delta Kappan* 77,1:33–36.

Fox, Jerald L. 1995. "Generative Language Research and Whole Language: Theory to Practice." *Frameworks Issues Papers*. Nebraska Foreign Language Standards/ Frameworks Project. Lincoln: Nebraska Department of Education.

Heining-Boynton, Audrey L. 1996. "Higher-Order Thinking Skills," pp. T50–51 in *¡Ven conmigo!* (annotated teacher's edition). Austin, TX: Holt, Rinehart and Winston.

LaBouve, Robert. 1996. "Standards for Foreign Language Education," pp. T44-45 in *¡Ven conmigo!* (annotated teacher's edition). Austin, TX: Holt, Rinehart and Winston.

Met, Myriam. 1994. "Are America's Schools Ready for World-Class Standards?" *Educational Leadership,* May, pp. 86–87.

Met, Myriam, Richard S. Sayers, Carol Eubanks Wargin, and Harriet Schottland Barnett. 1997. *Paso a Paso: A.* Glenview, IL: Scott Foresman.

Mitchell, Ruth. 1996. "Bravo, Bravissimo! The Standards for Foreign Language Learning." *Basic Education* 40,5:2–4.

Moeller, Aleidine J. 1995. "Teacher Development: An Effective Life-Long Model." *Frameworks Issues Papers*. Nebraska Foreign Language Standards/Frameworks Project. Lincoln: Nebraska Department of Education.

O'Neil, John. 1993. "Can National Standards Make a Difference?" *Educational Leadership* 50,5:3–8.

Phillips, June K. 1994. "The Challenge of Setting National Standards for the Study of Foreign Languages," pp. 1–5 in Robert M. Terry, ed., *Dimension: Language '94, Changing Images in Foreign Languages*. Valdosta, GA: Southern Conference on the Teaching of Foreign Languages.

Rodríguez-Pino, Cecilia. 1996. "New Perspectives for Native Speakers," pp. T54–55 in *¡Ven conmigo!* (annotated teacher's edition). Austin, TX: Holt, Rinehart and Winston.

Samaniego, Fabián A., M. Carol Brown, Patricia Hamilton Carlin, Sidney E. Gorman, and Carol L. Sparks. 1994. *¡Dime! Dos.* Extended Teacher's Edition. Lexington, MA: D.C. Heath.

Shanker, Albert. 1994. "Making Standards Good." *American Educator,* Fall, pp. 15, 20–27.

Smith, Nicole. 1995. "Methodologies for Tomorrow." *Frameworks Issues Papers.* Nebraska Foreign Language Standards/Frameworks Project. Lincoln: Nebraska Department of Education.

Standards for Foreign Language Learning: Preparing for the 21st Century. 1996. Yonkers, NY: Standards for Foreign Language Learning Project.

¡Ven conmigo! 1996. Austin, TX: Holt, Rinehart and Winston.

Wilson, Jo Anne S. 1996. "Using Portfolios in the Foreign Language Classroom," pp. T52–53 in *¡Ven conmigo!* (annotated teacher's edition). Austin, TX: Holt, Rinehart and Winston.

Zéphir, Flore. 1995. "Meeting the Demands and Challenges of the Foreign Language Methodology Course," pp. 47–63 in Robert M. Terry, ed., *Dimension '95: The Future Is Now.* Valdosta, GA: Southern Conference on the Teaching of Foreign Languages.

Appendix

Standards for Foreign Language Learning: Preparing for the Twenty-First Century

Following are goals, standards, and an abbreviated sample of the progress indicators for grades four, eight, and twelve as they appear in "Standards for Foreign Language Learning: Preparing for the 21st Century."

Communication

1.1 Students engage in conversations, provide and obtain information, express feelings and emotions, and exchange opinions.

This standard focuses on interpersonal communication, that is, direct oral or written communication between individuals who are in personal contact. In most modern languages, students can quite quickly learn a number of phrases that will permit them to interact with each other. In the course of their study, they will grow in their ability to converse in a culturally appropriate manner.

Sample Progress Indicators

Grade 4: Students ask and answer questions about such things as family, school events, and celebrations in person or via letters, e-mail, or audiotapes and videotapes.

Grade 8: Students exchange information about personal events, memorable experiences, and other school subjects with peers and/or members of the target cultures.

Grade 12: Students exchange, support, and discuss their opinions and individual perspectives with peers and/or speakers of the target language on a variety of topics dealing with contemporary and historical issues.

1.2 Students understand and interpret written and spoken language on a variety of topics.

This standard involves one-way listening and reading in which the learner works with a variety of print and nonprint materials. The context in which students experience the language and their ability to control what they hear and read may affect their development of comprehension. As a result, the ability to read may develop before the ability to comprehend rapid spoken language. In addition, content knowledge will often affect successful comprehension, for students understand more easily materials that reflect their interests or in which they have some background.

Sample Progress Indicators

Grade 4: Students comprehend the main idea of developmentally appropriate oral narratives such as personal anecdotes, familiar fairy tales, and other narratives based on familiar themes.

Grade 8: Students use knowledge acquired in other settings and from other subject areas to comprehend spoken and written messages in the target languages.

Grade 12: Students demonstrate an increasing understanding of the cultural nuances of meaning in written and spoken language as expressed by speakers and writers of the target language in formal and informal settings.

1.3 Students present information, concepts, and ideas to an audience of listeners or readers on a variety of topics.

This standard focuses on the formal presentation of information, concepts, and ideas in spoken and written form and is concerned, in most cases, with one-way speaking and writing. Students with little or no previous language experience are likely to produce written and spoken language that will contain a variety of learned patterns or will look like English with words in the other language. This is a natural process and, over time, they begin to acquire authentic patterns and to use appropriate styles. By contrast, home-background students will write in ways that closely resemble the spoken language. Moreover, they will control informal oral styles. Over time these learners will develop the ability to write and speak with more formal styles.

Sample Progress Indicators

Grade 4: Students prepare illustrated stories about activities or events in their environment and share with an audience such as the class.

Grade 8: Students prepare tape or video recorded messages to share locally or with school peers and/or members of the target cultures on topics of personal interest.

Grade 12: Students prepare a research-based analysis of a current event from the perspective of both the U.S. and target cultures.

Cultures

2.1 Students demonstrate an understanding of the relationship between the practices and perspectives of the culture studied.

This standard focuses on the *practices* that are derived from the traditional ideas and attitudes *(perspectives)* of a culture. Cultural practices refer to patterns of behavior accepted by a society and deal with aspects of culture such as rites of passage, the use of forms of discourse, the social "pecking order," and the use of space. In short, they represent the knowledge of "what to do when and where."

Sample Progress Indicators

Grade 4: Students use appropriate gestures and oral expressions for greetings, leave-takings, and common classroom interactions.

Grade 8: Students use appropriate verbal and nonverbal behavior for daily activities among peers and adults.

Grade 12: Students identify, analyze, and discuss various patterns of behavior or interaction typical of the culture studied.

2.2 Students demonstrate an understanding of the relationship between the products and perspectives of the culture studied.

This standard focuses on the *products* of the culture studied and on how they reflect the perspectives of the culture. Products may be tangible (e.g, a painting, a piece of literature, a pair of chopsticks) or intangible (e.g, an oral tale, a dance, a sacred ritual, a system of education). Whatever the form of the product, its presence within the culture is required or justified by the underlying beliefs and values (perspectives) of that culture, and the cultural practices involve the use of that product.

Sample Progress Indicators

Grade 4: Students identify and observe tangible products of the culture, such as toys, dress, types of dwellings, and foods.

Grade 8: Students experience (read, listen to, observe, perform, respond creatively to) expressive products of the culture (e.g., stories, poetry, music, paintings, dance, and drama) and then explore the effects of these products on the larger community.

Grade 12: Students identify, discuss, and analyze such intangible products of the target culture as social, economic, and political institutions and explore relationships among these institutions and the perspectives of the culture.

Connections

3.1 Students reinforce and further their knowledge of other disciplines through the foreign language.

Learning today is no longer restricted to a specific discipline; it has become interdisciplinary. Just as reading can have applications beyond a particular segment of the school day, so too can foreign language build upon the knowledge that students acquire in other subject areas. In addition, students can relate the information studied in other subjects to their learning of the foreign language and culture. Foreign language instruction thus becomes a means to expand and deepen students' understanding of, and exposure to, other areas of knowledge. The new information and concepts presented in one class become the basis of continued learning in the foreign language classroom.

Sample Progress Indicators

Grade 4: Students demonstrate an understanding about concepts learned in other subject areas in the target language, including weather, math facts, measurements, animals, insects, and geographical concepts.

Grade 8: Students discuss topics from other school subjects in the target language, including geographical terms and concepts, historical facts and concepts, mathematical terms and problems, and scientific information.

Grade 12: Students discuss topics from other school subjects in the target language, including political and historical concepts, worldwide health issues, and environmental concerns.

3.2 Students acquire information and recognize the distinctive viewpoints that are available only through the foreign language and its cultures.

As a consequence of learning another language and gaining access to its unique means of communication, students are able to broaden the sources of information available to them. They have a "new window on the world." At the early levels of language learning, students can begin to examine a variety of sources intended for native speakers and extract specific information. As they become more proficient users of the foreign language, they can seek out materials of interest to them, analyze the content, compare it to information available in their own language, and assess the linguistic and cultural differences.

Sample Progress Indicators

Grade 4: Students read, listen to, and talk about age-appropriate school content, folk tales, short stories, poems, and songs written for native speakers of the target language.

Grade 8: Students use sources intended for same-age speakers of the target language to prepare reports on topics of personal interest, or those with which they have limited previous experience.

Grade 12: Students use a variety of sources intended for same-age speakers of the target language to prepare reports on topics of personal interest, or those with which they have limited previous experience, and compare these to information obtained on the same topics written in English.

Comparisons

4.1 Students demonstrate understanding of the nature of language through comparisons of the language studied and their own.

This standard focuses on the impact that learning the linguistic elements in the new language has on students' ability to examine English and to develop hypotheses about the structure and use of languages. From the earliest language-learning experiences, students can compare and contrast the two languages as different elements are presented. Activities can be systematically integrated into instruction that will assist students in gaining understanding and in developing their abilities to think critically about how languages work.

Sample Progress Indicators

Grade 4: Students can cite and use examples of words that are borrowed in the language they are learning and their own, and they pose guesses about why languages in general might need to borrow words.

Grade 8: Students hypothesize about the relationship among languages based on their awareness of cognates and similarity of idioms.

Grade 12: Students recognize that cognates have the same as well as different meanings among languages and speculate about the evolution of language.

4.2 Students recognize that cultures use different patterns of interaction and can apply this knowledge to their own culture.

As students expand their knowledge of cultures through language learning, they continually discover perspectives, practices, and products that are similar and different from their own culture, and they develop the ability to hypothesize about cultural systems in general. Some students may make these comparisons naturally, others may not. This standard helps focus this reflective process for all.

Sample Progress Indicators

Grade 4: Students compare and contrast tangible products (e.g., toys, sports, equipment, food) of the target cultures and their own.

Grade 8: Students speculate on why certain products originate in and/or are important to particular cultures by analyzing selected products from the target cultures and their own.

Grade 12: Students analyze the relationship between the products and perspectives in the target language and compare and contrast these with their own.

Communities

5.1 Students use the language both within and beyond the school setting.

This standard focuses on language as a tool for communication with speakers of the language throughout one's life: in schools, in the community, and abroad. In schools, students share their knowledge of language and culture with classmates and with younger students who may be learning the language. Applying what has been learned in the language program as defined by the other standards, students come to realize the advantages inherent in being able to communicate in more than one language and develop an understanding of the power of language.

Sample Progress Indicators

Grade 4: Students communicate on a personal level with speakers of the language via letters, e-mail, audio, and video tapes.

Grade 8: Students perform for a school or community celebration.

Grade 12: Students participate in a career exploration or school-to-work project which requires proficiency in the language and culture.

5.2 Students show evidence of becoming lifelong learners by using the language for personal enjoyment and enrichment.

Each day millions of Americans spend leisure time reading, listening to music, viewing films and television programs, and interacting with each other. By developing a certain level of comfort with their new language, students can use these skills to access information as they continue to learn throughout their lives. Students who study a language can use their skills to further enrich their personal lives by accessing various entertainment and information sources available to speakers of the language. Some students may have the opportunity to travel to communities and countries where the language is used extensively and, through this experience, further develop their language skills and understanding of the culture.

Sample Progress Indicators

Grade 4: Students play sports or games from the culture.

Grade 8: Students listen to music, sing songs, or play musical instruments from the target culture.

Grade 12: Students consult various sources in the language to obtain information on topics of personal interest.

Sample Learning Scenario: Newscast

Targeted Standards

1.1 Interpersonal Communication

1.3 Presentational Communication

2.1 Practices of Culture

3.1 Furthering Connections

5.1 School and Community

5.2 Lifelong Learning

Description

In the Spanish II class in Williamston High School, a small, rural community in Michigan, students worked in groups to write, produce, and videotape a fifteen-to-twenty minute Spanish language news show that included news events; a live, from-the-scene report; weather; sports; and commercials. The news events included items from the Spanish-speaking world, the United States, the state, and local areas.

Reflection

1.1 Students work cooperatively in groups using the language to produce the newscast.

1.3 Students produce the newscast in the language studied.

2.1 Students present news stories that reflect a perspective from the culture studied.

3.1 Students develop news items on a variety of topics.

5.1 Students use the language in the classroom.

5.2 Students develop insights necessary for media literacy.

If the students were asked to view taped newscasts and commercials from two Spanish-speaking countries and use them as models for their project, an emphasis could be placed on Standards 1.2 and 4.1 (in preparing for the project, students view newscasts and compare and contrast language styles) and Standard 4.2 (students note cultural similarities and differences in the videotapes they viewed). This type of preparation for the project would also provide the opportunity to target Standard 2.2 with students analyzing a product of the culture studied. This scenario could be applied to any language at a variety of levels.

Sample Learning Scenario: Chinese Calendar

Targeted Standards

1.2 Interpretive Communication

2.2 Products of Culture

4.2 Culture Comparisons

Description

In Ms. Chen-Lin's Chinese class in urban Springfield, MA, eighth graders are learning about the Chinese calendar. Students listen to the folkloric tale of how the years got their names, which the teacher explains using story cards. The students then use artistic expression to recall the details of the story by making posters that announce the race of the twelve animals in the story. They are encouraged to include on their poster the date, time, location, and prize in Chinese. On the next day, the class explores the importance of a calendar in the students' own culture and in others. The students discuss the differences found in the Chinese and American calendars. They then make a calendar using Chinese characters to be used in their homes. They include birthdays, family celebrations, school activities, and other special events.

Reflection

1.2 Students comprehend the story of the Chinese calendar told in the target language.

2.2 Students read about and discuss products of the culture.

4.2 Students compare and contrast products found in the two cultures.

In this activity, the students understand the calendar explanation more easily because the teacher accompanies the story with visuals. The use of artistic expression to check for their understanding allows students with various learning styles to be successful in showing what they understood from the story. The follow-up discussion helps students reflect on the importance of a calendar within a culture and the role that the calendar plays in American culture.

Index to Authors Cited

Index to Topics Cited

German, 52, 104, 126, 128–29, 178, 199
Gerstner, Louis, Jr., 11
Getty Center, 136
Goals 2000: Educate America Act (P.L.
    103–227), 15, 16, 17, 28, 32, 137,
    140–43, 169, 188, 202–3, 205
Golden State Exams, 173
Grade inflation, 11

H, I

Harvard Project Zero, 177
HEA. *See* Higher Education Act (HEA)
Heritage languages, 106–16
Higher education, institutions of, 50
Higher Education Act (HEA), 31, 32
Holmes Group, 42, 79, 82–83
Holt, Rinehart and Winston, 199, 200
Honig, Bill, 15
Immersion programs, 99–106, 110–114
Immigration, 172–73
Improving America's Schools Act, 32
In-service education, 23, 58, 68–71. *See
    also* Professional development, of
    teachers
Indiana, 146, 151–65
Indiana University of Pennsylvania, 70
Individual differences, 47
Induction, of new teachers, 84
Industrial-era school, 122
Instructional materials. *See* Materials of
    instruction. *See also* Textbooks
Instructional strategies, 47
Interactive satellite, 125
International economic competition, 204–5
International Education Exchange, 32
International Education for a Competitive
    America, 32
International Public Policy Institute, 32
International studies, 30
International Visitors Program, 31
Internet, 34, 78, 122, 125
Internship, for teacher candidates, 42
Interstate New Teacher Assessment and
    Support Consortium, 36–37, 46–48, 51,
    53
Iowa, 49, 68
Isolationism (international policy), 30
Italian, 52

J, K, L

Japanese, 52, 87, 104, 112, 126–28
Japanese Technical Literature Translation
    Center, 32

JNCL. *See* Joint National Committee for
    Languages/National Council for
    Languages and International Studies
    (JNCL-NCLIS)
Johns Hopkins University, 34
Joint National Committee for Languages/
    National Council for Languages and
    International Studies (JNCL-NCLIS),
    27, 30–34, 35, 57, 82
Journals, 180–81
Kansas State University, 134
Kentucky, 17
Korean, 112, 113
Language associations. *See* Foreign
    language associations
Latin, 52
Lau vs. Nichols, 29, 38, 111, 117
Learner-centered education, 47, 122–23,
    131–32
Learning logs, 180
Learning Outcomes Framework, 144
Legislation, affecting language teaching,
    31
Less commonly taught languages, 178
Licensing, of teachers, 23–37, 46, 48
Local organizations, 87
Longitudinal assessment, 177
Los Angeles, 200
Los Angeles Unified School District, 44
Louisiana, 146, 147, 149, 198, 200
Louisiana State University, 43

M

Madison, James, 28
Mandates, 146–47
Marlborough County, South Carolina, 49
Maryland, 44, 68
Massachusetts, 49
Materials of instruction, 75, 156. *See also*
    Textbooks
Math Online Resource Center (MORC),
    78, 91n
Mathematics, 12, 14, 48, 53, 75–78, 140,
    141–43, 147, 148, 157, 183
McGill University, 100
McLuhan, Marshal, 125
Mentoring, 84
Miami, Florida, 200
Michigan State University, 43
Middle School Math Project, 78, 91n
Mississippi, 44, 49
MLA. *See* Modern Language Association
    (MLA)
Modern Language Association (MLA), 26,
    36–37, 70